HEALERS
AND THE
HEALING PROCESS

Cover art by *Jane A Evans*

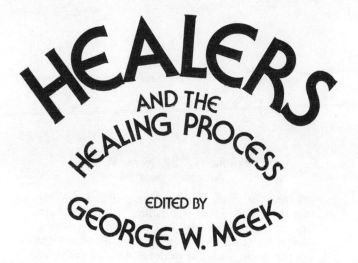

HEALERS
AND THE
HEALING PROCESS

EDITED BY
GEORGE W. MEEK

A report on 10 years of research by 14 world famous investigators

A Quest Book

This publication made possible with the assistance of the Kern Foundation

The Theosophical Publishing House
Wheaton, Ill. U. S. A.
Madras, India/London, England

A Quest original. Third printing, 1982. Published
by the Theosophical Publishing House, a department of The Theosophical Society in America.
Inquiries for permission to reproduce all, or portions
of this book, should be addressed to Quest Books,
306 West Geneva Road, Wheaton, Illinois 60187.

ISBN: 0-8356-0498-5
Library of Congress Catalog Number 77-5251
Printed in the United States of America

DEDICATION

To all those men and women who down
through the ages had the moral courage,
love, compassion and inner wisdom to
alleviate by one method or another, the
pain, illness, and disease of their
fellow human beings
and to those
of the new generation who,
traveling some of the paths
discussed in this book, will add
valuable new dimensions to medicine,
the church, and science.

CONTENTS

PREFACE

A new scientific truth does not triumph by convincing its opponents and making them see the light, but rather because its opponents die and a new generation grows up that is familiar with it.

— Max Planck

This comprehensive study by competent observers is intended to throw new light on the healing processs itself, and on the pros and cons of what has been called psychic, mental, faith, spirit, spiritual and paranormal healing, and to provide evidence for a more considered evaluation on the subject.

Whenever anything new or unorthodox is discovered in any field of endeavor, established authorities tend to "condemn without investigation" or be content with only a superficial investigation. This has been particularly true in the area of psychic phenomena in general, and all types of unorthodox healing, in particular. In recent years there has been a tendency to refer to all such healing as "paranormal". We accept that term as a useful catch-all. However, we do hasten to point out that all such healing is PARAnormal only to the extent that it is outside the capability of present medical and material science to explain fully just what is going on. In no sense does paranormal healing imply miracles or the miraculous.

Because these healing processes defy our present "belief system", and because our extensive personal study of the healers practicing them disclosed a degree of fraud and sleight-of-hand, we can understand why parapsychologists, medical doctors, and material scientists have decided that the work of so-called spiritual and psychic healers is not worthy of their time or attention.

The American and foreign press, television, and radio have failed to tell the public that the deceptive practices are confined largely to perhaps two dozen healers living in one small island in the Philippines. The fact that tens of thousands of healers all over the world treat several million patients yearly without any need for resorting to deception is not, apparently, the stuff that sells books, builds circulation, or appeals to radio and television audiences.

However, the findings of my fellow researchers over the past decade in the field of paranormal healing have brought to light irrefutable proof that there are dimensions of the subject that cry out for serious scientific attention. These findings constitute a veritable Pandora's Box filled with phenomena that will force us, when confronted, to rethink our concepts of the universe and the nature of man's mind and spirit as well as the cosmic energies manifesting through him.

While not as pessimistic as Max Planck, we realize that some areas remain largely for the new generation of parapsychologists, medical and material scientists, and religious leaders. They must carry on the research now undertaken by those who have recounted their experiences and convictions in this book. Fundamental changes in psychology, medicine, science, and religion will be suggested by this new knowledge once it has been refined, developed, and utilized. In my world travels I have been heartened to find present-day workers in these fields who have the strength and conviction to proceed quietly in their studies of paranormal healing. From them we may expect further demonstrable evidence that these powers do, in fact, exist. Several of these researchers are represented in this book.

We hope you will find stimulation and challenge in the material; that it will inspire you to "lift the lid of this Pandora's Box" and thoroughly consider the information assembled. Perhaps several chapters herein are primarily of interest to professionals in the fields of science and medicine, so the non-scientific or general reader may want to skip some or all of Chapters 7, 8, 13, 18, 22 and Appendix C. If you are a professional, perhaps you may visualize beneficial changes which can be made in the fields of medicine, religion or science in the decades ahead. Whether you are a professional or a layman, we hope you will use this material to prevent many minor and major illnesses and add to your useful life span.

What has been assembled herein presents a picture as complete as facts permit. All who have worked on this material have paid a willing price in time, effort, and resources, with one thought in mind — the elimination by mankind of much illness and suffering, and the achievement of vibrant health.

Paraphrasing Max Planck, I am confident that the new generation will grow up knowing far more about psychic, mental, faith, spirit, spiritual, and paranormal healing than my generation.

George W. Meek
Ft. Myers, Fla.
December, 1976

ACKNOWLEDGMENTS

The cooperation of many individual healers in the U.S.A., England, Brazil, and the Philippines is gratefully acknowledged. They permitted close observation of their daily activities in spite of frustration caused by extensive movie and still photography. Without their patience and understanding, this book would not have been possible.

The editor is appreciative of the cooperation of the following co-authors whose devotion to a common goal has resulted in a unified presentation of the subject of paranormal healing:

Gilbert Anderson	London, England
Forrest J. Cioppa, M.D.	Oakland, California
David Hoy, L.H.D.	Paducah, Kentucky
Hiroshi Motoyama, Ph.D.	Tokyo, Japan
Hans Naegeli-Osjord, M.D.	Zurich, Switzerland
Michael Wynne Parker	Norwich, England
Andrija Puharich, M.D.	Ossining, N.Y.
Jeanne P. Rindge	Buffalo, N.Y.
Sigrun Seutemann	Karlsruhe, West Germany
C. Norman Shealy, M.D.	LaCrosse, Wisconsin
Sir Kelvin Spencer	Devon, England
Alfred Stelter, Ph.D.	Dortmund, West Germany
William A. Tiller, Ph.D.	Palo Alto, California
Lyall Watson, Ph.D.	London, England

It is to be understood that each of these authors assumes responsibility for only the material he or she supplied and is in no way responsible for, nor necessarily endorses the material contributed by others.

Since the authors researched the subject largely without compensation, and often at their own expense, it is worthy of note that they have stipulated that royalty income shall be utilized for the purpose of financing further scientific research on the subjects covered by this book.

Acknowledgment is made of the crucially important research of the Brazilian healer, Arigó, by Andrija Puharich, M.D., Henry Belk and the many medical and scientific team members who planned and executed the studies.

Special thanks are extended to Harold Sherman who, with Henry Belk, pioneered the study of the Filipino healers and who did much to lay the groundwork for the researchers who followed them.

Foreign travel expenses during the last two years of the research on which this book is based were defrayed in part by contributions from Mr. and Mrs. Julian Burnette, Oliver Colvin, Jr., Joaquin Cunanan, Albert Mevi, Maximo T. Kalow, Jr. and the Caliraya Foundation, Loren Parks and Donald Westerbeke.

We acknowledge editorial criticisms and suggestions of the more than thirty individuals who so kindly took time to read and comment on the entire manuscript or portions thereof.

We express our appreciation to Random House, Inc. and author Doug Boyd for permission to quote copyright material from the book, *Rolling Thunder*; to Doubleday & Co. and author David St. Clair for permission to quote copyright material from the book, *Psychic Healers*; to Macmillan London Limited and author Prof. John Taylor to use illustrations from the book, *Superminds,* and to Doubleday & Co. and author Dr. Lyall Watson for permission to quote copyright material from the book, *Supernature*.

Marcus McCausland of London, England, made important contributions to the chapter on theory.

Mary Scott of Swindon, England provided the important Fig. BB and the valuable comments on same.

Jeannette D. Meek assisted greatly in coordinating portions of the extensive foreign travel by the editor and some of the co-authors; in handling the heavy correspondence required to produce this book; in editing and typing the manuscript in its various drafts; and in proofreading.

Acknowledgment is made of the work of Leslie Price in compiling the bibliographies.

1

PERSPECTIVE — AN OVERVIEW OF PARANORMAL HEALING

Jeanne Pontius Rindge

From unremembered time, accident and disease have been with us. Dinosaurs had bone tumors; paleolithic man TB of the spine. In Neolithic times, trephination—removal of pieces of the skull—perhaps relieved epilepsy, or permitted demons to escape.

As we gaze back through history, noting the human struggle to gain foothold on this planet and to evolve toward mankind's ultimate destiny, we observe the consuming effort to pit human weakness against what seemed to be the overwhelming powers of the universe.

If we are to understand the developing attitudes toward health and healing throughout history we must appreciate mankind's changing experience of "reality".

For primitive man, wherever found, the line of demarcation between self and not-self was extremely thin—perhaps non-existent. He had yet to become a differentiated, individual being. His immersion in, and experience of, the "out-there" was more real than his experience of himself as a person, separate and distinct.

Experience of and control of the "out there" are, however, two different things. More often than not, primitive man was awash in the overpowering energies and *entities*—both beneficent and malign— which totaled his daily experience. Upon these, as upon a vast moving picture screen, he projected his undifferentiated inner experiences.

The relationship with, and control of, these illusive, universal forces became highly personalized and frequently fraught with terror. Positive procedures for dealing with these invasions were, it seems, surprisingly similar in all parts of the world. Having projected the causes of accident and disease upon exterior forces, material and non-material, it behooved the sufferer to find means to destroy, neutralize, appease, cajole or importune them so that healing could take place.

Gods, demons, departed human beings and forces of nature received overriding consideration. The veil between this and the after-life was as thin as between inner and outer experience. When a person passed on he continued to exert his chosen influence, good or bad, as part of the community life. All of these forces had to be reckoned with. Living persons, plants, objects—all of which had a life of their own—also could exert evil influences to be parried by the unfortunate victim.

Certain individuals, through innate ability or training, were found more capable than others in dealing with the denizens of the unseen world. They became the shamans, witch doctors, sorcerers and, later, the priests in all early cultures.

There were in many places special castes of witch doctors embracing chiefs or headmen. Tibetan lamas, shamans of Siberia, Zululand, North and South America, Philippines, Borneo, Melanesia, Sumatra, Polynesia—all underwent severe initiatory rites and ordeals as they were held responsible for the well-being of the tribe. The consistently unsuccessful shaman was short-lived.

Sorcerers were thought to have the power to leave their bodies and enter those of others. They were taught to flatter, wheedle, and even threaten the spirits to do their bidding. Placation through bodily sacrifice in many parts of the world may have derived from observation that dangerous wild life became quiescent on a full stomach.

During this period—by far the longest in history—the gods were approached to grant requests, to ameliorate misfortune and (but not always) for worship. In Egypt, gods and goddesses, some of whom inflicted disease, also healed. (Isis early caused, later healed disease, especially of children.)

Everywhere talismans and chants were used against demons. In Africa even today, millions believe that death is due to "interference", either human or from *Mizumu*, spirits of the dead.

As ethical considerations and religious principles developed in the evolutionary process, the priesthood often dressed up to play the part of the celestials, saying, "It is not I who says it, it is Isis who says it."

There was, frequently, another brand of healer, the medicine man, although he and the witch doctor could be synonymous. The medicine man had the task of handling misfortune due to mundane, but no less difficult, causes. His problem was complicated by the widespread belief that one's person extended to anything belonging to that person—objects, hair, even his own shadow, or his name. Any damage done to any possession damaged the owners as well. For example, in Australia sharp stones placed in footprints could lame the maker.

Magic attack had to be met with magic treatment. Discovering the name of the living opponent could reverse the evil. When the supposed human cause of a person's illness was discovered (often a suspected witch or wizard—usually a woman), death was the punishment if the patient died. The medicine man also could cure by proxy—treating the effigy instead of the patient or the disease, mumps, for example in Africa could be transferred to a rat. In Kashmir, bulls were driven through the streets to absorb cholera.

The medicine man, in time, came to depend not alone on charms, amulets, and his own volatile version of the bedside manner, but also upon a remarkable array of medicinal herbs, remedies believed to have been revealed to him by the gods. Increasing numbers of these herbs are implementing modern pharmacopeia (thus being retrieved from "magic"). Chaulmoogra, quinine, curare, and reserpine are among them.

In 2000 B.C. according to the code of Hammurabi, money was given for successful surgery, with death to the doctor if the patient died. This doubtless kept experimental surgery to a minimum! In Egyptian papyri, there are two groups of texts, magical and scientific. The magical included knowledge of the enemy, words of power, and drugs to use as charms and with incantations. The scientific texts revealed a high level of sophisticated medicinals and practices.

A growing division of healing practices into the pragmatic and the metaphysical suggests an increasing split between the undifferentiated world of primitive awareness and a developing trend toward material discrimination and I-that separation. In Mexico today the dichotomy is complete. According to Mexican historian Rolando Guillermoprieto, as told to this writer, there is the white, sterile, impersonal hospital, the ultimate in a physicalistic approach to healing; while behind hundreds of adobe walls lie thousands of years of magical traditions, creating magical healing daily. At least 180,000 *curanderos*, or healers, in Mexico are curing diseases, many of which defy present-day medical practices. A brain tumor is released in hemorrhage after the patient breathes fumes from a certain berry crunched in hot water. Hernia is cured by tying bark from a certain tree over the spot for three weeks. In Mexico City a streetside curandero will extract an excruciatingly impacted wisdom tooth without pain, using a secret family formula.

Similar situations exist in all parts of the world where natives have remained in close touch with "separate realities", including the documented healings of Arigó and others in Brazil, the apparent healings in the Philippines, and the resurgence of American Indian *medicine power* which emphasizes harmony with universal forces.

As the evolving human being in more complex societies became more differentiated from his surroundings, he began to withdraw a few projections from the unseen world and to accept some responsibility for his relations with those forces—still considered to be outside himself. Although the Old Testament makes it clear that God is the arbiter (*It is I who deal death and life, when I have struck, it is I who heal and none can deliver from my hand.* Deuteronomy 32:39), sickness in Biblical history was considered a breach between man and God for which man himself was increasingly responsible.

For this reason, perhaps, the early Jews and also the Greeks, tended to shun the ill, although the Hippocratic school was born in Greece. In Greek thought, there was growing division between mind (nous) and body (physis), brilliantly criticized by Plato whose insights sound like advanced thinking today: "If the head and body are to be well, you must begin by curing the soul; that is the first thing . . . the great error of our day in the treatment of the human body (is) that physicians separate the soul from the body." (*Dialogues*)

Jesus of Nazareth undertook to heal this dichotomy and to add new dimensions to healing. His concern for the total physical, mental and spiritual health of individual persons was a revolutionary departure. Although He has been called a "shaman" due to his role as a mediator between God and man, this was not to appease a vengeful and arbitrary deity, but rather to channel *love* as a healing energy emanating from the Source of all being which He described as Loving Father.

Jesus taught the importance of realizing individual at-one-ment with this loving Source, but also demonstrated that healing energy could be administered through himself and others. The Gospels record 26 individual healings and 27 group healings by Jesus, and nine multiple healings by his Apostles. Methods used were touch, words, prayers, exorcism, faith of person, family or friends, use of saliva, and natural compassion.

Dr. Wade Boggs points out in *Faith Healing and Christian Faith*[1] that the medical debt to Jesus has been overlooked:

> *Without his spirit, medicine degenerates into depersonalized methodology and its ethical code a mere legal system. Jesus brings the correction of love without which true healing is rarely actually possible. The spiritual father of medicine was not Hippocrates of the Island of Cos but Jesus of the town of Nazareth.*

Two thousand years later, the promise of Jesus, *All these things I do, ye shall do and more*, has yet to be believed or implemented. However it is interesting to note that in April, 1975, the theme of a high level conference of medical doctors and government health personnel held near Washington, D.C. (the second annual May Lectures) was designed to investigate new approaches to health and healing which could overcome the sobering medical trend toward insulation and "depersonalized methodology".

Superstition and ignorance were the twin handmaidens of the Dark Ages. With the dawn of the Age of Reason and the flowering of science, medical orthodoxy, firm in its growing acquaintance with the physical universe, closed ranks against the possible efficacy of "magic"—its own cupping and leaching notwithstanding. It assumed zealous stewardship over scientific "facts" appropriate to Newtonian mechanistic, and increasingly physicalistic, views—hypotheses now challenged by advanced thinkers as incomplete descriptions of Reality.

It is a curious observation—especially since Pasteur's elucidation of the germ theory—that the causes of disease were arbitrarily transferred from outside evil entities to outside evil micro-organisms and the cures from the shaman's incantations to the pharmacist's chemical decoctions! The patient continued to be the victim of invading forces.

The Christian churches, in tune with the times, increasingly de-emphasized Christ's healing ministry. Protestant theologians such as Bonhoffer, Tillich, Bultman, and Bishop Robinson have called the idea mythological, finding no basis for the influence of "higher powers" or Christian healing.

Down through the centuries (orthodox trends to the contrary) have come consistent reports of medically unorthodox healings, both within and without the churches. Around the world, no matter what the religious background, there is indication that high spiritual attainment often is accompanied by purported power to heal. The list is long of Christian, Sufi, Hasidic and other saints, Tibetan lamas, and Hindu gurus.

Holy shrines and relics long have been considered agents of healing. Among the thousands traveling to Lourdes, the most famous shrine, only a few have been certified by medical and ecclesiastical commissions, as miraculously healed.

In 1778, Fredrich Anton Mesmer took Paris by storm with apparent healings by hand passes, which, he claimed, channelled a space-permeating "magnetic fluid" into the body. In spite of medical denunciation, Mesmer-trained practitioners fanned out over Europe, England, and America.

In the intellectual insularity of the West, no one seemed to notice a certain similarity of this theory to the long-held Eastern belief in "prana", an omnipresent life force which the strict application of Yogic disciplines could activate for physical well-being and the harmonizing of body, mind, and spirit.

The Marquis de Puysegur, discovering the power of his will over the patient's mind, discounted Mesmer's theory and claimed healing was due to "the actions of thought upon the vital principle of the body."[2] By mid century, Braid, in England had named the suggestive therapy "hypnotism". Another half century passed before the "power of suggestion" achieved medical recognition.

Hand passes and suggestion frequently entranced the patients, some of whom in this somnambulistic state "saw" what their physical eyes were incapable of seeing including, reportedly, their own internal organs with diagnosis (often erroneous) and prognosis (often correct) of cure. Further, many claimed to see, converse with, and be healed by departed spirits. This trend mushroomed into the rapidly spreading Spiritualist movement, and was accepted by millions. It absorbed many of the Mesmerists who claimed collusion with departed spirits for the purpose of healing.

During the past decade, as the research reported in the following chapters progressed, one very intriguing fact emerged. The only large concentrations of healers seem to be in countries where the belief systems involve what is generally known as Spiritualism or Spiritism. This belief postulates, in part:

> The Fatherhood of God, the Creator of all that is,
> The Brotherhood of Man,
> The continuous existence of the soul or spirit, and
> Communion of the individual with both Creator and spirits.

Although anathema to science, serious investigation of paranormal developments including telepathy, clairvoyance, discarnate contact, and paranormal healing, began in 1882 with the founding of the

British Society for Psychical Research followed shortly by the American Society. Both organizations were founded by intellectual giants courageously determined to discover order in the controversial chaos. In this century, Dr. J. B. Rhine at Duke University and other intrepid investigators (including authors of this book) have pioneered objective scientific investigation of unorthodox claims, risking hard won professional prestige in the effort to sift wheat from chaff. Their efforts are only beginning to be recognized (but not necessarily accepted) by open-minded peers.

The remarkable capacity of patients in hypnotic trance to recall details of long-forgotten life events led F. W. H. Myers,[3] a founder of the British Society to hypothesize an unconscious reservoir of the mind. On this foundation Sigmund Freud built his psychoanalytic edifice from which have sprung other ramifications of depth psychology.

Modern medical orthodoxy is preoccupied with disease "invasion" rather than with health. It concerns itself with crisis intervention through prolific chemical and brilliant surgical procedures rather than with prevention. It specializes in parts rather than with the whole person. However, investigations of consciousness suggest that the patient frequently is less the victim of invading forces and more the accomplice—through ignorance, negligence, or motivations deeply buried in the unconscious.

The task of various current psychotherapeutic approaches is to extricate the maturing ego from its primitive unconscious matrix and to help the patient stand forth as a separate, individuated self with increasing control over his states of being. Through biofeedback training, meditation, bioenergetic and other therapies, individuals are taught to become their own channels of psychological and frequently of physical healing.

While reading each chapter which follows, the reader would do well to keep in mind the enduring wisdom of the American Indians who, except where demeaned and degenerated by their white brothers, long have known who and what they are and from whence comes *their* medicine power. Mohawk Indian Ranihokwats put it this way, *"The whole is contained in each part. You are not only part of that whole, the whole is part of you."*[4]

Advanced theoretical physics is saying the same thing! It is probable that the question of healing, whether inner- or outer-directed, is embedded in this larger gestalt or worldview.

REFERENCES

1. Wade Boggs, *Faith Healing and the Christian Faith*

2. Marquis De Peysegur. *Du Magnetisme Animal* (Paris: Desenne, Cellot, 1807).

3. F. W. H. Myers, *Human Personality and Its Survival of Bodily Death* (London: Longmans Green, 1903).

4. Brad Steiger, *Medicine Power* (New York: Doubleday, 1974).

Other Background Books

Assagioli, R. *Psychosynthesis.* New York: Hobbs, Dorman, 1965.

Castenada, Carlos. *The Teachings of Don Juan: A Yaqui Way of Knowledge.* Berkeley, California: University of California Press, 1968.

_____. *A Separate Reality.* New York: Simon and Schuster, 1971; London: Bodley Head, 1971.

_____. *Journey to Ixtlan.* New York: Simon and Schuster, 1972; London: Bodley Head, 1973.

Puharich, Andrija. *The Sacred Mushroom.* New York: Doubleday, 1959.

Sigerist, H. E. *A History of Medicine,* Vols. 1-2. New York: Oxford University Press, 1951, 1961.

Thompson, R. C. *Assyrian Texts.* London: 1924.

I

PARANORMAL HEALING IN BRAZIL, ENGLAND, U.S.A. AND U.S.S.R.

Since the practice of psychic, faith, and mental healing has been considerably more prevalent in countries other than the U.S.A. our researchers of necessity had to supplement their studies in the U.S.A. by extensive research abroad.

2

THE HEALERS IN BRAZIL, ENGLAND, U.S.A. AND U.S.S.R.

"The art of Medicine consists of amusing the patient while nature cures the disease."

—Voltaire, 1750

"I do not think we cure anyone! People cure themselves. I think that with God we provide an environment in which healing can take place."

—Robert M. Bradley, M.D., 1973
(Pres. Acad. of Parapsychology
and Medicine)

George W. Meek

What actually takes place between the healer and his patient? To understand this, it is necessary to make systematic observations of many healers in several countries over a long period of time. The case histories presented in this chapter illustrate the work of six healers whose activities over many years are representative of the great service being rendered by the better healers.

The reader will note great differences between the healers' procedures and techniques. These differences have made it difficult to isolate common factors in the healer-patient relationship.

In additional case histories, found in the following chapters, overall observations as to similarities, differences, education, training, personality, age, temperament, belief systems, etc., will be found particularly in Chapters 5 and 12.

When one travels the world and watches healers at work, it is soon obvious that THE HEALER DOES NOT CURE DISEASES. In a unique way, just like the physician, he provides an ENVIRONMENT in which healing can take place. But, as will be developed in later chapters, the "environment" provided by a good healer has dimensions totally ignored by academic medical and material science. These new dimensions are explored in this book.

The field trips to Brazil, England, the Philippines and throughout the U.S.A. which provided much of the material for this book brought us into contact with many persons considered by their peers as healers. In studying the healers, whose patients exhibited the full spectrum of human ailments and suffering, we observed obvious successes and obvious failures of the healing process.

We have traveled around the world to meet and study typical healers introduced in this and in the next two chapters well-known healers from Brazil, England, the U.S.A. and the U.S.S.R. (*See* Chapter 6 for Philippine healers). All of them have had many years of experience and the work of each has been studied in depth.

M. H. TESTER (England)

Tester was a professional man who in middle life experienced a slipped and ruptured disc between the fourth and fifth lumbar vertebrae and other serious complications in his spinal column. Months of surgical jackets of different designs, traction, and sedation were of no avail so it was decided from numerous X-rays that an operation would hold at least some small hope. Mr. Tester decided, instead to go to Fricker's Healing Center. After six visits over as many weeks, Tester's spinal problems had disappeared. But to Tester, perhaps the most surprising thing was that Ted Fricker said, "You yourself are a born healer. You can do for others what I have done for you."

Tester was in a good position to know what benefit could come from unorthodox healing. He decided to give up his professional life and become a healer. His accomplishments in the years since that decision are a matter of public record.[1] The case of Tom Pilgrim, one of his patients, is given here in Tester's own words:

> He told me his name was Tom Pilgrim. He could not speak very well. One side of his face was distorted. It was twice the size of the other. He was a man in his early sixties. He said he was sorry he could not speak clearly. His face was distended by a massive growth on the jaw. He could not wear his dentures. He asked for healing as he was scheduled for an operation and he did not want to have it.
>
> Tom Pilgrim lived then at 19 Ladies Mile Road, Patcham, which is just outside Brighton in Sussex, a seaside town about fourteen miles from Haywards Heath where I live. He had developed this growth over some months. His doctor had sent him to see a specialist at The Royal Sussex Hospital at Brighton. They did a number of tests including X-rays of the head. They diagnosed a growth on the jawbone. They told Pilgrim he would have to come into the hospital as soon as they had a bed, which they expected to be in a week or two. They then intended breaking his jaw, removing the growth by surgery and then putting his jaw

in a temporary splint for some weeks to maintain drainage. They would then operate again and restore it to as normal as they could get it. There was no information as to whether the growth was malignant or benign. But the proposed operative treatment seemed drastic and the post-operative treatment not too pleasant.

I seated him on the stool and put my right hand on his jaw and the left on the back of his head and then sought attunement. This is the state in which I heal. I go into a light trance and let myself be used as a healing channel. In this case the healing was drastic. There was a great deal of vibration and some heat. I do not know how long the healing lasted, but it could only have been a few minutes. Tom Pilgrim said he felt as though a hand had been right into his jaw and had tugged at the growth. It certainly looked less distended.

He came back a week later. The jaw line was much nearer normal. He was wearing his dentures. There was still some swelling. I gave him more healing. After the third visit his jaw seemed to be the same size on both sides. His dentures were comfortable. He had no pain. He could speak and eat normally. He expected to have a letter any day asking him to go into the hospital for the operation. He asked what he should do. I told him to see his doctor.

His doctor, a Brighton general practitioner, examined him. He said the jaw looked well enough, and that the operation that was planned now seemed unnecessary. He sent Pilgrim to see another specialist. This one was at Guys Hospital in London. Here he was thoroughly examined and a new X-ray was taken. They could find no growth. There was a small amount of fluid present and he submitted to a minor operation with a local anaesthetic in a dentist's chair to drain the fluid away. It only lasted half an hour. He went home afterward, sore but otherwise happy.

That was two years ago. Tom Pilgrim never had the major operation that was planned. He was changed by his experience and decided to see what he could do to help sufferers. Tom Pilgrim is a natural psychic, and he has developed into a fine spiritual healer himself. He now has a healing centre of his own at 20 Sackville Gardens, Hove, Sussex, England. But that is another story.

OLGA WORRALL (Baltimore, Md., U.S.A.)[2]

Probably no other healer in the world has been the subject of as much study by medical and material scientists as Olga Worrall.

John Carlova, senior editor of *Medical Economics,* gave (in the June, 1973 issue) details of some of Mrs. Worrall's work in his report on a conference attended by four hundred physicians and scientists at Stanford University:

> Between formal sessions, a number of doctors took patients for treatment to one of the participants in the seminar, a sixty-seven-year-old faith healer named Olga Worrall. The patients, a total of ten, all had afflictions that had failed to respond to medical care. Seven of the ten, their doctors reported, either improved or were cured after the "laying on of hands" by Mrs. Worrall.
>
> A few years ago, reports on the exploits of a faith healer would have drawn little more than snorts of derision from the medical community . . . but scores of M.D.'s in the U.S.A. and in foreign countries have gone to Olga Worrall for treatment of their own ailments and many more have unofficially referred "hopeless" patients to this faith healer.
>
> Physicians, in fact, form a large part of the 1400-member American Academy of Parapsychology and Medicine, the organization sponsoring the Stanford Seminar. Robert Bradley, a Denver obstetric and gynecology specialist, who is president of the Academy, comments, "How does this healing work? What are the mechanisms? A lot of doctors want to know the answers—they just might add greater dimensions in the field of healing."

That is the purpose of this book—to begin to answer these important questions. With capable healers like Olga Worrall who are anxious to cooperate to the fullest extent with medical science, we can make headway with these studies, provided we can assemble enough open-minded and qualified scientists to carry through a greatly expanded series of research programs, and find the necessary funds to support this research.

Carlova's report continues to quote Dr. Bradley:

> When I say I have come to the conclusion that Olga is a sincere person who possesses a decided gift for healing, I know that I may leave myself open to criticism by other doctors. We just are not supposed to talk about such things. I call this peer fear—the apprehension that other doctors will denounce us, or that our practices will suffer. This is a lot of nonsense. I make no secret of my interest in such healing and it has not hurt my practice a bit.
>
> Nevertheless, many doctors are leery of venturing into the ethical area separating them from the healers. Asked to define this area, a spokesman for the American Medical Association quoted from Section 3 of *The Principles of Medical Ethics*: "A physician should practice a method of healing founded on a scientific basis, and he should not associate with anyone who violates this principle." The

A.M.A. spokesman added, "Now if it can be proved that a faith healer is practicing a method of healing founded on a scientific basis, hip, hip, hooray!"

The A.M.A. spokesman should be gratified by the contents of this book. The chapters by Motoyama, Watson, Spencer, Naegeli, and Stelter, in their entirety, and parts of many other chapters are the forerunners of work which is oriented toward establishing a scientific basis for paranormal healing.

One example of Mrs. Worrall's cooperation reported in Chapter 13, is the sophisticated scientific experiment by physicists Robert N. Miller and Philip B. Reinhart in using the Atomic Laboratory Model 71850 Cloud Chamber to sense the energy flow when Mrs. Worrall was engaged in healing six hundred miles away.

Mrs. Worrall is, and rightly deserves to be, taken seriously in scientific circles. Increasingly she is being invited to lecture before scientific groups and at colleges, both in the U.S.A. and abroad. In endeavoring to explain the basis of the healing which she and her aeronautical engineer husband (who was a healer until his death at the age of seventy-two) carried on as a team for many years, Mrs. Worrall turns back to a statement made 1900 years ago by the Apostle Paul in I Corinthians 15, *There is a physical body and a spiritual body*. Mrs. Worrall continues:

> The physical body is a mirror of the spiritual body.
>
> The spiritual body is a matrix around which the physical body is formed.
>
> Health and healing are the results of bringing into physical manifestation the spiritual perfection, the imprisoned splendor, slumbering within.
>
> This is accomplished by focusing the mind or consciousness upon creative force or God power within by regular disciplines of prayer and meditation.
>
> Finally, healing is simply a matter of accelerating the working of the marvelous but perfectly normal ability of the body to automatically repair, rebuild, and maintain itself in perfection.

ROLLING THUNDER (U.S.A.)

Recently, we have begun to learn of the tremendous accumulation of healing skill possessed by the medicine men of the American Indian tribes. This healing capability is used to treat both mental illness and malfunction and disease of the physical body. Research into the treatment of mental illness by witch doctors and medicine men in many countries led Dr. E. Fuller Torrey of the National Institutes of Mental Health to say,[3] "I learned from these healer-doctors that I—as a psychiatrist—was using the same mechanisms they were, and getting about the same results. Witch doctors and psychiatrists are really the same behind their exterior mask or pipe."

Rolling Thunder, spiritual leader, philosopher and acknowledged spokesman for the Cherokee and Shoshone tribes, was a principal speaker at the Menninger Foundation's Third Annual Conference, on October 15, 1971, when eighty-five medical doctors, scientists and lay people from five nations met to discuss the emerging science of consciousness. As a medicine man or shaman, he is guardian of a wealth of secret and mysterious knowledge which has been passed down through countless Indian generations. This knowledge includes the power to cure disease and heal wounds. Doug Boyd[4] tells of the healing activities carried on by Rolling Thunder before the assembled group of eighty-five observers:

> Rolling Thunder walked down the center aisle carrying the old suitcase which was his medicine bag. He approached the chair where one of our staff members sat with a painful, discolored and infected leg injury. Rolling Thunder performed a short ritual which involved inhaling four times as he verbally addressed the four points of the compass. Then, after the patient had taken four puffs on the pipe, Rolling Thunder asked him, *"Why do you want to be relieved of this condition? Do you just want to feel better or what are you going to do? Is there anything else you would like to improve or change? Whatever you say now, that is the way it is going to be."*
>
> After the patient answered and was further questioned, he was placed on his back as Rolling Thunder began a high wailing chant. Suddenly he thrust his head on the wound and sucked it with his mouth. . . . He lifted his mouth, and with lips tightly closed moved a few steps away where he leaned over a basin and vomited violently. The sniffing, wailing, sucking and vomiting was repeated several times. . . . Twice Rolling Thunder rubbed his hands together vigorously and placed both palms at once upon the injured area. . . . With the feather he removed from his hat band, Rolling Thunder made long, sweeping motions over the patient's body. [Just as the Spiritista healers in Brazil do when cleaning and sealing the aura.] These passes never touched the body and several times with snapping motions he shook the feather at a piece of raw meat he had brought in his bag.
>
> When Rolling Thunder repacked his bag and had instructed that the meat not be touched before it was burned to ashes, several of the medical doctors came forward to examine the patient's leg. The consensus was that the color had returned to normal, the swelling had decreased, and the flesh around the wound was flexible where it had been hard. The young man reported the pain was gone. In a few

minutes the patient, who had been in bed and in great pain, was able to participate in physically active sports.

I thought of countless Indians who for centuries held healing rituals. Rolling Thunder had explained that he got his power from the Great Spirit. This seemed to me to be an appropriate expression when I considered that the Great Spirit is a name, when there must be one, for the collective conscious will-energy of the universe and that one who is sufficiently prepared and purified becomes a clear channel for this purpose.

HENRY A. MANDEL (St. Petersburg, Florida, U.S.A.)

The two case histories I am about to report differ from all others in this chapter in that the patients had relapses. Because of this, these cases teach two important lessons.

Now 81, Mr. Mandel has been a healer since the age of 63. I have observed his work closely for the past six years and have taken friends and relatives to him.

A businessman friend of mine, aged 48, developed cancer of the lungs. After the maximum amount of radiation therapy, John was advised that his was a terminal case. I took him to visit Henry. After three healing sessions, Henry pronounced him cured. One month later when his radiologist took new X-rays, he shook his head in amazement and said, "John, you are a lucky fellow. Perhaps the radiation therapy did the job after all." (John did not have the courage to tell the radiologist he had visited a healer or to remind the radiologist that he had judged John to be a terminal case.)

Three months later John died. What had happened? In the subsequent two years it was discovered that there had been some indiscretions and frustrations that had been repressed and kept from public view. After the reprieve by the intervention of the healer, some deep level of John's mind rebelled and sought a graceful way out by a disease in the spleen. He wanted to die. This illustrates what every doctor and every healer learns very quickly: a patient cannot be kept well if at some deep level he wants to be *ill* more than he wants to be *well*.

Another case: Betty, a 45-year-old woman developed partial paralysis, was forced to give up her job as teacher of retarded children, and became bedridden. Over a period of months, at what my colleagues assure me is one of the best diagnostic clinics in the U.S., she was given just about every test they had, including a psychiatric examination and a muscle biopsy, at a cost of $2,500. The results? Nothing, not even a clue as to what had caused the difficulty and no suggested therapy. Over the passing months the prospect of becoming a "vegetable" filled the patient's mind with terror.

Betty and her husband agreed that they had nothing to lose by following my suggestion that they visit Henry. She was taken to the airport in a wheelchair and was met with a wheelchair and taken to Henry's home. On the seventh day after three treatments, she walked three quarters of a mile. On the eighth day after the fourth treatment, she flew to her home city and gaily pushed the empty wheelchair that her husband had brought to the plane ramp. Four nights later she attended a Christmas dance, and in the following days walked long distances in crowded streets and stores.

Three months later she had a serious relapse, suffering considerable pain, and was largely confined to her bed. What had happened? Had Henry done a poor job?

Two things had happened, one physical and one mental. She had made two trips to a physical therapist in the hopes of more rapidly rebuilding the weakened leg muscles. Perhaps the activity was too strenuous for her condition. The only other thing which seemed to relate to the situation was the newspaper clipping that she enclosed with a letter telling of her relapse. The clipping told how a well-known American surgeon, after making a one-man study of the public healing services of Kathryn Kuhlman, had "proved" that the patients of Miss Kuhlman usually had serious relapses. (Betty had been a great admirer of Miss Kuhlman).

Once again Betty visited Henry Mandel in Florida, this time bringing her sister to help manage the transportation. The sister hoped to get relief from a back condition of long standing. Henry's treatment of the sister's back problems brought the desired improvement and his efforts on behalf of Betty again made her functional to the point where she could resume her daily routines. As of the time this is written she is in the process of learning that every person has the God-given right and responsibility to decide in favor of good health—or illness and disease.

How had Henry been able to produce such dramatic initial results in the face of the complete failure by Western medicine? Could a newspaper clipping trigger such a serious relapse? How was Henry able to accomplish what he did with both Betty and her sister, as well as with my friend John? Chapter 19 will make a start at supplying the answers.

While these two cases were selected to illustrate the part the patient's own thoughts and emotions play in relation to efforts of the healer, it would be unfair to Henry Mandel not to give just one example of the *lasting* quality of the healing in those cases where the "seed falls on fertile ground." Often the most dramatic results of healing occur with children and animal pets. They know only that there is something wrong and they want to get better. Children have yet to build a belief system based on the idea that most healing comes from pills, injections, prescriptions or adjustments. Consider the case of my little friend Christina in Australia.

When Christina was old enough to stand in the play-pen it became obvious that her right knee did not function properly. When she began to walk she had a noticeable limp. Soon it became painful for her to walk. Her parents took her to the best orthopedic specialists they could find in Australia. Injections had no effect. By the age of two and one half she wore a cast each night and took full-strength aspirins daily to keep the pain down. Her eyesight began to be affected, apparently from this proportionately heavy aspirin intake. Because every indication was that Christina would grow up to be a cripple, the parents started for Europe to see if they could find surgical help. En route from Australia to Switzerland, they stopped in my town to visit Christina's grand-parents. The grandmother, knowing of my research in the healing field, asked if I could help. I put Christina and her parents in my car and drove them to St. Petersburg Beach to visit Henry.

After a thirty-minute session, Christina walked out of Henry's treatment room with only a slight limp. Ten days later, after a total of five treatments by Henry, Christina and her parents went on to Europe for a vacation, but they felt no need to seek surgical help. Christina never again wore the cast, nor did she need to take pain pills for her knee. Six months after their return to Australia the mother wrote and said, "How I wish you and Henry Mandel could have stood beside me this morning as I looked out of the window. Christina was running all the way around the cricket field with children much larger than her-self."

Two years later Christina again visited her grandmother and the only momento of the congenital defect was a thin "lift" which she wore on the heel of one shoe to make up for the delayed growth of the bad leg during her formative years.

Taken together, these three patients of Henry Mandel begin to give us a clue as to the role of thoughts and emotions in healing, a subject we will explore in great detail later, in the chapter, "Toward a General Theory of Healing".

HEALERS IN THE U.S.S.R.

Alexi and Victor Krivorotov, a father and son living in Tbilisi, Georgia, work as a team. Their healing activities have been reported in many Soviet newspapers and scientific magazines. Their work has been investigated by Russian scientists, including Victor Adamenko, physicist at Moscow's National Institute of Physiology. Dr. Adamenko reported on a test of the Krivorotovs' healing ability as conducted by himself and a team of seven physicians:

> This was a carefully controlled experiment conducted at Republic Hospital in Tbilisi, the city where the Krivorotovs live. It was ordered by the Ministry of Health there.
>
> The physicians on the special commission began by per-sonally diagnosing the illnesses of 30 patients, confirming that these people were suffering from real ailments. They found such problems as light paralysis in arms and hands, chronic headaches, backaches and diseases of the nervous system.
>
> For a week the Krivorotovs treated these patients. They received no other treatment. At the end of the week the

patients were re-examined by the commission which reported that all the patients showed improvement in their condition, and several were cured.

To offset the possibility that the Krivorotovs' spoken instruction might aid the healing processes, doctors had chosen several people who could not speak Russian.

Further tests at Tbilisi University in July, 1974, revealed that the Krivorotov hands normally radiate only ordinary amounts of energy in the ultraviolet portion of the electromagnetic spectrum. When the men focus their thoughts and emotions on the task of healing a patient, their hands emit many times as much of this particular energy. (For more about such energy exchange, *see* Chapter 19.)

Alexi, the 77-year-old father, a retired lieutenant-colonel, says that patients travel hundreds of miles to see them. He reports:

Usually the patients come to us only when they have been unable to get help from the regular medical profession. One example was a five-year-old child who was suffering terribly from a tumor behind her right eye. It caused the eye to protrude. The doctors had started to operate but when her heart stopped beating under anesthesia, they refused to proceed further. I treated her seven times in a few days. The pain stopped, she was able to sleep normally, and by the end of one month the eye had returned to its proper position. I examined her at intervals for another three years and the tumor never returned.

HARRY EDWARDS (England)

The existence in England of the National Federation of Spiritual Healers with its thousands of healers, and the fact that governing authorities of 1,500 hospitals permit entry of Federation members to visit patients, are both a tribute to the many decades of pioneering work in the field of healing by Harry Edwards. His sensible and statesmanlike conduct in the Federation for more than a quarter of a century did much to gain entry for healers into the hospitals to treat patients who desire their services. In his eighties Mr. Edwards was as busy as ever at his healing sanctuary and handling more than 10,000 written requests per year for absent treatment. Harry Edwards died in England in December, 1976, after this manuscript was completed.

When asked to single out just one recent case history for inclusion in this chapter, Mr. Edwards sent the following (complete documentation available in my files):

In July, 1974, the parents of Jayne Smith, living at 2 Curborough Rd., Lichfield, Staffordshire, approached me seeking spiritual healing for their daughter. She had cancer of the left upper leg and the other leg and buttock were solid like wood. The surgeon and the doctor at a hospital in Staffordshire had been planning to amputate the leg, but

when examination showed the disease had penetrated into
the hips and pelvis so that nothing more could be done, they
advised to the effect that the only help lay in spiritual
healing.

Mr. and Mrs. Smith consulted the rector of their church
and he personally brought Jayne to our Sanctuary. I shall
always remember that leg, enlarged and bone hard. Within
a month it had started to soften. Healing was continued at
roughly monthly intervals, being maintained by prayerful
absent healing. Within six months the symptoms were
overcome, the joints could be bent, she was walking and
keeping up with her school friends, and was ready to take
her driving test.

Jayne's recovery dated from the commencement of
spiritual healing in which the rector joined. Medically,
Jayne was scheduled to die. She has not died. The diseased
cancer cells are being replaced with healthy tissue. The
tendons are lengthening, the paralysis is yielding and
coordination is returning.

Mr. Edwards concludes, "There must be a reasoned process to account for all of the facts in this case."

The current state of knowledge about the reasoned process is the subject of Part V of this book.

REV. WILLIAM C. BROWN (U.S.A.)

Any study of healers immediately brings the investigator face to face with the concept that spirit intelligences (variously referred to as guides, controls, or protectors) are working through the minds of healers to supply information of which the healer himself has no conscious knowledge. In no case is this more apparent than in the work of Rev. Brown as he, in deep trance, performs "surgery" on the etheric body.

Although I have personally visited Rev. Brown and his present wife, Maria (who works with him very closely), I am of the opinion that an excerpt from a chapter in the book, *Psychic Healers,* by David St. Clair[5] gives one of the best accounts of a typical "operation" by Rev. Brown, assisted by his wife Nancy (now deceased) and his doctor "guides". In this account, Mr. St. Clair's friend Chuck has asked for help:

On the small table between the chairs that Rev. Brown and
Nancy sat in, rested an open Bible. The Bible is kept open to
the Book of Isaiah. Rev. Brown claims that the only place in
the entire Bible where spirit teachers are mentioned is to
be found in Isaiah 30:20-21.

Chuck came in and sat beside me, and as soft music
played, Mrs. Brown took her place in a chair at the foot of
the table and Rev. Brown sat in a chair against the wall, on
the opposite side from me. The chair was about two feet
from the operating table.

He asked us to repeat the Lord's Prayer in unison but to pay attention to the words and what they were saying. Then he began the Affirmation of Faith, which we repeated after him. I glanced at Chuck. He was fidgeting in his chair.

The music stopped playing and there was silence. I kept my eyes glued to Rev. Brown's face. His eyes were closed and he was breathing deeply. His hands were palms-down on his knees. His feet were flat on the floor and slightly apart. I glanced at Nancy; she was sitting in the same attitude but with a pencil and notebook on her lap.

Then suddenly Rev. Brown fell over. It was a quick and unexpected movement. He just doubled from the waist, his head down between his knees. It was almost like the motions of a puppet whose string had suddenly gone slack.

Then slowly, but very slowly, his head came up again. Finally he was back in an upright position but his face seemed somehow changed. His eyes were still tightly closed. His mouth opened and a deep voice came out. Nancy greeted it as "Dr. Spaulding", her husband's protector.

Rev. Brown's face grimaced for a second and then relaxed.

"Top of the morning to you," the thick brogue came out of Rev. Brown's mouth. Nancy and Chuck both greeted Dr. Murphy (who acts as the head of a team of doctors working through Rev. Brown). "Who is that sittin' over there?" Dr. Murphy wanted to know, pointing a finger at me.

"It's a researcher, Dr. Murphy," Nancy said. "He's come to watch us work. He's writing a book."

"A researcher is it now? Why are you wastin' your time this lovely Sunday morning sittin' here when you could be outside with the pretty colleens?"

I explained that I was writing a book and that I had come for information not colleens.

"That's the pity of it," he said. "When you are young enough for colleens you prefer your books. Someday when you're old, you'll prefer the colleens to your books but it won't be any use at all." He laughed. "Anyway, I'm glad to meet you and happy that you are here. Be welcome."

"Thank you," I said. I was surprised to see Rev. Brown act like this and to speak with the light Irish voice. While he has a sense of humor and likes to tell jokes, he is just not the type to put on an accent and call attention to himself.

"Dr. Murphy" asked who was going to be operated on that day and Nancy said it was Chuck, but she had been having trouble with her big toe and would he look at it? He told her to get up on the table. Bending down to look at the toe—but with his eyes shut tight—Dr. Murphy told her that it was infected. She said she didn't think it was because it didn't feel like that.

"Now, Nancy," he said, "don't be tellin' me my business. That thing is infected and I am going to have to give it a shot."

He looked down past the end of the table and seemed to be searching for something. "There it is," he said, "under that other stuff." He reached down and lifted an object from the table. An invisible object from an invisible table, I must add. He held it like a hypodermic syringe and, lifting it up, he squirted against the light as his finger pushed a drop up and out of the needle. Then he told her to lie still. With his eyes closed he came within a few inches of her aching toe and forced the invisible liquid into the toe of her etheric body. He pulled out the needle and placed it back on the invisible table.

"That'll hold ya for a while," he said, and motioned for Nancy to get off the table. "Now who's next?" he asked.

"It's Chuck, Dr. Murphy," said Nancy. "He's had trouble with an old operation that some physical doctors performed on him. He hopes you can help him."

"I hope so too," he said. "All right, my lad, get up here now. Let's have a look at ya."

Chuck took off his bathrobe and swung himself onto the table. Nancy covered him with the white blanket. Dr. Murphy told her, "I'm going to have a look at his private parts, Nancy, if you don't mind." She left the room and he pulled Chuck's gown up to his chest; then he pulled the blanket down to just below the groin. "You've a lot of scar tissue in there," he said. "No wonder it's been causin' ya troubles." He looked at Chuck, "But why are ya so nervous, my boy? You've been here before and we didn't hurt ya, did we?"

"Not on the table," Chuck answered. "But it sure ached later."

"But it's the fire that tempers the steel, haven't you ever heard of that?"

"I've heard of it, Dr. Murphy, but I'm not made of steel and I don't like being tempered."

Dr. Murphy put his head back and laughed. "Well, we'll calm you down a bit with some of this." He reached over and picked up another invisible hypodermic syringe. Deftly he injected its unseen contents into the young man's neck. Then he put it down and picked up another. This one was injected into the other side of the neck. Then to me, "You, Mr. Researcher, come over here and feel this young man's pulse."

I rose and came over to the table. Reaching down, I took his wrist in my hand and placed my fingers on his pulse. It was beating strongly. I told Dr. Murphy so.

"Well, just wait a few moments and see how fast it's beatin'," he said. "I put enough material into him to calm him all the way down."

Sure enough, as I stood there, my thumb pressing firmly on Chuck's pulse, I could feel it getting weaker and weaker and weaker. Finally it was almost impossible to find.

Dr. Murphy motioned me back to my chair. Rev. Brown's

body was returned to the chair and sat down. His hands fell to his sides. Then his features relaxed and his hands began to move again. "Good morning," said a soft voice with a definite British accent. "I'm Dr. Thorndyke. Shall we begin?"

He worked quickly and silently. Like a skilled surgeon, with an invisible assistant who knew his every move in advance, he picked up a knife, made an incision, and clamped it open.

Dr. Thorndyke pulled something out of the wound. I could see Rev. Brown's hands going through the motions. Then he was handed something so thin that it must have been a needle. He ran the fingers of his left hand down the invisible thread attached to the needle and began to stitch up the incision. Then he patted Chuck's abdomen and pulled his gown down as he pulled the blanket up to cover him. He began to tell him what he wanted him to do. Things like no running or high reaching, etc.

Chuck sat up on the table, looking whiter and weaker than he had before. He said that he had felt as if a rubber band had been stretched across his stomach. Aside from that, the operation was painless. He shuffled off to one of the three post-operative rooms and in a few moments he was fast asleep. In the weeks which followed, Chuck said he had benefited from the work of Rev. Brown and his helpers.

An interesting incident which related to Rev. Brown's "invisible" helpers is related by Jeanne Rindge (author of Chapters 1 and 13) as follows:

I had received a letter from Rev. Brown. I handed this letter, still sealed, to a psychic whom our research had shown to have excellent clairvoyant abilities. We told her nothing about the envelope. First, she said she saw a long table with someone lying on it and a person standing nearby. Then she got confused and said she did not understand it, but there were other figures she could "see through" standing around the table. She described these other figures as ghostly figures.

It is worth bearing these details in mind when reading the accounts of Dr. Fritz at work in Brazil (Chapter 3) and Dr. Lang of England which follows.

GEORGE CHAPMAN (Aylesbury, England)

George Chapman is selected for inclusion in this chapter because his daily fulltime work as a healer may provide additional insights into the admittedly sticky question of spirit helpers or discarnate entities. In the preceding pages you were introduced to the concept that Rev. William Brown claims to get all of his diagnostic abilities from a group of spirit doctors. The same applies to the work of Henry Mandel. But healer Olga Worrall disclaims any such specific source of guidance; and Harry Edwards obtains guidance from what he characterizes as the "Healing Intelligences". This subject of spirit helpers most certainly is an important, although highly confusing, area for serious scientific study!

The more than twenty psychiatrists, clinical psychologists, medical doctors, parapsychologists, psychical researchers and scientists who have been associated in the research reported in part in this volume are a long way from understanding whether the view of the healer or that of the skeptic is correct. (*See* Appendix C)

A careful reading of the Old and New Testaments shows that the idea of "spirits" was already established 2,000 to 4,000 years ago. (*See* Supplementary Bibliography C) There is some evidence that in the early versions of the New Testament there were perhaps even more such references. It is also a possibility that much of man's inspired writings down over the centuries in both East and West may have come from such sources.

Research in progress during the last several years is beginning to throw important light on this subject, but as of now none of the researchers involved in preparing this book have sufficient data at hand to feel competent to write a chapter detailing the role of discarnate entities. In the absence of firm scientific data, it may be useful to present a serious "conversation" between a purported spirit guide and one of our researchers, Robert W. Laidlaw, M.D., formerly head of the Department of Psychiatry at Roosevelt Hospital, New York, and former president of Life Energies Research, Inc., New York. On December 31, 1969 Dr. Laidlaw visited George Chapman at his home in Aylesbury, England for the express purpose of talking to "Dr. William Lang", the discarnate spirit entity who purportedly guides Chapman.

Chapman, a former fireman, has been so successful in diagnosing and treating illness that patients come to him from all over the world and new patients usually must wait six months to get on the schedule. Dr. Laidlaw's account of his visit with "Dr. William Lang" follows:

> When I entered the consultation room in George Chapman's home in Aylesbury, a middle-aged man in a sports jacket was sitting with his back to the window with his eyes closed. He greeted me with a high, somewhat quavery voice of an old man, saying, "I'm glad that you've come to see me, Doctor."
>
> I replied (as I was somewhat confused at being so suddenly precipitated into this situation), "Am I talking with George Chapman or with Dr. Lang?", to which he answered, "You know, Doctor, in England we surgeons are known as Mr. and I would prefer that you address me as Mr. Lang."
>
> He then asked me to sit down on a chair alongside a long settee and he sat down on the settee so close to me that in

the course of our interview he, as a way of emphasizing what he was saying, could reach out and touch me on the arm.

I greatly regret that I did not have a tape recorder. The following notes were scribbled by me during the ensuing talk which lasted about an hour and a quarter.

"When I was alive, I lived in the east end of London. All the things in this room belonged to me while I practiced. The curtains are by Wm. Morris. Then I moved to Cavendish Square. The furniture that you see here was collected and given to me by my parents in 1872. I was not famous but I was well-known and well-liked. At my death some of my possessions went to my colleagues. After I came through to my colleagues by means of my medium, they arranged for some of my possessions to be brought back here. . . . Sir Henige Ogilvie was an associate surgeon in London. . . . He was interested in psychiatry. I was a down-to-earth surgeon. Psychiatry was looked down upon until recently. I liked to examine the body as a whole and to explain to my patients local difficulties. I felt that many of them were due to a state of mind. . . . My son would be ninety were he living today. . . . In the 1870's, the poor type of student who did not do well in medical school was sent into psychiatry. My father was a merchant. I had a number of brothers and one sister who married into the clergy. When I entered medicine in the London Hospital, I assisted Israel Zangwell, the writer who lost his sight. He recovered and wrote a book of poems about his experience in the London Hospital.

"I was a general surgeon. I wanted to make a special study of vision and I worked ahead. I became a consultant. In the spirit world I wanted to come back. I had always loved helping people. I was told in the spirit world that I had to go to school in order to come back. I preferred to work on the spirit body. I wrote a number of papers and edited material for the London Hospital. I kept my papers simple. I and my son wrote books on the eyes. I use simple explanations when I talk with patients. I break them down into (1) the physical and (2) the spiritual which contains energies and gives life to the physical body. I am able to operate on it. After death the spirit body dies. [Ed. comment: For simplicity in talking to the patient Dr. Lang avoids introducing the concept of the "etheric" body. What he calls "spirit" body is termed "etheric" body in Chapter 19, dealing with theory.] The spirit self (i.e. the mind) remains. This is the part of you that is the driving force. When it is upset it can give rise to mental difficulties.

"Some diseases, such as fractures, require treatments on a physical level. Other diseases come from the spiritual body. I have to diagnose the source of the trouble. If, after a successful operation, pain remains, the trouble is with the spiritual body or in the mind. Many people call the spirit body the etheric body. Many people have perfect organs but are always ill. I find them lacking in energy. They are depleted from giving off, like a depleted battery. I draw energy from my medium and give healing rays. . . . Retrobulbar neuritis is often called a purely physical disease but I find that patients with unhappy life experiences or too active a conscience may build up tension which manifests as retrobulbar neuritis. This comes from the spirit self. One must look into the patient as a whole. One can put the patient into a light trance, have him inhale deeply until he is completely relaxed and then ask him questions and discuss his problems. Then one can treat him through the spirit body and remove the fibrous trouble in the physical body. . . . *The only part of you that can travel is the mind.* Like the pigeon it can travel miles and miles and always return home. *The spirit body can travel only a few feet,* attached by a cord, *as it gives life to the physical body.*

"One must treat the physical body by separating the spiritual body from it."

Then there was much technical language which I was unable to record, but the implication was that the physical body and the spiritual were separated a matter of inches which allowed the spirit surgeon space enough in which to operate.

"Not every condition is curable. I tell patients I can only do my best. My medium emphasizes this. The clergy feel that laying-on-of-hands won't help. God won't do it without the patient's desiring help. It is necessary to instill the desire to live despite handicaps, and to eat appropriate food."

He spoke of the way many advanced arthritic patients give up and lead sedentary lives and eat the wrong foods.

"Alexander Cannon wrote books on psychiatry. In 1928, he offered me a partnership as he said that there were so many conditions that were related to the mind. I said that I had retired in 1914 and wouldn't risk it. In 1935 I was quite feeble. I had an increase in a tremor of my hands. I was a tiny man who liked golf. In 1937, Cannon said he was going to help me but I was worn out and dying. He tried to get me to relax. He felt that I had the gift of healing. I passed over."

"Many years later my medium cooperated with him in experiments. He was a fine person. He passed over a few months ago. He'd come to lunch and say, 'All I want is a potato and a poached egg.' He was a vegetarian. I'm not. I'm very fond of fish cakes. I treated Shaw's uncle. I tell some patients to eat meat. They need a balanced diet."

He then discussed leukemia in a way that indicated his medical familiarity with it.

"George (Chapman) likes light wine as I do. He takes

only two meals a day. The body must be empty on going into trance.

"I haven't heard of Dr. Fritz (in answer to my question) but I have known of Arigó. The spirit world is immense and there are many spirit doctors. I am part of a team of doctors I knew. The team expands as their sons or friends pass over."

There followed a discussion of the ethics of medical practice.

"I'm just the same William Lang I was on earth."

"Many people talk about spheres. They speak of having guides who are on the 7th-sphere, for instance. This is nonsense. There is just one sphere. I come back and I am William Lang. I talk with my colleagues. These guides at times take on other names. This is rubbish. One should use one's own name. I was never a formally religious man but I believe in the universal mind and that one should do as much good as one can. A lady patient recently called me an earth-bound spirit!

"I will remain here in contact until my medium joins me and then for some time thereafter my son Basil will be the medical helper to George's son Michael. I enjoy coming back as myself and talking with my friends. The young spirits should do the work and the older spirits should assist. George started at 25 and is now 49.

"My medium is now tiring."

The entranced medium then arose, felt his way to the door and asked Michael to give him a copy of *Healing Hands* and to put on the kettle for tea. "For the two of us." He crossed the room and groped about the desk. He said, "I can see you but I cannot see objects." He then sat down, inscribed a copy of *Healing Hands* to me and signed it "William Lang". We then bade each other farewell.

And with this report by Dr. Laidlaw we drop detailed discussion of discarnate entities and spirit guides. Readers interested in pursuing the subject further will find considerable additional detail in Appendix C. We will, however, touch upon the subject again in Chapter 19 where we set forth an overall theory of paranormal healing.

ARIGÓ (Jose Pedro de Freitas)

No introduction to the *healers* would be representative if it did not include reference to the work of José Pedro de Freitas, the Brazilian healer, known internationally as Arigó. It is the opinion of the editor and some of his co-authors that Arigó was the most versatile and accomplished healer encountered in our researches to date. For this reason Andrija Puharich, M.D. has prepared the following chapter as a testament to the work of Arigó, and as a challenge for all medical and scientific researchers to seriously consider doing additional research in the field of paranormal healing.

REFERENCES

1. M. H. Tester, *The Healing Touch* (London: Barrie and Jenkins, 1970).
   _____, *How to be Healthy, Wealthy and Wise* (London: Psychic Press, 1974).
2. Ambrose and Olga Worrall, *The Gift of Healing* (New York: Harper and Row, 1970).
   _____, *Explore Your Psychic World* (New York: Harper and Row, 1970).
   _____, *Your Power to Heal* (New York: Harper and Row).
3. E. Fuller Torrey, *The Mind Game: Witch Doctors and Psychiatrists* (New York: Emerson Hall, 1972).
4. Doug Boyd, *Rolling Thunder* (New York: Random House, 1974).
5. David St. Clair, *Psychic Healers* (Garden City, New York: 1974).
6. Bernard Hutton, *Healing Hands* (London: W. H. Allen, 1966). *See also* Supplementary Bibliographies—A (Paranormal Healing)

3

PARANORMAL HEALNG IN
BRAZIL — ARIGÓ

"Even before he died last year in an automobile accident at the age of
49, the peasant known as Arigó had become a legend in his native
Brazil. Claiming to be guided by the wise voice of a long-deceased
physician whom he had never known personally, the uneducated
healer saw as many as 300 patients a day, diagnosing and treating
them in minutes. . . . He treated almost every known ailment, and most
of his patients not only survived but actually improved or recovered.

"A few years ago, reports on the exploits of such miracle workers
would have drawn little more than derision from the scientifically-
trained. Now, however, many medical researchers are showing a new
open-mindedness toward so-called psychic healing and other methods
not taught in medical schools."

Time Magazine
October 16, 1972.

Andrija Puharich

I have a dream of what I call the *complete* healer. The complete healer
has not been seen, and may never appear, yet to discuss such a person
will give us an idea of what is meant by the term, healing. "Healing" is
used very freely in non-medical circles but it is not so commonly used
among medical men. Physicians don't always pretend to heal, and
speaking as a physician, I can candidly say that we mostly patch things
up. I think this is because we do not have a complete philosophy nor a
complete practice of medicine, nor do we have a model of the complete
healer before us. I will try to give you an idea of what I envision as the
complete healer, and how Arigó, the late Brazilian healer, demonstrates that such a person could indeed exist.

The FIRST characteristic of the complete healer is the ability to diagnose illness, whether the patient is present or absent. Arigó used two
basic methods of making a medical diagnosis which were extremely

impressive in their accuracy. One method was to simply look at the patient and immediately give a diagnosis, even though the condition was invisible or inaudible to Arigó. In one case, a patient informed Arigó that he had leprosy, and Arigó replied, "No, you in fact have syphilis, and you shouldn't lie to me!" Our subsequent medical examination confirmed this to be true. In another case, Arigó quite casually mentioned that we should check the blood pressure of a patient because at that instant it was 23 over 17, which in English parlance meant a blood pressure of 230 mm. of mercury over 70 mm. of mercury. We found that this indeed was the case. These are but two examples of the diagnostic skill that a complete healer should possess.

Another aspect of Arigó's diagnostic ability has become, for me, a paradigm of certain extrasensory perception phenomena. I uncovered this while observing Arigó perform a series of approximately 1,000 diagnoses, in which a phenomenal number were accurate. I was particularly impressed with his command of precise medical terminology. For example, rather than saying that the patient suffered from eye trouble, Arigó diagnosed it as retinoblastoma, or retinitis pigmentosa, etc. When Arigó saw my amazement, he said, "This is one of the simpler tasks for me because I simply listen to a voice in my right ear and repeat what it says."

Arigó died on January 11, 1971, in his 49th year. As a boy, he had no education except for two years in a parochial school from which he was dismissed because, in his own words, he was too stupid to continue.

His subsequent career involved hard labor, either in the fields or mines, and later, a clerical job in a social security office. Nobody ever saw Arigó read a book, or even attempt to read one, as we discovered in an extensive sociological study of his background. For all practical purposes, Arigó could be considered an illiterate. Thus, we had to consider very seriously the hypothesis that there indeed may have been a voice presenting itself in his head. The important question is, what was its source?

The SECOND characteristic of the complete healer is his ability to heal by the process of "laying on of hands", which I prefer to call manual healing. Although medicine should have been aware of manual healing hundreds of years ago, it is only beginning to be recognized today. Through the work of Dr. Bernard Grad of McGill University in Canada and Sister Justa Smith of Rosary Hill College, N.Y. we are beginning to understand some of the mechanism of "laying on of hands". Dr. Grad worked with a healer named Col. Estebany. In one experiment, Col. Estebany treated coded jugs of water by placing his hands on them, and then poured the water in random fashion onto plants which were set up in statistically controlled manner. The plants which received the benefit of "treated" water grew much more rapidly and had a greater net weight within a given period of time than those plants which received "untreated" water.[1]

Sister Justa Smith extended this study to show that in using water to dilute certain enzyme systems that break down polypeptides into amino acids, the Estebany treated water produced about a 15% increase in the hydrolytic activity of that enzyme.

A THIRD characteristic for the complete healer is his ability to heal himself. This is one of the rarest skills in a healer, and I have yet to encounter it. This statement stands even though I have had extensive experience with practicing Christian Scientists. These, of course, do not themselves claim the ability to heal, but claim, rather, to function as a channel for a higher power.

I never saw Arigó heal himself, and to my knowledge, in the twenty years in which he practiced, he was never able to heal any organic illness in any blood relative. This is a curious aspect of healing which is difficult to rationalize.

A FOURTH characteristic is the ability to use molecular medicine. This is not radically different from that which occurs in orthodox medicine, i.e. the use of chemicals, molecules, etc. added to the organism, human or animal, which affect that organism in such a way that functions are modulated, and diseases are either mollified or disappear. A good example of this would be the intake of aspirin, or insulin, or any other common chemical manipulation. A good healer, and I do not limit this to Arigó, has the ability to match, in his head, a knowledge of what is wrong in the chemical nature of an individual with the right chemical to correct it. In Arigó's case, he demonstrated this ability to an extraordinary, and even to a superlative degree.

Arigó was able to prescribe every known modern pharmacological agent, and often what he prescribed had no rational connection with the ailment, in the light of conventional medicine. Our medical research team was highly impressed by the range of knowledge which Arigó demonstrated in using this molecular matching procedure, and in particular, with his ability to treat not only the immediate problem, but the root cause of it.

In contrast, the modern physician will generally treat stomach ulcers locally, i.e., by giving an antacid, or an agent to slow down the vagus nerve, and perhaps a tranquilizer if he thinks the patient's mental or emotional state contributes to the problem. Arigó, however tended to ignore the stomach as the problem area, and instead prescribed a series of pharmacological agents which treated the cause which may have originated in the brain, or the liver, or through a parasite, or some other supporting function for which the stomach was only a front manifestation.

A point of interest is Arigó's prescriptions calling for massive doses of vitamins for certain illnesses. We are all familiar with the work of Dr. Humphrey Osmond, Dr. Abraham Hoffer, and others in treating certain so-called organic mental problems, such as schizophrenia, with megavitamin therapy. Arigó had been prescribing this as far back as the early 1950's in cases of epilepsy, schizophrenia and other such illnesses.

The FIFTH characteristic is the healer's ability to produce anesthesia by non-chemical means. I don't wish to argue whether this is hypnosis, or telepathy at a distance or any other similar technique. The fact is that a good healer, as Arigó, can place a very sharp knife into an unanesthetized patient's eye, and can manipulate the knife in the eye without causing either damage or pain. I have witnessed hundreds of operations, both major and minor, in which he used a knife, scissors or other such instrument, without causing pain. As an experiment I offered my arm in which a lipoma was present, for surgery. Arigó removed it very quickly, and I felt nothing. This is documented on motion picture film.

A SIXTH characteristic is the healer's ability to perform what I call instant surgery. Surgery as it is carried out in hospitals, requires a great deal of preparation. The room and all of the equipment have to be sterilized, the instruments arranged and prepared, etc. Arigó, however, simply borrowed any locally available knife, usually a pocket-knife belonging to another patient waiting in line, performed the surgical procedure hastily, wiped the knife on his shirt, returned it to the owner, and went on to the next patient. This is my definition of instant surgery. The patient did not experience pain, the surgical problem was corrected, there was no post-operative infection or shock, and the surgical wound healed more quickly than normal.

The SEVENTH characteristic for the complete healer is what I term the "bacteriostasis" treatment ability. A true healer should be able to violate every known surgical principle of antisepsis. Arigó did this repeatedly as indicated in examples of his healing described above.

The EIGHTH characteristic is the ability to perform what I call "action at a distance". Classically it is known as "absent healing". The patient and the healer are separated by distance, and the patient does improve or is healed. This is the second criterion in which I have no clear evidence of Arigó's ability. This is practiced quite commonly by many spiritual and prayer groups in many different churches.

The NINTH characteristic concerns the role of a "guide" in the healer's practice. This guide may be a voice. It may be a spirit which the healer identifies by name and who is constantly with him in his work. This is one of the great frontier areas of healing research which should be clarified.

Arigó, as I have previously indicated, always worked with a voice in his right ear, which he identified as Dr. Fritz. Without Dr. Fritz, Arigó claimed that he could not work at all. It is one of the great frustrations of my life that I was never able to devise an objective research method which would clearly distinguish between Arigó's own native genius as a healer and physician, and the presence of an alter ego, or second personality, whom he identified as a spirit. In attempting to identify the root behavior of the mind, we confront great difficulty in pinning down the concept, scope and location of the mind itself.

The TENTH characteristic for the complete healer is the ability to regenerate tissue. This may be an organ; as an ear that does not function because the nerves have been destroyed; an eye, a limb, or, based on cases in literature, even life itself, when all indications confirm that the person has definitely been dead, for as long as several days in some cases. I have never seen any evidence of this ability in any healer. I include it as a part of the lore and the literature of man's history in this area, and I do believe this ability should be actively sought after, especially since it is subject to experimental enquiry using amphibia and other lower organisms.

Of these ten criteria for the complete healer, Arigó demonstrated seven. The three which he lacked were (1) the ability to heal himself; (2) the ability to heal at a distance, or lack of evidence thereof; and (3) lack of evidence of his ability to regenerate tissue.

In the two medical research expeditions which I organized (1963 and 1968) to study Arigó, the quality which impressed me most was his commonness, the earthiness expressed in his body. He certainly was not the conventional image of a spiritual person. In trying to establish whether he had unusual physiological abilities, we could not confirm that he could control his blood pressure, or brain waves, or body temperature, or any physiological variable which we normally work with in autogenic training. Thus, Arigó can be considered to have been a perfectly normal individual, as determined by modern medical standards.

Arigó saw 300 to 400 patients during an ordinary work day, in a simple wooden building which he called his clinic. He never asked his patients what was wrong, although they sometimes volunteered this information. Arigó wrote prescriptions as though taking dictation from the voice in his right ear. These he wrote in a particular shorthand illegible to everyone but his assistant Altomiro, who then typed them out.

Our medical research team witnessed and documented on film, many of Arigó's surgical procedures. One shows Arigó scraping with a sharp knife the cornea of an unanesthetized patient's eye, simply to demonstrate that there is no pain, no damage, even though the knife is actually cutting into tissue. Our subsequent examination confirmed that whatever incisions may have occurred, they had been immediately healed.

We also witnessed Arigó using a very dull knife to treat an abscess on a patient's back. The patient did not feel any pain as Arigó cut through the abscess, but as Altomiro cleaned out this same wound later, the patient felt strong pain. Arigó then performed another operation on this patient, to again demonstrate that there was no pain. In this instance he treated a sebaceous infected cyst of the scalp, using his hands to squeeze the capsule and then actually pull it out without surgically dissecting it from the scalp or from the periosteum of the skull, which from a surgical standpoint is an almost impossible feat. Arigó normally did not bother with such cases, as they were simple minor surgery: "Don't waste my time, your own physician can do a better job than I." Arigó performed these only for research purposes.

I might add that Arigó had the ability to stop a patient's bleeding, simply by using a cloth or rag to wipe the wound.

Once I witnessed a fly land on a patient's nose during eye surgery. The patient noticed it and brushed it away. However, when the fly landed in the area of the surgery, the patient was not aware of it at all.

Arigó's great genius lay in treating illnesses diagnosed as "incurable". I can personally testify, as can my medical colleagues, that he was eminently successful with practically every type of cancer that is known to man. He usually treated it with chemotherapy, and in some extreme cases, surgery. Although I did not witness this particular case, we have reliable testimony and X-ray documentation concerning a patient with a very advanced cancer of the stomach, who was not given much time to live. When Arigó arrived at the clinic, he spotted this man out of a line of hundreds. "You, come in immediately. You are really sick." Arigó diagnosed immediately that the man had a cancer of the stomach, and quickly wrote out a prescription, instructing him to take a certain number of drugs continuously over a 24-hour period, and advised him to return the next day, all of which the patient did. The following day, Arigó performed a procedure which was rare in his practice. He put his hands through the patient's abdominal wall without using a knife, and extracted a lot of bloody tissue. The patient returned to his doctor, and subsequent X-rays of his stomach, etc. confirmed that his cancer was eliminated.

Although Arigó was able to treat every known type of "incurable" illness, he turned many patients away for a number of reasons. I've previously stated that patients who could be successfully treated by their own physicians were told not to waste Arigó's time. Patients with malingering illnesses, either brought on by themselves for personal gain, or for psychological reasons, were also turned away. There were also patients whom Arigó could not treat. "Your time has come. I cannot do anything for you. God bless you," he would say.

To my knowledge, Arigó never charged for his treatments during his entire career, and always had a full-time job to support his family.

Let us examine some of the inner workings of the Arigó phenomenon. We have Arigó's thesis and claim that everything he did was programmed by a guide, a voice, a spirit entity. This is one of the great problems challenging us. I cannot discount this thesis because I cannot disprove it and because, certainly, the weight of evidence, particularly in the area of medical diagnosis, leads me to believe that Arigó was working with intelligence far beyond that which Arigó possessed in every other situation, and beyond that of the great medical diagnosticians whom I have known in my lifetime. One of the problems before us is to try to determine whether this is indeed an aspect of mind as related to individual brain, or whether this is mind unrelated to a specific brain, in the true sense in which spiritists, for example, teach and believe.

Human beings are invariant products of a production line, and while each may differ in individuality, we more or less come out of the same mold. This invariance of biological reproduction is certainly a fact of medicine. If we accept this premise, we acknowledge that the healer, as well as the patient, has a complete blueprint for some 60 trillion cells which is reflected in a mental or parallel structure to the cell structure. A cooperative effect is created between the two; you might call it resonance. If for example, the healer, who has a healthy heart, can transfer his heart field to the patient's ailing heart, then a lining-up effect is created with the healthy field, and the patient will improve.

This can be supplemented by molecular deficiencies as I've indicated. If for example, you do not—as a patient—produce a certain type of enzyme, the master blueprint could induce it in you. While this is a nice hypothesis, it did not hold true for Arigó. However, it could be rigorously tested in the case of manual healing.

This leads us to the consideration that there may be common characteristics throughout all life forms. For example, water is common to all life and is a very important carrier. It may, in fact, be a vehicle for the type of blueprinting which I have just described.

Another hypothesis which we may consider, and I think we must be very imaginative in these areas, is that other civilizations have existed elsewhere. Other civilizations may have reached our planet with abilities that can direct/program/influence human beings, animals, weather cycles, etc., very much as we do with certain earthly types of telecommunications and teleaction equipment. I certainly could not discount this possibility without further evidence. I mention this possibly because our research team, while in Brazil, witnessed many UFO sightings in Arigó's vicinity. We also photographed them. The mere fact that they appeared in Arigó's proximity, and that the area in which he lived was unusually active with UFO's, calls for further investigation.

The last hypothesis to consider is related to the first—the parallel to the known genetic programming of cells that reproduces an organism and sets up all the equivalent parallel genetically coded instructions which are not actual molecules, but some kind of parallel mind effect, an isomorphic field, which I call psi plasma in my book, *Beyond Telepathy*,[2] which may, in fact, give rise to the phenomena that we see in healing. I put this out as a hypothesis to be tested.

In creating the model for the complete healer, I do not feel I have exhausted all possibilities. Some of the great religious literature of the world, for example, may also provide possibilities, and in true scientific tradition, we must keep all these in mind while assessing this phenomenon.

REFERENCES

1. A. Puharich, "Psychic Research and the Healing Process". In *Psychic Exploration*. Edited by John White. (New York: Punam, 1974), Chapter 14.
2. *Beyond Telepathy* (London: Darton, Longman and Todd, 1962).

4

PARANORMAL HEALING
IN GREAT BRITAIN

Gilbert Anderson

Today's Reality

Great Britain has perhaps the best organized spiritual healing program in the world. Three thousand persons, members of the National Federation of Spiritual Healers are regularly engaged in healing. Government approval has been granted for qualified members of this organization to treat patients in 1,500 national hospitals in Great Britain, despite what was originally very strong opposition from the British Medical Association. It is estimated that 1,000,000 were treated during the past year in Great Britain by the above-mentioned members, and approximately 17,000 non-members. Treatment was by absent healing or by laying on of hands.

An ever growing bond of trust and co-operation is manifesting between spiritual healers, medical doctors and scientific researchers due to the growing recognition of the reality of spiritual values in healing that have hitherto been disclaimed by orthodox medical practice. As doctors see daily proof of the efficacy of spiritual healing in specific cases where medical science has failed, more and more are turning towards healers, not only seeking help for their patients, but often also for themselves.

Through the tireless efforts of Harry Edwards and the National Federation, healing from a spiritual or divine source has become accepted by the layman as a perfectly natural part of his life. Through public demonstration, Mr. Edwards and others have shown (often with medical doctors present to examine patients both before and after healing) the dramatic change that takes place in the chemical composition of the body with the freeing of calcified arthritic joints, dispersal of growths, restoring sight and hearing, overcoming of paralysis, etc. Often the change takes place in a matter of minutes—something which seems completely inexplicable to medical science. It is the activities of healers day after day throughout all of the principal towns and cities of Great Britain that has made this the readily acceptable therapy that it is today.

The National Federation of Spiritual Healers which is just 21 years old, has been largely responsible for this progress, by drawing together the hundreds of isolated individual healers and small groups of healers throughout the country. This permitted them to learn from each other, whereas previously they had remained outdated in their practice, simply through isolation.

In 1971 the N.F.S.H. decided that it should organize research in the healing field. It was agreed at a meeting of doctors, scientists and healers that since cancer constituted one of the worst scourges in modern life, the initial research should concentrate on the causes and alleviation of this disease.

A very intimate 130-item questionnaire was compiled with advice from the medical profession, to be circulated to as many cancer sufferers as possible and the results computerized. It was not until these forms were ready to go out that it was found that although thousands of people had cancer, only about 1% had been told by their doctors the actual nature of the disease. Finally a sufficient number of patients were found and a corresponding control group contacted of healthy people who did not appear to be cancer prone, and comparisons were made. As anticipated, the test showed a strong destructive stress element present in all the cancer patients. In the case of the control group stresses were present, but of an entirely different nature and did not impair their health.

As a result of these findings, a pilot study into the cause and cure of cancer was then introduced. Now, a year later, the results indicate that stress appears to play as large a part in triggering cancer as it does in initiating other illnesses. These studies also show that removal of stress is a strong factor in overcoming and often in preventing illness.

Fourteen months ago the writer, together with a medical doctor, set up a pilot study group of terminal cancer patients, similar to that of Dr. Carl Simonton in America, except that instead of radiation therapy, we substituted spiritual healing. Otherwise, we used similar techniques involving group therapy relaxation, mental imagery, and directed thought. It is significant that after thirteen months, four of the original seven patients have not only survived the original three months life expectancy given by their respective specialists fifteen months ago, but have been told that no trace of cancer can now be found! As a result of the success of this initial pilot study, eight other experimental groups are being set up in different parts of the country. There are now a number of medical consultants working closely with these groups and it is hoped that by the time this book is published, the British Medical Council will have eased certain rulings and thus allow doctors to work in closer co-operation with many of the non-medically registered therapies, for the overall benefit of the patients.

The Path Of Progress

Success is not achieved easily and the N.F.S.H. has fought hard and long to reach the position of respect that it enjoys today. Thirty years ago spiritual healing was frowned upon as something "not quite nice" and indeed was being conducted by a few healers in a way that brought discredit to the practice as a whole, not through any ill-intent, but simply due to their ignorance of what was really necessary and how much of what they were doing was not only unnecessary but often objectionable to the patient and to onlookers.

The first task of the Federation was to stage mass healing services in large public auditoriums. Following the public demonstration, up to 300 healers would then treat the many patients needing attention. Many unacceptable practices were noted which would tend either to frighten off a would-be patient or would hold spiritual healing up to ridicule. However, by close and constant supervision of healers, their practice has become simple, dignified and natural, and cannot offend, no matter what beliefs one holds.

We believe that this better and more natural healing is partly responsible for the close liaison between healers and doctors during the past two years. Another contributing factor is the growing knowledge that stress and one's mental attitude are largely responsible for modern disease.

It was not until after World War II that healers in Great Britain were free of the stigma of the Witchcraft Act and liable to punishment under this outdated law. It was finally repealed only after lengthy pressure.

As with many new organizations, there was the initial tendency for the Federation to cultivate quantity rather than quality. However, when undesirable results of this tendency became apparent, steps were taken to ensure that healer-members of the Federation maintain a high standard of efficiency and conduct. When a healer completes his training (described later) he receives a certificate of acceptance as a N.F.S.H. Practicing Healer. Through the hard work and determination of the late Gordon Turner when he was Chairman, N.F.S.H. healers were finally granted government approval to treat patients in 1,500 hospitals throughout Great Britain and later the Federation was given corporate membership in the United Nations Association.

Training And Beliefs Of Healers

For 17 years the Federation and other organizations have held schools and seminars for intensive study by groups of 100-400 under expert supervision. These are held in holiday camps, hotels, universities, and at local headquarters for both home and overseas students. Training courses in relaxation, meditation, mind control and contact healing are offered as an evening study at headquarters throughout the winter months. Tape recorded meditation instruction and exercises are available for those not able to attend instructional classes.

Over the years correspondence study courses have been introduced which have been a tremendous asset in helping the development of healing in all parts of the world. These courses cover four different aspects of healing: absent healing and meditation; theory and practice of spiritual healing; scientific approach to spiritual healing; and anatomy and physiology. Other courses are being prepared.

The Federation is a non-denominational organization and most world religions are represented in its membership. Each healer realizes that he himself is not doing the healing but rather is being used as a channel through which the healing is to manifest from a higher source of intelligence. Members believe that healing is God's gift to everyone no matter what his color or belief system might be and hence they make no distinction regarding the color or religious belief of a patient. The healer-members are bound, as is the orthodox medical practitioner, by the oath of Hippocrates regarding healer-patient relationship.

Compensation For Services

The Federation is opposed to the charging of fees by its members for treatment given. However it does appreciate that in many instances the healer's cost of travelling to a patient should be met by the patient, unless the healer is in comfortable financial circumstances and can afford to travel about at his own expense. If a patient wishes to make a donation in appreciation for help received, the healer should accept and in the event he does not require this contribution for the upkeep of his own sanctuary, it should be passed to headquarters whose cost of maintaining an adequate healing service throughout the world is an ever increasing problem. The greatest compensation to any healer for the time and effort given to this work is seeing the joy one is able to bring to so many medically helpless cases. When a healing takes place as so often happens with medically terminal conditions, it does not just react on the patient himself; rather the joy and happiness extends out to the whole family and friends in ever widening circles. It is seeing these reactions that warms one's heart and really makes life a wonderful experience.

Attitude Of The Established Church

The "closed shop" attitude of the average clergyman is still very much in evidence within the orthodox church, possibly because the clergy do not feel competent to fulfil the healing part of their ministry. Yet, to date they have been generally unable to widen their vision and attitude to Christianity sufficiently to accept that healing can be brought to bear *outside* their church. It has been the orthodox church's disregard of this vital part of its ministry over the years that was responsible for the rebirth of healing amongst Spiritualists in the early part of the century. There must be many thousands of people alive today only because of what was done by Spiritualists with the wider knowledge and understanding of life in its entirety. These pioneers not only extended life for these patients, but changed their lives from misery to happiness through their healing ministry. Sadly, the majority of orthodox ministers still look upon spiritual healing done outside the orthodox church as witchcraft and associated with the devil!

In this connection, it is perhaps significant that the churches which have the fullest congregations are the few which include the laying on of hands as part of their ministry [*See* Chapter 21 for a detailed comment on this subject.]

Attitude Of Medical Science

To protect its members and the general public, many years ago the British Medical Assoc. introduced legislation as a safeguard against a "quack" or charlatan or other unqualified person being set up in practice as a doctor. These laws also forbid registered medical practitioners from associating with any non-medically registered practitioners or therapies. If a doctor felt that spiritual healing or any other form of non-medical treatment might be beneficial to his patient he could not contact a non-registered practitioner, else he might be disciplined for breaking the rules. It is understandable that the Medical Council should take all steps to protect the good name and well-being of its members and the general public. However, the proven merit of therapies previously non-acceptable in their fields has aroused tremendous interest within orthodox medical and scientific research circles, and sooner or later will result in some updating of the medical practice act. For the time being this has led to the "I'll take a chance" attitude being adopted by individual doctors today who wish to cooperate with spiritual healers.

Attitude Of Individual Doctors

If a doctor has the well-being of a patient truly at heart and feels that medical science has done all it can and without success, it would surely be inhuman to deprive the patient of any possible means of help that was available. The scientific mind is rapidly becoming aware that man's knowledge has its limitations but there is a supreme being (God, or any other name one cares to use) that can, and often does, make the seemingly impossible possible in the curing of medically incurable diseases.

Four years ago when the National Federation contemplated researching into stress in relation to disease, it offered a substantial case for investigation by the British Cancer Council and other medically sponsored research councils. The very idea was ridiculed because it was "contrary" to their school of thought. In reality it was probably not as ridiculous as the outdated existing medical laws.

Over the past two years, however, the writer has been invited to speak on this approach to cancer research to medical and scientific conferences with highly successful results. Even the small initial pilot study with the relaxation/positive thought/healing therapy group reported earlier in this chapter created much interest on the part of doctors and consultants. Now they are offering their services to assist in the formation and continuation of additional experimental groups being set up in other parts of the country. Dare we hope that in two or three years this research devised by the N.F.S.H. may produce the answer that medical science has spent millions of pounds and over half a century searching for? If we allow research and indeed life itself to be directed by more spiritual motives, maybe the world will yet be a place fit for heroes and humans to live in.

We are today witnessing an explosion of scientific understanding which dwarfs anything seen before. This is taking place on a world-wide level. The very thought of scientists contemplating anything spiritually oriented in relation to their work would have been quite unbelievable even a few years ago, but now, not only are they showing an ever growing interest but are offering their knowledge and experience in helping to explore this new avenue of research.

The Merging Of The Paths

The policy of the National Federation of Spiritual Healers has, from its inception, been one of seeking closer co-operation with medical practice. It has been the aim of the Federation to break down, wherever possible, the prejudices that have existed for so long. These prejudices were partly due to the misconception of spiritual healing held by orthodox churches and medicine; and partly to the poor presentation of healing by many Spiritualists in the early days when healing was so often linked with seances, darkened rooms and inferior mediumship. It would seem that the world is at last sickening of the destructive influences of materialism and is seeking more understanding and more compassion in the healing of mankind's ills. We detect a rapidly changing attitude and broadening outlook amongst the scientific and medical minds, with their invitation of closer liaison in the work of healing on all levels.

To date medical science has looked upon man as a purely physical being and hence has concerned itself solely with the maintenance of a physical body. Spiritual healers however believe that man is a *spiritual* being as well as a physical one and this spiritual counterpart is the eternal life force within us. It is this spirit or soul or mind that is often sick and needing healing. Briefly then, it is believed that medical science treats the effect of disease, often like pruning of branches from a tree with diseased roots hoping that the disease will not continue to spread. Spiritual healing, on the other hand, goes first to the cause— the diseased roots, and having removed this cause, the body's natural metabolism will rid itself of the effect. With the failure of medicine to overcome so many medically classified terminal diseases, and with the proliferating adverse side effects from prescribed drugs, doctors and scientists are demonstrating their willingness to investigate other channels which seem to be achieving success where they fail.

Let us hope that man is reaching the stage when he can believe that all forms of healing have something of value to offer to humanity and a closer liaison between them can only be for the good of all people.

In late 1975 the N.S.F.H. sponsored the formation of a World Federation of Healing with the object of drawing together all non-medically registered forms of healing. The Healing Research Trust which is an affiliate of N.F.S.H. is concerned with the goal that ultimately it will be possible to direct enquirers to whichever type of healing is considered to be most suitable to the individual. This activity and the developing of a scientific/medical network throughout the country suggest that in the not-too-distant future non-medically registered and registered practitioners will be working side by side for the healing of the whole person, not just the physical body. Considering how far spiritual healing has come in Great Britain during the past two decades, this does not seem to be an unrealistic goal.

5

OBSERVATIONS

George W. Meek

The import of the preceding chapters is that paranormal healing is "an idea whose time has come."

The brief introductions we have just had to the healers indicate that their work poses a goodly number of mysteries. Just *how far* science will have to go if it is to unravel these mysteries of paranormal healing is shown by these four well-documented items in the life of the relatively uneducated Brazilian healer, Arigó, who:

- Made almost instantaneous on-the-spot medical diagnosis of each of 500 patients with an accuracy of 95% as determined by a team of American medical doctors.

- Treated as many as 1,500 patients a week in his spare time—patients with the complete spectrum of human ailments—patients from all walks of life including members of the family of the President of Brazil.

- Wrote prescriptions for a wide variety of materials—some of which had not been dispensed for many years, and some European drugs so newly developed that they were not yet on the druggists' shelves in Brazil.

- Performed minor and major surgery in minutes with only a pocket knife, stopped bleeding almost instantaneously, and caused greatly accelerated closure of the opening with few, if any reported cases of infection.

It will be a long time until the rank and file healer can be trained to a level of performance equaling that of Arigó! Therefore let us assemble such observations as can be made at this time about the *typical* healers working today in Brazil, England and the U.S.A. The work in the Philippines is treated separately in Part II.

1. A healer may be of either sex; of any race or color; and he may or may not adhere to any organized religion.

2. Lack of formal education is NOT a barrier to development as a good healer—it may well be a positive advantage.

3. Healing abilities may be developed at any time of life, from adolescence to past 60.

4. Once developed, healing abilities need not decrease with age.

5. The patient does not need faith in the healer. However, it seems to help if the patient has a strong belief system of his own.

6. The healer does not necessarily need to have physical contact with the patient but such contact may be of help in situations involving joints or the skeletal structure.

7. Some healers do not need to be in the immediate presence of the patient.

8. The level of healing ability varies greatly between individual healers and is dependent on native abilities, desire for service (love), attunement with the cosmos, and experience with and understanding of human nature.

9. Some healers are more successful with certain types of ailments than with others.

10. Most, and perhaps all, of the healing "miracles" attributed to Jesus of Nazareth in the New Testament are daily performed in various parts of the world by the healers, collectively, if not individually.

11. No healer has a 100% success record with his patients any more than the best of Western medical clinics, but the healer often has success with patients who received no help from conventional medicine.

12. The healing can take place practically instantaneously, but most often takes days and, in some cases, several weeks or months.

13. A profound, intuitive knowledge of human nature enables some healers to help persons who could not otherwise be helped.

14. Healers are almost invariably warm, loving people with a great concern for their patients. (Often the emotional make-up of the healers is in pleasant contrast to that of the patients seeking help!)

    Additional tentative observations:

15. It is probably difficult for a selfish, power- or money-hungry person to achieve his full potential for serving as a healer.

16. Some successful healers who became preoccupied or obsessed with ego or money making, appear to suffer a decline in healing abilities.

17. The healer does not need faith in himself as a healer. The overwhelming majority of healers whose work has been studied in depth have a strong, personal belief system in a higher power—even if it is just being "simpatico with nature".

While this book is primarily about healers, we will comment briefly on the patients and their doctors. One observation about the patients stands out above all others: in 99% of the cases they have not even the slightest knowledge of the part *their own thoughts and emotions* played on triggering the cellular malfunction or dysfunction.

What observation can be made about orthodox medicine which for one reason or another did not provide the results which the patients rightly or wrongly expected? A viewpoint often expressed by the medical profession is epitomized in this statement taken from private correspondence with the head of the Dept. of Psychiatry of a large American medical school:

> "Many patients who go to healers maintain they have been abandoned by orthodox medicine, when in fact,
>
> a. They have never been properly examined, or
> b. They refuse to accept the diagnosis made, or
> c. They refuse to accept the treatment offered."

Certainly no part of this statement applies to the ten cases selected by doctors for submission to Mrs. Worrall; to Mr. Edwards' patient whose leg would not need to be amputated; nor to the greatly accelerated healing of the bruised tissue by Rolling Thunder before the assembled doctors and scientists; nor to most of the other cases mentioned.

Although some medical doctors may have patients whose conduct prior to visiting a healer is described in the above quotation, a fact infinitely more important is that our present technological medicine is almost entirely based on the treatment of *symptoms*. This is largely a result of the fact that, in the case of many patients and many types of illness, the medical doctor, *no matter how well trained,* is in ignorance of what actually induced the malfunction in the first place.

And as to claims about the accuracy of clinical diagnosis, it must be admitted that it, in fact, is not all that good, as several cases reported in Chapter 2 demonstrate. In this connection a 1974 bulletin from Life Extension Institute, 1185 Avenue of the Americas, N.Y., N.Y., 10036, (which has had 50 years of experience in making health examinations of business and government leaders) announced that the accuracy of its diagnoses with relation to heart and circulatory disorders had, as a result of newly purchased equipment, been raised from 15% to 25%!

* * *

Interesting and informative as has been the review of paranormal healing in Brazil, England, Mexico, and the U.S.A., this book would be incomplete if it did not include an in-depth study of the highly controversial work of just a few dozen healers in a small area of the island of Luzon in the Philippines.

II

PARANORMAL HEALING IN THE PHILIPPINES

Until recently the Espiritista healers in the Philippines have provided one of the best research laboratories in the world for the study of psychic, faith, and mental healing. For that reason we present the results of six years of on-the-spot research by specialists in several fields.

Contradictory and controversial reports have circulated in various aspects of paranormal healing in the Philippines. The phenomena are significant and merit examination in some depth. The next seven chapters offer a basis for understanding this admittedly bewildering area.

6

THE HEALERS

George W. Meek

We will meet some of the better known healers and learn about the types of patients who spend time and money to travel long distances to seek their help.

Native Filipinos, like the healers whose work was reported in the preceding chapters, often have outstanding results in their healing efforts. In past times many of these healings would have been labeled "miracles".

There are minor differences, of course. Against the many thousands of healers in both England and Brazil there are, in 1975, fewer than 30 Filipino healers who regularly work with foreign patients. Many of these healers have a limited command of the English language and most have had only a few years of formal schooling. These two factors combine to a point that researchers quickly learn that they can obtain very little insight from the healer himself as to what is going on in his work with the patient. Another important point is that until recently these healers have had to receive their patients in native surroundings which bore little resemblance to the hospitals, clinics and doctors' offices with which the patients have had life-long association. With a few foreign patients this had an adverse psychological impact.

Why have serious scientists and other researchers taken the time and money to travel literally halfway around the world and put up with tropical heat, earthquakes, typhoons and other discomforts when they could have researched paranormal healing projects in their own countries? What did they find so interesting that collectively 18 of them have spent the equivalent of 120 weeks on the other side of the planet? Were they so naive that they just disregarded the many reports of other observers as to the amount of deception and sleight-of-hand said to be prevalent in the Philippines? Was the 90-minute British TV documentary (?) film correct in suggesting that the whole healing scene in the Philippines was an outright farce designed solely to reap tourist dollars?

What the scientists found of such compelling interest is known as materialization, dematerialization and apport phenomena—each of which we describe briefly:

Materialization—The appearance of temporary, more or less organized substances in various degrees of solidification and possessing human, animal or mineral properties.

Dematerialization—The disappearance of temporarily or permanently organized substances in various degrees of solidification.

Apport—An object, either animate or inanimate, which, after apparent penetration through matter such as buildings, often arrives at the scene of action following a seemingly instantaneous transmission or teleportation from nearby, or from thousands of miles away.

Since the death of Arigó, these phenomena exist in Brazil only on a limited scale. They have not existed in any substantial way in England for almost 50 years and the few scientists there who risked their reputations to investigate these matters early in this century lacked the present level of scientific understanding necessary to give any credence to their work. Such phenomena are reported to exist in some parts of Africa, and in very small areas in India but the travel, living and communication problems in those areas are even less inviting than in the Philippines.

"But what," one asks, "is so interesting and important about materialization, apport and psychoenergetic phenomena?" It is as simple as this: In the light of present scientific knowledge, such phenomena CANNOT exist. THEY VIOLATE WHAT SCIENCE KNOWS ABOUT THE MATERIAL UNIVERSE.

If these phenomena *do* exist then much of what we *think* we know in the fields of medicine, religion, and science needs immediate revision.

So, in brief, that is what this book is all about. The many researchers who have collaborated on these investigations now state, "These phenomena *do* exist, and we had better get on with the job of taking a new look not only at medicine, religion and science, but also at our whole concept of Man and his place in the Cosmos!"

It is fortunate that these studies took place when they did. For various reasons, conditions have developed within the past two years which would make it extremely difficult to carry through these studies today. (These reasons will be developed in Chapter 10.)

Now, before detailing the work of these seven healers from the Philippines, we will introduce each of them to you.

JOSEFINA SISON

Josefina is a woman in her early thirties who has been healing since the age of eighteen. She lives with her husband and three children in a rural area in the heart of the rice fields of northern Luzon. She and her neighbors live about as close to nature as possible, with water buffalo, ducks, pigs, goats and chickens free to wander the area around her home and her small Spiritista chapel. There is no electricity and no running water. The literal translation of the name of the street on which she lives is, "New Pig-pen Road".

Josefina had perhaps the equivalent of two or three years of schooling. She has no notion of the inner working of the human body and, as with practically all native healers, it is a total waste of time to ask her how she knows what to do with all of her patients. Yet she works seven days a week, making herself available to all native Filipinos as well as to the busloads of foreigners who drive up the dusty road to reach her chapel. She seems to be able to help many people, some of whom, like the Australian whose case we have chosen to report, feel amply repaid for the time and money it costs to travel thousands of miles to reach New Pig-pen Road. The Australian, who drives a Jeep in the roadless out-back country, gave us these comments:

> I have had great pain from a cyst growing at the lower end of my spine. This is a condition prevalent among Jeep and truck drivers who work only on the rough roads and areas in Australia where we have no roads. The operation usually performed is to cut out the cyst and make a dish-shaped area which is then packed with cotton wool. This is to make the wound heal from the bottom near the spine to the top. Otherwise, it would not heal over with a strong skin and there might be an infection. It is not a big operation but a painful one. You would need to lie on your face for a few days and then remain in the hospital until the wound healed sufficiently.
>
> I have had this complaint for some fifteen years and I have periodically gone to doctors who have opened it to give relief from the pressure built up at the base of the spine. They always advised me to do this and put up with the pain rather than to have an operation.
>
> The pain was not too bad when I left Australia but the constant sitting and shifting from side to side to relieve the pain during the seven-hour plane ride, the airport buses, and the four-hour drive from Manila to Josefina's house resulted in misery. I came to this woman in great pain and agony. I walked in to her, told her what it was, laid face down on the wooden table, and within thirty seconds she removed a cyst which looked like a pigeon's egg. When I stood up the pain was all gone and there was no scar. That was three days ago and I have not had pain since, even though we drove to Manila and then drove back here again this morning so that Josefina can give me a second treatment on an eye condition.

When Josefina was asked how she knows what is wrong with the patients, she said, "There are three stages of knowing. In most cases, I can tell with my 'third eye'." [Ed.: clairvoyantly] "In more difficult cases, I feel that my hands are guided to the area needing attention and I hear a voice in my ear. In extremely difficult cases, I do both of these and in addition I sit down and do some automatic writing. As soon as the pencil moves along the paper, I know what the pencil is writing and it may be a great surprise to me."

FELISA MACANAS

On January 29, 1975, I drove through the rice fields in northern Luzon with Dr. Alfred Stelter,[1] Alex and Betty Bull from Sydney, Australia, and Benjamin Singson—a Filipino who has probably spent more time than any other person searching out and becoming acquainted with the native healers in these outlying areas. We stopped, unannounced, at the home of Felisa Macanas in a small village where the rice fields suddenly end and the lush green mountain juts upward.

As we entered late in the afternoon, Felisa was sitting with her husband and four of her six children. I sat beside her on the settee where she was nursing the baby whom she had been carrying in the womb when our medical research team had observed her working on a patient at the Merciful Endeavors Center in Quezon City on the outskirts of Manila some months earlier. As we chatted, Ben recalled that six days previously he had brought to Felisa a high school student from Guam where a laboratory explosion had put glass fragments in his face and eyes. Ben proceeded to give details, telling how Felisa had removed three pieces of glass.

Alex Bull listened attentively and then said, "Eight years ago when I raised a window sash, the glass shattered and my palm became embedded with many slivers of glass. We removed at that time what we could and over the following months I cut out several more sharp splinters. The spot at the base of my thumb has occasionally festered but, try as much as I could, I have never been able to dig out the piece of glass that must still be embedded below the muscle fibers. Do you think you could take it out?"

After the nursing was completed, a low stool was placed in front of Felisa, and Alex sat down facing her, with his hand, palm up on her knee. After a few moments of attunement, Felisa's altered breathing indicated she had entered into a very light trance state. She placed two fingers of each hand over the area of the palm indicated by Alex. She gently moved her finger over the area for perhaps half a minute. Then she asked her husband to hold the open Bible, face downward, about a foot over her head for perhaps the next twenty seconds.

Within two minutes of the time Felisa started, Dr. Stelter, Alex and I observed, with our eyes only eighteen inches from the action spot, the sharp point of a piece of glass appear on the surface. Felisa took this between thumb and forefinger and held it out to show us. It was very sharp and slightly over one half inch in length.

There was no blood on the palm or on the glass.

There was no sign of a "hole" in the tissue of the palm. We walked outside and with the use of a supplementary closeup lens, the photograph in photo section Fig. C1 was taken.

A glass sliver had apparently been removed without surgery, drugs, anesthetic or pain, just as the glass had been removed from the student a week previously. However, we must say from a scientific standpoint we have no way of knowing whether this was or was not the particular piece of glass which had been embedded in Alex's palm. All that can be reported factually is that in correspondence later, Alex reported he had not had pain in the area on which the glass sliver appeared between Felisa's fingers.

The mechanism by which the glass was seemingly transferred through the muscle fibers and the skin is totally outside the understanding of science. In any event, the experience adds an additional dimension to our introduction to the healers and the range of their activities. (In the following chapter, Dr. Stelter considers the problem of building a scientific base, as does Tiller in Chapter 18 and Meek in Chapter 19. The possibility of deception and sleight-of-hand will be taken up in Chapter 10.)

TEAM HEALING—ROMY and JOE BUGARIN, JOSÉ MERCADO, MARCELO JAINER

At the age of 39, Mrs. Noeline Stein of 321 Devonport Road, Tauranga, New Zealand was seriously injured in an automobile accident and was hospitalized. Among numerous complications, she was unable to see. The doctors told her that the retinas of both eyes were damaged, and that there was a serious bleeding condition. She was given six laser beam treatments. Her ophthalmologist reported that the retinal bleeding had stopped but that the scar tissue was extensive and accounted for the lack of vision.

For the next four years Mrs. Stein was blind, but continued to cook and do the homework for her husband and two children. She was given a "talking book" machine by the New Zealand Foundation for the Blind. After her husband read an article on "psychic surgery" in the *Bay of Plenty Times* she got in touch with persons who were organizing a group to visit the Philippines and with these 38 other persons flew to Manila.

The party put themselves in the hands of a group of four healers who rendered their services in a large hotel in downtown Manila, remaining two weeks, with each patient having several sessions with one or more healers. Healer Romy Bugarin, assisted by his brother Joe worked with Mrs. Stein. During the two-week period, the group attended several lectures given in their hotel by Joaquin Cunanan, the purpose of which was to give each patient an insight into the process by which his own negative thoughts and destructive emotions can adversely affect the cells and organs of his body, opening the way for illness, and dis-ease; and conversely how his positive thoughts and emotions can work with the vast natural healing capability of the body to restore the body to health and wholeness.

On the closing day of their visit in Manila, Mrs. Stein stood before the assembled group and summarized her experience: "After the first treatment, I just could not believe it. I looked and saw my walking stick and my purse lying nearby on the dresser. Someone helped me to the door and I remember thinking, 'but I can *see* the door.' " She continued her remarks by telling of the additional improvement which followed on subsequent days, and demonstrated that she could now read the newspaper. She told of the thrilling anticipation of being able to look into the faces of her family upon her return to New Zealand—faces she had not seen for four years. She then presented her white "blindman's cane" to the healer's staff, saying, "Obviously I have no further need for this and I give it as a token of appreciation to Romy, Joe, Mr. Cunanan and the staff."

A letter in the editor's files from Mrs. Stein, written months after her return home, tells of the delight in resuming her normal life, including gardening, driving the automobile, and "catching up on my reading." Her letter reports that the majority of the other members in her group were benefitted by their visit to the healers.

A few days after writing the above paragraphs about the New Zealand patient, my research for some portions of the chapter dealing with theory of healing took me to Puerto Rico. While in San Juan, I visited Mrs. Maria J. at her home.

Like Mrs. Stein, Mrs. J. had become totally blind, and after having made an unsuccessful effort to get relief through the best available medical services, joined a group of patients flying to the Philippines. She arrived three days after Mrs. Stein and was under the care of the same group of healers.

When Mrs. J's vision had first become affected she promptly put herself in the hands of an ophthalmologist. He detected that the retina of each eye was deteriorating but could give no reason for the condition. He told her she would be completely blind in one to three months if the condition persisted. As intense headaches developed she went to an internist for a complete physical examination. Nothing of significance was detected and Mrs. J. was adjudged to be in excellent health.

Mrs. J. then went to another ophthalmologist twice each week for drops in the eyes. Eventually he gave the same prognosis as the first eye specialist. Determined to get help, Mrs. J. went to a third ophthalmologist. By the time he decided that nothing could be done, Mrs. J. had no sight in the right eye and could see only through the upper portion of the left eye. This doctor's wife kindly led Mrs. J. to the Centro Medico (American Medical Center of Puerto Rico). The ophthalmologist in charge called in three additional ophthalmologists for consultation, (now a total of seven) each making his own examination. One of these said to the patient, "The fissures or marks in the retina look almost as though they were writings in Chinese characters." They decided to make a complete X-ray examination to see if there was a brain tumor. Results negative. Finally Mrs. J. was told, "There is nothing we can do. It would be useful for science if you would go to a certain clinic in the U.S.A. and let them see these retinas. It would be interesting if science could learn the cause of this relatively sudden and complete deterioration of the retinas. However, we must say there is no expectation that you will regain your sight."

Mrs. J., now completely blind, flew to the Philippines with a group from Puerto Rico and was assigned to the same healer who was then helping to return eyesight to Mrs. Stein. Romy was assisted by two very experienced healers, Marcelo Janier and José Mercado. For the seven days following the "psychic operation" by the three healers, Romy visited Mrs. J. daily to put drops into her eyes, massage the facial muscles, and give her encouragement. In the evening she was led to the dining room where after dinner she could hear Mr. Cunanan discuss mind-body-spirit relationships.

After the second "operation", on the eighth day, Mrs. J. began to see large objects indistinctly. At the end of the third "operation", on the ninth day, much of her vision had returned. When she arrived home, her vision was back at the very satisfactory level it had been years earlier. In concluding her remarks she said that every step of the foregoing could be documented for anyone inclined to investigate. She concluded, "My husband and my three daughters are most happy that I was not content to be a scientific guinea pig."

* * *

The other side of the coin—Since the foregoing are the only references in these reports to *organized groups* of patients going to the Philippines, it is necessary to point out that the editor's files contain letters reporting that in certain groups *not even one* patient considered his trip was worthwhile. In the editor's opinion such dissatisfaction is at least in part a result of:

A. Running from one healer to another day after day, hoping that one of them can "press the magic button."

B. The failure of the group or tour leaders or organizers to *supplement the work of the healers* by:

    a. Giving the patients psychological and spiritual insights which will help them to have *greater rapport with the healer* during their time together.

    b. Making less of a circus of the whole affair with night-life and with driving day after day from one "side-show" area to another.

    c. Giving the patients with psychosomatically triggered illness,*

---

*The portion of any particular group falling into this category could vary from a low of perhaps 40% to a high of as much as 90%.

insights into their responsibility for continuing their healing
and recovery upon returning to their home environment. This
involves the positive orientation of their thoughts and emotions, adequate rest, proper diet, and the avoidance of habits
which are deleterious to health. In other words, they must learn
that *keeping* well is *their* job, not the healer's.

TONY AGPAOA

Just as no compendium of healers would be complete without mention of Arigó, it would be incomplete if it omitted reference to Antonio
Agpaoa of the Philippines. While it is very difficult to separate fact
from legend, it seems that Tony, with very little schooling, started
traveling among the villages of northern Luzon at approximately the
age of twelve, to act as a healer of his fellow Filipinos. Now, in his
middle thirties, he and three assistant healers handle a flow of patients
from all over the world who come to the Dominican Hill Clinic in
Baguio City. This clinic, perched at an elevation of one mile, in the
rugged mountains, a five-hour bus ride north of Manila, looks down
toward the China Sea from a site whose natural beauty rivals that of
any health resort in the world.

In the two decades it took Tony to climb from the rice fields to this
position of achievement, his activities, escapades, and accomplishments have become a living legend. The many facets of his personality
and character and his diverse abilities read more like fiction than fact.
Saint, sinner, healer extraordinary at times, genial host, inspirational
leader, and construction superintendent to his one hundred Filipino
workmen who labored sixteen hours per day at low pay to convert a
long abandoned Dominican Monastery into a luxury hotel and
clinic—he is all of these and more. (The most complete portraits of Tony
presently available are given by Harold Sherman[2] and Tom Valentine[3].)

In recent years, Tony has had the help and guidance of a young
German psychic and medical practitioner, Sigrun Seutemann, who
herself was restored to health with Tony's assistance and who subsequently has taken more than twelve hundred patients from central
Europe to Tony for healing (Chapter 9).

The case chosen to serve as an example of Tony's work is one that I
have investigated thoroughly and followed for a period of two years.
This case of A.L. was brought to my attention by her writer-
photographer husband who had taken a photographic record of the
case. In her thirties, she was losing a 13-year battle with cancer. The
condition had started in the pelvic area but had progressed to the lungs.
The maximum program of radiation therapy had been administered.
The surgeons had given her six months to live. She had developed a
serious infection, had lost much weight, and was being kept alive by
intravenous antibiotic therapy and feeding as she lay in her hospital
bed in California. Her internist, a lung specialist, who had visited the

Philippines and had seen some remarkable work by the healers, told the couple of his observations there.

They discussed the matter and concluded that even though she might die on the long, hard journey, they had nothing to lose. She was removed from her hospital bed, taken to the plane and eventually was "operated" on by Tony. In fact, a series of eight "operations" were performed over several weeks.

Five weeks after arrival in the Philippines, A.L. had put on weight, was able to eat well and was sufficiently recovered to return to the U.S. unaccompanied. Gradually her strength returned. Such problems as remained were confined largely to excessively irradiated tissue in the pelvic area caused by the cobalt treatment. Her lungs have remained clear to this day.

A.L.'s improvement must, in part, be attributed to her own increasing level of spiritual and intellectual enlightenment. She feels she has reached a level of understanding on which she KNOWS that thoughts and emotions can trigger and accelerate the growth of cancerous cells in the body and that her thoughts and emotions determine to a great extent the environment in which healing can or cannot take place. (*See* Chapter 19.)

Like Olga Worrall, Tony Agpaoa has been studied extensively by scientists, including Dr. Hiroshi Motoyama (Chapter 14), Dr. Alfred Stelter (Chapter 7), and others.

Sigrun Seutemann, the German medical practitioner who wrote Chapter 9, is a psychic with excellent clairvoyant abilities. Based on her observations of several thousand individual treatments being performed by Tony, she said at one of our research meetings:

> While I watch Tony during healing, I see remarkable changes in his energy body. Clairvoyantly I note that he radiates energy from his body to the patient. He cannot work without a patient—he requires a living field of energy in order to work efficiently. Around his body there are many bright points of light, a turbulence of colors—blue, yellow, etc.—and as his hands approach the body, each hand has a different color with a ray from each. The better Tony's concentration, the better the ray. The energy he exchanges with the patient depends on the body of the patient, i.e. if the patient is not receptive, the energy exchange is low. [Ed. note: This description correlates well with the description of Karagulla.[4]]
>
> The main problem for Tony is attuning with Europeans, who are different from Filipinos. The Europeans are not so receptive because of their intellectual hang-ups. Tony can treat 100 Filipinos a day without any difficulty, whereas only 50 Europeans require much greater effort.
>
> If a patient is anxious or fearful on arrival, this affects the physical and the energy body. Tony aims to remove blockages in the system and rebalance and correct the flow of energy to the organs. When balanced, the patient feels much better.

After this brief contact with a few of the Filipino healers, we will turn in the following chapters to observations made of various aspects of their work, by persons who collectively have spent more than two years in detailed studies.

REFERENCES

1. Alfred Stelter, *Psi Healing* (New York: Bantam Books, 1976).
2. Harold Sherman, *"Wonder" Healers of the Philippines* (London: Psychic Press, 1966; Los Angeles: De Vorss, 1974).
3. Tom Valentine, *Psychic Surgery* (Chicago: Henry Regenery Co., 1973).
4. Shafica Karagulla, *Breakthrough to Creativity* (Los Angeles: De Vorss, 1967).

7

PSYCHOENERGETIC PHENOMENA

Alfred Stelter

One of the most important realities of our physical world is "energy". There are many forms of energy which modern physicists have traced back to four basic forms of energetic interactions. In order of decreasing strength these are:

1. The "strong interactions" which work at the subatomic level of the elementary particles and which cause also the cohesion of the atomic nucleus to the end that we have a material world to live in.

2. The electromagnetic interactions, to which the biggest part of our everyday physics can be traced.

3. The "weak interactions", which one also sees only at the sub-atomic level of the elementary particles and radioactivity.

4. The gravitational interactions which we continuously experience as gravitational pull and which paradoxically is the weakest form of all interactions. It assumes so much importance for us because the mass of our earth which is reacting with our bodies and other material aggregates, is so immense.

In addition to these scientifically acceptable interactions, there seem to exist other energetic effects, the existence of which is implied by research discussed in other portions of this book.

In Chapters 18 and 19 mention is made of "non-physical" energies. Energy forms which lie outside the physically comprehensible terrain, and are therefore non-physical will probably be viewed as physical in the growing physics of tomorrow. (When non-physical energies are mentioned in this chapter it is with this expectation.) Non-physical energy forms will play a large role in our future understanding of biological systems, and will also be closely connected with mental-spiritual happenings. They are probably working in every human being, although up to now they have been mostly overlooked. In some especially gifted people, known as mediums or sensitives, these encrgies come into interaction with our physical world, and offend our everyday scientific knowledge and so-called common sense. They are here described as *psychoenergetic manifestations*. It is possible that the non-physical energies responsible for these manifestations are produced in people and/or directly received from outside and transmitted.

I will now describe some of the psychoenergetic phenomena displayed by healers whom I have studied during the forty weeks I have spent in the Philippines since 1970. One form of expressing these psychoenergetic powers is psychokinesis, several examples of which will now be given.

Pulling Teeth

Paranormal pulling of teeth, more frequent and better in past years than today, was nevertheless demonstrated in my presence by some of the healers. With his bare fingers, sometimes with matches placed between them, the healer touched the tooth to be pulled, concentrated his mind on an "injection" against pain, and without any effort at all lifted out the tooth with thumb and index finger, even though the tooth was sitting in the jaw tightly. Frequently teeth located in hard-to-reach places were pulled, and sometimes molars which were imbedded deeply in the gums. These offered the healer a limited area for contact, so that, as mentioned above, he placed two matchends between his fingers and the hard-to-reach tooth crown, and then extracted the tooth. I observed this several times in February, 1971, with the healer Marcelo Jainar. There is no doubt about the fundamental existence of this phenomenon, although it cannot be observed very often any more, as present-day attempts by healers to pull teeth frequently do not succeed.

That this is a true paranormal action and not simply pulling teeth by means of a strong arm or a strong thumb, can be seen in the fact that the healer, in the case of some patients (especially Filipinos with impacted molars) has no trouble, but the same healer may fail in pulling the already loose tooth of a Western foreigner, especially if the patient is a skeptic.

It seems to me that the accomplishment of this act, which in my mind is psychokinetic in nature, depends on the unanimity or rapport between healer and patient. This is easier to achieve with a Filipino than with people from the West.

The strength of the thumb is not important, but psychological-parapsychological factors *are* important. This statement is based on repeated observations in 1971. Prof. Hans Bender and Dr. Wartenberg of Germany, after a short visit with Tony Agpaoa in May, 1971, adopted a negative point of view with regard to the *surgical* performances of Agpaoa, but agreed that Tony pulled deeply rooted molars without trouble with his bare hands, in cases where a dentist in the West would have had considerable trouble even with the help of pliers. (See *Stern*, June, 1971)

Taking Out An Eyeball

I observed another form of psychokinesis in September, 1973—the paranormal taking out and replacement of eyeballs. Without any instruments to help in reaching behind the eyeball, healers were able to take it out completely. When I saw this done by Alex Orbito and by Marcelo Jainar, I was always very close and was accompanied by a veterinary doctor who specialized in animal eye surgery and who also had a vast knowledge of the human body. (He gave lectures comparing the anatomy and physiology of animals to humans at an English-speaking university.)

The whole thing was a puzzle to him. A trick with a glass eye or an animal eye was absolutely impossible. I hasten to point out that not all eye "operations" of Philippine healers are real, as were those just described. As an example, I recently saw a film of an eye "operation" by another healer, and I certainly would not guarantee it to be genuine. It did not have any similarity to the operations we observed.

Injections

A third kind of psychokinesis can be found with the so-called magnetic or "spiritual shots" or injections, which are frequently done by both Juanito Flores and José Mercado in the province of Pangasinan. This I personally experienced quite often. The procedure is as follows: The healer reaches into the air for an imaginary hypodermic needle which he places on the Bible, in order to "charge" it. Then he aims it at the patient, moves a finger as if he were giving a shot, often without touching the body, and sometimes from a distance as much as one meter. At times this is pointed to the exposed skin and at other times through the clothes toward some specific spot on the body. Dr. Theo Locher, editor of *Swiss Bulletin for Parapsychology*, wrote in May, 1973:

> In February, 1972, the Italian neurologist, Prof. F. Granome of Vercelli undertook an extended investigation of nine healers in the Philippines with a team of scientists and camera crews for fifteen days. Spiritual injections were applied by hand without touching the body.
>
> These injections made the seven Europeans of the team feel needles or electric shock at the particular place on their body. Three members experienced bleeding. The analysis of one of the blood samples, made by Medical Institute of the University of Turin, showed that it was not human blood. In spite of movie cameras, infrared photos and other observations of the entry point, nothing suspicious was found. The analysis of the blood running down the leg of another team member was not blood either, which the research team could not understand.

[Ed.: Clues as to one reason why the blood does not test out as human are given in Chapter 10.]

A piece of paper placed under the shirt of one of the scientists showed three small holes where the injection was made. [Ed.: This type of experiment is also reported by Dr. Watson in Chapter 20.] The hands of the healer were constantly under observation of the team's cameras and never came closer than one-half meter to the patient.

At one time I myself received an injection in my left lower thigh without the healer coming closer than one meter. At this treatment quite a bit of blood ran from the entry point, and had to be wiped up several times with cotton before the bleeding could be stopped. We will return later to the paradoxical aspects of the bleeding.

Small Cuts In The Skin

Since February, 1971, I have often seen a fourth variant of psycho-kinesis under many different conditions with healer Juan Blance of Manila. He produces a psychokinetic cut on the skin. Usually he takes the index finger of an observer, forms a fist of all other fingers and thumb of this observer's hand, and with it makes jerky motions 20 or 30 cm. above the skin of the patient. A cut appears on the skin underneath, such as would be made by a razor blade, and the healer sometimes withdraws a substantial amount of blood using a glass suction cup. The blood sometimes contains tissue substances. That this psychokinetic cut made by both Blance and David Oligani is genuine, is disputed by many observers with little experience. It is said the healers secretly used sharp objects such as slivers of glass or small pieces of razor blades attached to a false thumb in order to make an opening in the skin, the cut being so light as not to be noticeable at first. The blood would then come with time, making it look like a psychokinetic cut.

Since the attention of the patient and the spectators is not usually directed to the place until the blood was slowly trickling out, (often under pressure on the skin at the sides of the cut) skeptics say that the healer previously wiped the place to be opened with a cotton swab which concealed some mechanical aid and it was this item which caused the skin to open. For four years I frequently watched and studied Blance's psychokinetic cuts, both in Manila and during his visit to Germany during four weeks in January, 1974. The cut is not always done the same way. I often saw incisions appear without any contact or any previous treatment of the skin, where the skin burst open the moment the movement occurred in the air. In these cases the healer had very strong mediumistic powers. In other cases the healer apparently needed the contact with the skin, which opened after the healer placed a finger or thumb on the spot. (This recalls what may be a similar situation in the bending of metal by Uri Geller and by the British or Japanese children, sometimes without being touched, and when it is touched, the contact or stroking is so slight it could not possibly explain the bending of the metal).

In the case of many of the incisions, I felt the movement of the fingers through the air was symbolical and the cut happened independently from it, or was there before it. A skeptic would presume this was

sleight-of-hand or a primitive trick. Based on my studies, I take the
point of view today that Blance can (and the same goes for David
Oligani) under *favorable* conditions make the incision from a distance
without touching the body of the patient. I once saw Oligani open the
chest of a Filipino from a distance of one meter. Less favorable conditions mean that the power of the healer is not at its strongest, or that
the healer has hindering factors such as presence of some people with a
negative attitude. In that case he brings about the opening through
direct contact with his finger or thumb—psychokinetically—not with
razor blade or glass slivers. I think that it takes less effort for the healer
to produce an opening if his finger touches the patient, than when he
does it from a distance. Similarly, I think Uri Geller's psychokinetic
bending is easier if there is even a slight stroking with the finger. [Ed.:
Dr. Motoyama reports, in Chapter 14, of his research into the nature of
the cut made by Blance.]

As a scientist, I am interested in the fact that psychokinetic incision
is possible. I am not interested in investigating the question of whether
the healers sometimes use razor blades or never do so. I know from my
observations that they often do not grasp the difference between "paranormal" and "normal" as we know these terms. In fact, the *para*normal
is as normal to the Filipino healer as "normal" is to us.

I am not surprised that the healer, if he cannot open the body
paranormally, will instinctively and without feeling guilty, reach for a
mechanical aid, such as a razor blade which he may keep handy for
cutting tape. His whole motivation and attention is concentrated on
helping the patient and not on using a method which is genuine paranormal and interesting to an observer from the West.

In February, 1975, I checked to see if the psychokinetic incisions
have ionizing rays in strong measure. I used films which are used in
Germany to protect people working with radioactive materials. The
films, sealed in plastic film holders, were placed on the patient's skin
before Blance made his incision from a distance. After his fingers
moved through the air, the film was untouched at the top but the skin
was cut and the film was scratched on its under side.

Since Blance placed the films himself, a skeptic could say that he
skillfully scratched them when placing them. This unlikely possibility
was absolutely ruled out by me with the last of six experiments, which I
did in March, 1975. Blance, as usual moved my right index finger
through the air, after he had placed the X-ray film on the part of the
patient's skin to be opened. Right after completing the movement, he
announced that the cut was not successful and he was going to repeat
the movement. I insisted on removing the film and taking a look. There
was no cut in the skin nor scratch on the film. I then pressed the film
down again. Blance repeated the waving through the air using my left
index finger. I then removed the film, revealing a good clean cut from
which the blood seeped out strongly. The cut in the film and the cut in
the skin were the same length.

Another point which speaks for the genuineness of the phenomenon is the fact that Blance can transmit his energy through another person, for example, the German Heilpraktikerin Irene Lutz. For several weeks she produced practically all of Blance's phenomena in the presence of Blance and myself.

At the end of the year 1973, Juan Blance came to Germany and worked three weeks in the clinic operated by Mrs. Lutz. I myself was present during two of the weeks and saw all of Blance's phenomena which were already familiar to me from Manila. However, in the course of this period, they grew continuously weaker. At the end of the second week, Blance was exhausted. We think the German climate did not suit him. Since I could not be there for the third week due to professional commitment, I am forced to accept the reports of healer Irene Lutz and her husband Franz, both of whom I hold to be reliable.

During this third week a strange phenomenon happened in connection with the psychokinetic cut. The cut appeared *under* the bookmark hanging from the Bible (which Blance and other healers often have some person hold over the patient during the treatment) and was induced through it. Probably it was at this point that the usually controllable psychokinetic powers began to get out of control. Blance became very restless when the cuts became uncontrollable and continued to be made through the bookmark and appear where they were not supposed to appear—even on the back of the healer's hand. While he and Irene Lutz were working on the upper part of a patient's body, cuts also appeared on the hands of the assistant who was massaging the feet of the patient during the treatment! We can see here the distinct change of controlled psychokinesis to an uncontrollable form.

Two days later he had a complete breakdown with life-endangering heart and circulation collapse. Perhaps it is due to the magnetic healing powers of Irene Lutz that he is still alive. Since the healer refused any kind of medication or admittance to a hospital, his life was in danger for several days before he was able to return to Manila.

When I visited Manila a month later on my next study trip, Blance had slowly resumed work but was still very weak. He still had scars from the psychokinetic cuts on the backs of his own hands.

Often large tumors were brought out by Blance after he had made the incision. In 1971 I watched a tumor the size of a plum come out of the hip of a Filipino patient. This tumor was not separated by any mechanical method. It really seemed to jump into the hand of the healer. I never again observed such an impressive phenomenon at Blance's.

I make the following observations in connection with Blance's
work:
1. When he is in good form, the patients feel very little or no
   pain.
2. In some operations where heavy bleeding would be expected, very little flow is observed.
3. Usually there are no infections, although no sterilization has been done by conventional means. When the healer is

in poor condition, some small infections have been noticed.

4. Any effort to claim that these results are due to hypnosis
   is, in my opinion a "cop-out". (Of course, insofar as the
   healing is concerned, we readily agree that the effect of
   suggestion *can* be a very useful and contributing factor in
   healing, whether the healer works in the Philippines,
   England, Brazil or any other country.)

Materialization

This subject has been one of my main interests during the many
visits to observe the Filipino healers. I share the opinion of Dr. Andrija
Puharich that if science could really uncover the processes involved in
materialization and dematerialization, much of modern science would
be due for some substantial revisions and expansion.

Perhaps the easiest materialization to describe and to visualize is its
practice by Josefina Sison and others in making surgical cotton disappear and reappear on the surface of the patient's body. The cotton,
often moistened with consecrated coconut oil, is formed into a tight wad
and seemingly pressed into and through the skin, into the patient's
chest, abdomen, head, arm or leg, and when she opens her hands the
cotton is gone. Sometimes she will leave the cotton in place and other
times she may immediately—or on the next visit—seemingly remove
the cotton. If the cotton is removed on a subsequent visit, it is often red
with blood, while newly inserted cotton comes out as white as it went
in.

I am not so naive that I am unable to spot trickery. I have observed
this materialization by Josefina and other healers many hundreds of
times, under all kinds of conditions. Dr. Hiram Ramos and other companions of mine have repeatedly asked Josefina to open her hands
before starting to "stuff" the cotton and after it had disappeared. We
ourselves have handed her the cotton. One of the most revealing investigations was made by my colleague Prof. Dr. Werner Schiebeler
who filmed this action in high-intensity lighting with 16mm. color
film. Examination frame by frame shows the cotton actually dis-
appearing between her fingers and it does not appear to physically pass
through the patient's skin.

> [Ed.: Many American patients and some American
> researchers had opportunities to observe this effect without
> the long and costly trip to the Philippines. Rev. Harold
> Plume, prior to his death in early 1977, frequently demon-
> strated paranormal activities which he carried on in his
> healing chapel in Redwood City, Calif. Rev. Plume used
> tightly rolled facial tissue in much the same way Josefina
> uses surgical cotton. When we observed Rev. Plume we
> noted that in addition to the "disappearance" of the tightly
> rolled tissue, portions of Rev. Plume's fingers or hands
> "disappeared" into my wife's jaw and into my bared chest.]

Even though the literature of the last 100 years is replete with well-documented cases of materialization and dematerialization, one's mind still tends to reject what his eyes are seeing. Only after long experience of the phenomena does it become any more credible. In the case of the "cotton-stuffing" activity, I personally feel that one of the most convincing incidents is to see a healer remove what is apparently bloodsoaked cotton from a patient, cotton which had been put into that patient several days earlier by *another* healer, whose identity is immediately sensed by the healer who is removing the cotton. Where was the cotton in the interval between its "insertion" and its "removal"? Was it in a state of fine material structure in the bioplasmic body of the patient or was it in the astral level, outside of our space-time framework?

The statement made by Harold Sherman in 1966 to the effect that Filipino healers can open the human body is basically correct. In my nine months in the Philippines watching the work of the healers day after day, I had a few rare opportunities to see truly sensational dematerialization of body tissue of patients. In February, 1971, Tony Agpaoa dematerialized flesh of a 38-year-old patient to expose the leg bone which, broken 16 years previously, had not knitted properly. I saw clearly and took photos of the broken ends of the bone. There was quite a flow of blood but after the "operation" the leg looked the same as it had before, since none of the bloody tissue remained. A photo taken by me proved that I had not been hypnotized and had not hallucinated, but had observed correctly. (A report some time later indicated that the leg had not been healed.)

When Blance treats a patient with a skin disease he sometimes seems to be pulling through the skin, spindle-like pieces of a yellow substance that looks like very small grass blades. However, the texture is more like a wax. I have seen this phenomenon many times under conditions where fraud was absolutely impossible. For example, in Frankfurt, Germany, Blance was treating a long line of patients one after another as their turns came. Since they had the normal gamut of illnesses he never knew which ailment he would be treating next. A friend of mine suffering from shingles, climbed onto the table and Blance, with his eyes closed and apparently in deep concentration, ran his hands over my friend's body. When he found the affected area, he proceeded to "extract" the above described "grass blades". After six visits in a few days, the shingles had disappeared.

In September, 1973, I saw healer Romy Bugarin, accompanied by a medical doctor, perform what was to me a sensational abdominal "operation" on a Filipino woman medical doctor. Romy entered the body through the abdomen, separated the organs, and lifted some organs outside the body cavity. When Romy closed the body there was some tissue left outside and considerable blood-like liquid.

These and other "operations" I have witnessed in the Philippines are outstanding but it appears that this level of mediumistic work cannot be performed in the environment of a scientific laboratory in Europe or the U.S.A. However, with the passage of time, the relationship between the scientist and the healer may mature into a harmonious effort to expand the frontiers of scientific knowledge. Let us hope there will be more progress in this direction in the next decade than there has been since Harold Sherman called these matters to the attention of the Western world.

8

PSYCHIATRIC AND PSYCHOLOGICAL CONSIDERATIONS

Hans Naegeli-Osjord

The phenomenon of paranormal surgical intervention upon and within the human body is a subject which is so unusual for the scientist of the Western world that careful study of the psychic aspects and of the conditions that permit these surgical interventions is demanded.

Throughout the history of all peoples and cultures we find spirit-healers, spiritual healers, or psychic healers, as they are variously known. Their methods vary from the somewhat comprehensible emanations from the hands, (magnetic healing) to the immediately visible and seemingly magical action upon the body. The healing effect attributed to the hand is recorded in the vocabularies of numerous languages, as in the English words "surgery", "manipulate" and "handle"; in the French and English "maintenance"; and in the German "behandeln". "Chiromancy" is evidence of the conviction, or at least belief, that the hand could or did presage the future. Yet the transection of the skin and the penetration of the fingers or of the whole hand into the body that is to be healed transgresses the known laws of the material scientist. It is true that materialization and demateralization of particles are known now to nuclear physics, but are ascribed by the *non*-physicist to a world that is of the laboratory and not of the daily reality of experience. Nevertheless, physicians, psychologists and scientists have observed these natural phenomena in Brazil and the Philippines and found some of them to be genuine. Many patients from many countries have personally experienced paranormal intervention upon and within their bodies.

The Time Of Occurrence

What is the reason for the almost simultaneous and increasingly frequent occurrence in the countries mentioned? "Psychic surgery" with direct intervention into the bodily tissue, we met in the Philippines for the first time shortly before 1950. Then we also met it in Brazil in the person of Arigó, the most prominent exponent, although there were many other mediumistic Brazilian healers active in spiritualistic circles and hospitals. Scientific study of the Philippine phenomena was begun in 1965 by H. Motoyama of Japan and by H. Sherman of the U.S.A.; and in Brazil studies began in 1967 by A. Puharich of the U.S.A.; yet their reports did not receive an appropriate response from the circles of the laity and of parapsychology until 1971.

While the exact time of transition from the Age of Pisces into that of Aquarius cannot be established exactly by astrology, it is generally considered as occurring within the second half of our present century. The astrologically oriented person knows that with the coming of the Aquarian Age there will be an increased turning of the spiritual person to the cosmic process. Natural philosophy teaches the relationships between the entire cosmos and our planet. Cosmic forces have their effect within the human psyche and the "Zeitgeist", the aura or spirit of the age, resulting in turn, in a general emotional attunement. But these acausal events pose a problem to science which conventionally considers only the laws of causality. In fact, in 1975 more than one hundred American scientists issued a manifesto which in effect ridiculed the idea that forces or energies from the cosmos could have any effect on a human being!

It is significant that today, just at the beginning of the Aquarian Age, there is an increasing number of voices of distinguished scholars, among them Lyall Watson (See Chapter 20), Walter Heitler, Heinrich Zoller and Max Thurkauf, from diverse fields of knowledge speaking against the one-sidedness and dogmatism of purely scientific thinking.

At about the time of the astrologic transition from Pisces to Aquarius, the American Association for the Advancement of Science in 1969 accepted parapsychology as a branch of science with the same rights as the other branches. Tolerance of psychic healers, and their admittance into English hospitals did not come about until recently. In other civilized countries too, such healers are now appearing in public with increasing frequency. Thus it seems to me that the new orientation of cosmic forces which is now taking place may be a possible factor in man's increasing attention to psychic healing. All occurrence has not only a primal or causal root, a causal connection; but also a teleologic meaning, a final orientation or a meaningful striving, towards a goal. Within this thinking it is not astonishing that phenomena such as the increasingly frequent appearance of the paranormal will occur first when there is a fructifying response in the human spirit.

The Significance Of Spiritist Communities As Religious Minority

In both Brazil and the Philippines the healers have developed almost entirely in the confines of spiritualistic communities. The establishment of Filipino groups in 1903 coincided with the change from Spanish to American occupation which had brought freedom of belief; but still these communities had to maintain themselves as apostates against the dominant might of the Catholic Church. As stated literally in their confession of faith, the Spiritists recognized not the Pope, but God as their father; the Earth, their mother. Thus they began to establish their own contact with God and the godly numina, a procedure which is of great importance. Since most of these spiritists had had a strict Catholic rearing and the saints of the church play a great role in their emotional life, it is not astonishing that saints or archangels become their "spirit-protectors", tutelary divinities, and that the spiritist healers maintain a close relationship with them. I shall return to the importance of the direct spiritual contact with numen, in the sense of an entity of holy essence.

The whole spiritist community is, however, in a state of heresy and diaspora in relation to the church. It is my personal observation, resulting from my several trips to the Philippines, that this endangered position *activates* the spiritual forces of the community; otherwise there would be only slight chances of its survival. The religious acts and ceremonies must be intensive and impressive and encompass the whole range of life of the believers; and to this belongs also the healing of the sick. In the early days of Christendom healings by disciples were an integral part of the worship of God.

It seems that during the first fifty years of divine services of the Philippine spiritualists, only "magnetic" (no so-called "bloody") healings took place. However, shortly before 1950 we find that Terte, Gonzales, Sarmiento and others in rural—almost archaic—regions begin to penetrate the body with what then became known by the term "psychic surgery". It was reported to me that this healing art is still practiced by the Igorots and other Philippine mountain tribes which remain uncontaminated by civilization.

I gather from the biographical information given me by Terte, Agpaoa and Guttierez that an "inner voice" gave them, while in a trance-like state, the task of becoming a healer. The healer's unconditional belief in this task, plus the cooperation of the transmitting numen or discarnate entity or spirit, sets in action the emotional force of the medium to such an extent that paranormal effects upon the patient's body become possible. The investigator who holds to the animistic way of thinking will link this inner voice to the psychic energy potential of the healer. Yet the fact that the healer thinks "spiritualistically" assures much stronger emotional impulses. There is no doubt in my mind that an unbroken, absolute belief in numinous powers, spirit entities, archangels, and archetypes is a requirement for "psychic surgery".

Psychic Requirements

For the realization of the phenomena which are being considered, these psychic conditions are prerequisite:

1. An unusually strong mediumistic ability,
2. A deep (one might say "rooted") religious belief,
3. An *undeveloped* intellect. The intellect makes even the religious and strongly gifted person uncertain, in that he remains always *outside* and not *in* things, or more exactly, in the *essence* of things. Only the genuine mystic, who has learned to displace or inactivate intellect and ego, can escape becoming uncertain.

These prerequisite conditions are fulfilled in those social strata from which the Philippine healers come. They are also valid in the corresponding Brazilian circumstances. In Brazil, through intensive racial mixture with indigenous Indians and immigrated Africans there still exist the psychic attitudes similar to those of an archaic population. In consequence, much from animistic religions has intermingled with Christendom in both the Philippines and in Brazil. This yields a fortunate mixture of father-religion, monotheistic Christendom; and mother-religion, with animistic natural deities and worship of primal principles. Indeed the confession of faith of the Spiritists, mentioned before, begins with, "God is my Father, Earth my Mother." Possibly the adherence to this belief system in both the Philippines and Brazil explains the abundance of healers in just those two countries.

Another factor is the existence of small religious groups whose interdependence is close, since they all find themselves in the situation of being unaccepted by both government and by the Catholic Church. Often the main healer is the president but there is no rule requiring this. The suggestive force of the leader of religious instruction within the circle is often decisive for the development of new healing mediums. The entire group strives to become accomplished in concentration, meditation, self-hypnosis, trance, and automatic writing. Those who are called to healing must in addition fast and at times withdraw into hermitages. Only this training regime, along with the healer's own regulation of consciousness, yields the necessary psychic readiness to be open to the unconscious and to the potential transfer of cosmic energy. Thus healing occurs in the fulfillment of an order of the person's own extra-sensory and intuitive cognition or, if one thinks spiritualistically, by mediation of a transcendental essence.

With respect to the procedure itself, the imagination of the healer plays an important part. Every healer has his own technique, though it may differ only slightly from that of colleagues belonging to the same circle. His own imagination determines the type of items which he will manifest with those native patients who are considered by the healer to be bewitched. Apparently some of the healers have a conscious or unconscious idea that broken egg shells are symbolically connected with possession. Hence, the appearance of egg shells (as just one example) in exorcistic healing, is not due to possession but to the mental projection of the healer-exorcist.

Space does not permit me to go into detail regarding the Huna system of magic and healing practiced earlier in Hawaii. Hence I refer the reader to the very illuminating books on this subject by Max Freedom Long.[1] To me there seems to be the indication that the Huna concept of "lower self" (the emotional sphere of the human being) must connect and unite itself with his "higher self" (the cosmically conditioned properties) in order to achieve a modification of matter or of the patient's body. In this connection, one may recall the "unio mystica" of the alchemists.

The Cognitive Function Of Man

Over what cognitive functions—in the sense of Carl Gustav Jung— must a mediumistically gifted person dispose, to be able to fulfill extraordinary accomplishments? Jung distinguishes four principal functions: thinking, intuition, feeling, and sensation. Thinking as the predominant cognitive function of a medium does not come into discussion. This is because the intellectual cognition is *active* and bases itself upon a real or often only supposed factual material from which it proceeds to arrive at intermediate and concluding deductions. Since the function of thinking is connected strongly with the function of will it, for just this reason, hinders the free medial cognition, which should be free from expectation.

The root of the word "intuition" is the same as that of "tuition" and "tutor" and means "lucky, favorable, propitious," in the context of "guard, protect, watch, observe," as found in the Latin "tueri"; it is cognate, according to some etymologists, with the Gothic "thuith" which means "that which is good." Intuition mediates spiritual cognitions and interconnections of meaningful content spontaneously, without deductive mental effort; it is withdrawn from the will and accordingly passive. It is the "spirit which moves wheresoever it will," without deed or will of the person, but only in the presence of his openness.

Something similar is true for sensation which similarly is spontaneous but belongs more to the world of instinct; it can be defined as an unconscious experiencing and knowing of interdependences within the material world. Intuition and sensation, in their perceptory function, resemble each other in some respects so strongly that they are frequently confused, and mistakenly interchanged. Often we believe that we have recognized the facts of a matter instinctively, whereas actually, perception has been almost exclusively a function of our cognition. Intuition has its principal relation to the spirit or to the spiritual, under which we understand the universal principles and also the numinous and parts of the cosmic structure. If Friedrich August Kekule recognized intuitively the structural formula of the benzene-ring, this is genuine intuition; if however, the dowser recognizes a vein of water or the clairvoyant recognizes a diseased organ in a fellow human being, the act is one of sensation. To perceive the forces of the essence of nature and the outer world, that is sensation. Intuition proceeds, it may be surmised, by way of the mental body, while sensation proceeds through the astral or etheric body. It is possible that in certain cases both functions of cognition participate, yet I should like to attribute the major proportion of passive PSI achievements to the sensory function.

The feeling-function, as is also the thinking-function, is preponderantly active. It processes obtained impressions and also spiritual cognitions and forms them into emotions which can become enhanced in intensity. Exactly this process occurs among the healers. The contact with the numinous must be taken up actively, because without emotional powers, no typical activity of a poltergeist or of a healer will manifest itself to the level of performing phenomena of penetration, materialization, and dematerialization. It is, after all, *the emotions that affect matter!*

In the works of Thomas Aquinas, two ways of cognition are delineated: In the first, one recognizes something alien; in the second, one recognizes that which is one's own inherent participation and upon the basis of the inner sympathetic vibration the alien becomes that which is one's own inherent. Through this arises "connaturalitas" (relationship of essence), in contrast to the first way of cognition, "percognitionem" which sees the external.

The healer, who must acquire a vital familiarity with the essence of things also has need of the cognitive "per-connaturalitatem", a cognition that comes close to the "participation-mystique" as it is named by Lévi-Bruhl. The healers participate in the happenings of nature, and the happening of sickness too must be comprehended in like manner. Then, from their highly developed function of perception, they know of the therapeutic procedure. Active masculine and passive feminine mediality come to full effect with the healers and are a precondition of a successful healing event. Healers often have a childlike disposition, but more in the sense of immediateness. They exhibit an inner harmony, an equality of the forces of Yang and Yin. This assures also a robust physical health. A sick healer loses his credibility, a loss which has a much stronger consequence in a primal culture than it does in Western countries.

The Strength Of The Ego, The Weakness Of The Ego

It is interesting to consider the question of whether the spiritual healers belong more to the strong ego type or to that of the weak ego. Medially gifted persons frequently have a weak ego. They are not inclined to activity, but rather let events come and are "open to the winds." They are more practiced and gifted in perception and their experiences are predominantly centripetal. They are of a passive nature and apprehend the influences and the essences of the world about them better than do persons more inclined to activity. However, according to my experience, the most successful healers are not of this type. They are predominately active persons who master the ordinary problems. They find themselves in a healthy equilibrium of active and passive gifts, so that in the moment of a trance they can divest themselves completely of their egos.

The Role Of The Patient

Let us now draw the patient into our psychological observations. Is his belief in the healer or in a godly influence a precondition of his recovery of health? According to our observations, skeptics and atheists too, become healed. Conversely, someone who is a believer may find no recovery. Let us consider Lourdes. Alexis Carrel, Nobel Laureate in Medicine, and a person who knows the phenomena in this southern French town, expressed himself to the effect that it can suffice if someone prays near the occurrence of healing.[2] My understanding is that by this act someone thus consummates the "unio mystica" with numinous energies, which are conferred upon the sick person for the harmonizing of his "leptomeric", "leptohylic", or (as it is more commonly called) "etheric" body.

Hiroshi Motoyama writes in *Psychic Surgery in the Philippines*,[3] "The first and most important condition for psychic healing is to meet a god." My feeling is that this has in fact taken place with a Spiritist healer and those who pray together with him. But I must add that it is also important that the proximity to the godly *continues* to accompany the patient—the person who has been given healing impulses. Persons who return unimpressed and avaricious to the world of every day, (that world which caused the sickness in the first place) experience early relapses. For these relapses the healers are unjustly given the blame. I consider it probable that the proportion of persons cured among the native sick is much larger than that among foreign groups because the former groups have a strong faith and live with less haste. (A team which includes young Philippine medical doctors has recently begun investigating this matter.)

The healed person should recognize that his previous preponderantly rationalistic-materialistic view of the world is completely inadequate and that there should be a striving for more spiritual content. The previous wrong way of behavior and life, which causes sickness, should be corrected.

Reaction Of Western Doctors And Scientists

The reaction of many physicians and other educated Western observers toward "psychic surgery" is revealing. Since they have been educated in universities which stress natural sciences, and since only very few of them keep a genuine connection with any religious faith, their own confession of faith is philosophical materialism. They depend upon it believingly, thus emotionally. For such a person the collapse of a view of the world, which previously seemed to be valid and right, is always painful, for it makes him insecure. No wonder that there is insecurity when a new content of belief, a content that apprehends the entirety of the personality, spontaneously and visionarily replaces the previous one. For him an accurate rethinking is impossible. Even by actually viewing such phenomena, only excerpts from the entire course of events are transmitted, and so the entirety of the personality can never be addressed. A skeptical or even hateful reaction is the rule, and the resulting counter-arguments are often childish and betray undisciplined thinking even among supposedly intelligent and well-educated critics. Although a thoughtful person should know that every generation has its own basis of thinking and that all is subject to change, a rationalist persists in limiting himself to use of those bases of thinking which were given to him through school and university. It is this lack of critical attitude toward the methods of thinking which people have been trained to accept, which accounts for the vehement and emotional reactions which result in rejection by most medical specialists of all unorthodox therapeutic methods.

Psychologic And Parapsychologic Typology Of Spirit

The diversity of the unorthodox healing methods which we encounter in all parts of the world permits the surmise that we may well be dealing with different paranormal events. As one type, we might consider the *energetic form*—healing through leptohylic energies, energies of "fine substance", streaming from the hand. (Probably this concept should include magnetic healing.) The thinking of the East assumes that cosmic energy, *prana,* is collected in the chakras and ascends by way of Kundalini to the higher centers and from there is radiated by way of the hand and/or the breath. It is surmised that the cosmic prana is enriched by the person's own bioplasmic powers.

A second, *the magic form,* is the use of sympathetic gesture which corresponds to a mental concept of a goal. The intention is to affect a distant object. For example, at a short distance of 8 to 12 inches, movements corresponding to those of an injection or of an incision are executed above the body (Blance, Flores, Mercado, and others). At an intermediate distance an "operation" is performed symbolically above an empty operating table and the action affects psychoplastically the patient lying in the same room. (This has been observed in Brazil.) At a still greater distance, as reported by Hiram Ramos, Ph.D., the now deceased healer, Gonzales, treated in Baguio City, Philippines, by proxy, while the actual patient was in Seattle, Washington experiencing synchronous healing. Afterward Gonzales described exactly the room in Seattle in which the patient had been. This leads to the conclusion that there is an astral migration, an exteriorization, of the healer whose corpus subtile (subtle body) effects the healing.

A third form is the *cosmic-numinous.* The healer attains the spiritual union, the "unio mystica" with a spirit-protector, who is a saint of the church, or the creative cosmic field of force, the "high self" of the Kahuna philosophy. The hands penetrate the body through the medium of actions in four-dimensional space, penetration, dematerialization, and rematerialization. Practitioners of this form include some Philippine healers as well as Arigó, Edivaldo and others in Brazil.

It is to be conceded that these three forms often may intermingle.

A fourth form is the *spiritualistic:* A spiritual entity exercises a healing function through a medium who is chosen by the discarnate or spirit entity. For example, the deceased Dr. Fritz functioned through Arigó in Brazil; the deceased Dr. Lang through George Chapman in England. The post-mortal continuing existence of the leptohylic body and its ability to pursue certain goals on this plane of existence will not be discussed here.

Psychic Health Of The Healer

Let us consider the question of whether or not the healers present certain abnormalities in their own psyches. E. Fuller Torrey has pursued this problem in his comparative study of witch doctors and psychiatrists in the book, *The Mind Game* (Bantam Books, 1973). He established that in all cultures except in Japan, psychic health somewhat better than the average was an attribute of the witch doctors. Western psychiatrists, it seemed to both Torrey and me, perhaps do not rate quite as well as do the witch doctors in this respect. As for the healers in the Philippines, I could detect psychopathic or psychotic traits in only a few of them.

It is my conviction that paranormal accomplishments of the healer demand a positive and harmonious attitude toward the environment and the cosmos. It requires an unconditional confidence in a personal protective spirit in order to become one with him—to attain the "unio-mystica". Still another condition, mentioned already, is the harmony between the Yang potential and the Yin potential.

Mentally sick persons almost always have a strongly negative attitude toward the environment. They are paranoid, mistrusting, and sense evil everywhere. In some cultures they are held to be possessed by negative entities which preclude every effort to contact the godly-beneficent and to obtain therefrom healing powers.

The Healing Of Mentally Sick Patients

There remains the question of whether or not mentally ill patients, too, may be cured by the psychic healers. Two of my schizophrenic patients, by their own wish, were treated by Tony Agpaoa. One was "operated" upon in "bloody fashion" in my presence. It appeared as though strands of nerves were being cut out of the brain and removed, but it may be presumed that this was materialization. Cinematography of the process was permitted but I was not allowed to preserve the removed strands to have them examined. Both patients appeared to be very relaxed and normal immediately after the treatment and also on the following days. However, after 3 to 4 months, a relapse occurred, and today, after two years the situation is unchanged.

As to the success of treatment of mentally ill native patients, I do not know, but it is certain that those who undergo therapy repeatedly have a greater chance of cure than do patients of the West who return home after one or only a few treatments.

All of the Philippine healers consider mentally sick persons to be possessed and that the spiritual entity which is responsible for this, must be driven out. I was witness to a large exorcism by a number of prominent members of a circle before the assembled community during a religious service which lasted the whole night. The patient, a girl, entered into a cataleptic state. Wrapped in covers, she was carried away and placed at the side of the assembly room where the healer talked to her, or in his view, to the entity which possessed her. The answers, as well as the howling and grumbling of the possessed person gradually became more quiet until she finally fell asleep.

David Oligani is considered to be especially successful as a healer. For him, not only the psychically sick are possessed, but also many of those who are afflicted with functional organic ailments. He determines the problem and treats according to certain fixed methods. My native Filipino driver had been treated by Oligani and after three weeks felt relieved of obviously functional digestive difficulties and attacks of migraine. As a resident of the large city of Manila, he had heard little about bewitchings and was very skeptical toward the subject.

I am of the conviction (and this is confirmed by the researches of Nigerian psychiatrists trained in our orthodox fashion) that the therapy of mentally sick persons is often carried out better and more enduringly within "magic" cultures than in Western nations by means of medicine and laborious psychotherapy.

Could this conviction be a demonstration that our Western understanding of the sick psyche is after all not so very superior to that of peoples whom we regard as "not intellectualized"?

REFERENCES

1. Max Freedom Long, *Recovering the Ancient Magic* (London: Rider, 1936).
   _____. *The Secret Science Behind Miracles* (Los Angeles: Kosmon Press, 1948).
   _____. *The Secret Science at Work* (Los Angeles: Huna Research Publications, 1953).
   _____. *Self-Hypnosis* (Los Angeles: Huna Research Publications, 1958).
2. Alexis Carrel, *Journey to Lourdes* (London: Hamish Hamilton, 1950).
3. Hiroshi Motoyama, *Psychic Surgery* (Tokyo: Institute of Religious Psychology).

9

A PSYCHIC PHYSICIAN'S EXPERIENCES

Sigrun Seutemann is in a unique position to report on this facet of paranormal healing because:

She has a medical background.
She herself has been psychic since childhood.
She has received help from Filipino healers for her own very serious ailments.
She observed the "operations" of 29 healers on more than 3,000 patients during her more than 20 trips to the Philippines.

Here she reflects on her experiences in personally accompanying more than 1,200 patients from Europe to the Philippines for visits with native healers.

Sigrun Seutemann

As background for the thoughts which I shall present in this chapter, I should state that I have made more than twenty trips to study the work of the Filipino healers; have made visits to the U.S.S.R. to discuss this work with Russian scientists; and have cooperated in the research in the field of healing with many scientists from many other countries.

But perhaps of still more importance is the fact that I myself have been psychic since childhood and gradually developed these psychic abilities to the point where I could use them to diagnose illness. By observing the effect of minerals as well as herbs and homeopathic remedies on the human aura, I have been able to prescribe these in a way that is most effective for the patient.

When I was a child I did not know that most other people could not "see" or sense the aura of persons, plants and animals. It was beyond my comprehension that others could not talk to the spiritual essence of a plant!

By observations over the years of the auras around people and animals, and by meditation and concentration, I gradually began to understand where a patient needed to be treated: at the physical, mental-emotional, or spiritual level. Today I could not serve so many patients as the 90 per day who sometimes come to me, if this gift had not become so well-developed. One of the greatest factors in my own development was the unusual circumstances which allowed me, at the age of thirteen, to daily observe the patients coming to the homeopathic doctor who was later to become my husband.

My medical studies were planned so that as a physician I could better serve my fellow man in a way that would combine science with my psychic knowledge. From the start I took seriously the admonition by Paracelsus to the effect that the physician must first decide whether to treat the patient at the physical, mental or spiritual level.

When I first came in touch with acupuncture and electro-acupuncture in 1959, my psychic ability enabled me to note changes in vibrations around a person. I could "see" or sense a sudden change in the energies or vibrations which I associate with the aura, precisely as I had observed changes when a patient took a homeopathic remedy.

During my medical studies I was subjected to considerable stress. I was concentrating on educating my intellectual self but my spiritual and psychic self constantly told me that some of the intellectual teachings in the medical texts were in error. Adding to my personal problems was the fact that since childhood I had suffered from a congenital heart disease. As I grew older this caused increasingly serious limitations on my work until finally it became such a limiting factor that I was faced with a complete stoppage of my medical practice.

Having heard of Philippine "psychic surgery", I made a decision to travel to the Philippines, even though at this time some very negative publicity came out in Germany against the work of the Filipino healers. In July, 1971, I put myself in the hands of Tony Agpaoa and that act changed my life. The recovery was so quick and so complete that I just could not believe what had taken place. Back in Germany again, I was so completely astonished at what had happened, that after a few weeks I decided to return to the Philippines to verify what was taking place. What I found convinced me I could render great service to many European patients for whom neither I nor my German medical colleagues could provide relief. Consequently for the last four years I have made repeated trips to the Philippines and have now accompanied more than twelve hundred patients there to seek treatment.

My observations of these twelve hundred patients; my collaboration with physicists, biologists, parapsychologists, electronic specialists, medical doctors and psychiatrists; my interviews with theologians of Christian, Shinto, and Buddhist persuasions; my studies of Eastern religious, philosophic and occult literature; and my close contact with many Filipino healers will now allow me to begin to summarize my findings. This will take many months but I can at least present some observations in this short chapter which may contribute to the picture which is being assembled in this book. Naturally, I will refrain from giving names of the researchers with whom I have been associated in these studies as many of them would still come into cross-fire in their profession.

Healer Observation

I have observed the work of 29 healers and it is safe to say that I have seen more than three thousand "operations". However, since my initial experience was as a patient of Tony Agpaoa and since I was very impressed psychically by what I observed when Tony was with patients, I have concentrated my studies largely on his work.

The first thing I had to do was to take further steps to assure myself against fraud. Tony collaborated fully. This involved working in a room which was bare except for a plain table for the patient to lie on. Tony put on clothes we supplied. My assistant held a new package of cotton and the plastic bowl with water. Tony had to repeatedly show his hands for inspection. I myself assisted. This type of test was repeated several times.

Of course as a physician I was able to see that this type of "surgery" had nothing to do with conventional Western medical surgery. Often the "operations" were performed in cases where there was no medical indication for surgery, for example: organic dysfunctions, diabetes, skin diseases, nerve inflammation, etc. Occasionally I would see the ends of Tony's fingers disappear, or even much of the hand, but the great majority of the "operations" were entirely on the surface of the patient's body.

Often when I wanted to observe closely, I reached down between Tony's hands and touched what seemed to be a tight membrane. On occasion I could verify parts of organs, but they did not seem specific.

Of course this was very puzzling. Once I asked five scientists to observe an "operation" and then tell me what they had seen. All agreed in the description of having seen how Tony put the cotton (handed to him by one of the scientists) into the bowl of water and then put the watersoaked cotton on the body. They agreed upon the movement of his fingers. But each had a different description of the red blood-like liquid and the membrane-like tissue. There began the frontiers of the unbelievable.

We of course took blood and tissue specimens, but these only added to the confusion. In some cases the laboratory tests confirmed the blood and tissue specimens. On other cases there was no confirmation by the laboratory.*

I detected another curious thing. In those cases where Tony knew the blood and tissue were going to be examined, he worked longer to produce the phenomenon and he seemed to concentrate more deeply and then seemed to be more exhausted after the "operation".

During the treatment patients themselves were able to observe what Tony was doing. In some cases a mirror was provided. The "operation"

*Research reported in Chapter 13 shows that often the healer's energy brings about a change in the molecular bond between the hydrogen and oxygen in the water. (The blood is mostly water) We have reason to suspect that the energies emanating from or through the healer may cause additional modifications in the blood.

usually lasted only from two to five minutes. Because of the language barrier and the almost complete lack of conversation, there was no question of hypnosis, and almost no chance for suggestion or auto-suggestion.

After their treatments some patients became very tired and slept for many hours while others felt so strong they had to be reminded not to waste energy. Sometimes the patients were given specific diet instructions.

My experiences quickly taught me that Filipino healers are not the holy persons many people expect. As for Tony, at times I just could not understand how he could combine certain things in his life style with the image of being a healer. I had been taught that a healer is a spiritually developed person with negative and positive potentials, and that he must continuously change negative potential for positive, for the benefit of the patient seeking his help. Certainly some of the "escapades" in Tony's life do not square with this concept. On the other hand, no other Filipino healer has become so well-known that every detail of his life has been held up for inspection by critics in so many countries. I know from personal observation that some of the practices attributed to Tony were the responsibility of others on his staff and family. In this connection, I can state that I am totally unsympathetic with any advertising of "miraculous cures" just to make money for travel agents.

The Etheric Body And Diagnosis

The entire subject of the etheric body will be treated elsewhere in this book, however, I do want to register the fact that the etheric body influences all functions of, and controls the metabolism of, the physical body. The etheric body reacts to all the thoughts and emotions of the individual.

It is my conviction that most of the work done by the healer is at the level of the *etheric* body. Only after this body is restored to normal balance can the healing result in the organs of the *physical* body.

After the experiences I had in my own clinic in West Germany I got so I could trust my knowledge of what it was I seemed to "see" around the physical body. This ability helped me greatly in my observations of Tony's work. However, his technique of diagnosis is quite different from mine. He says that at first it is like seeing a reflection of his own body, but he has learned to protect himself by concentration so that the patient's problems will not be transferred to him. While he is thus concentrating, his whole metabolism is changing and the reactions in his nervous systems are completely different. He says that he works to concentrate the power in his brow chakra and in his hands. [Ed.: Motoyama in Chapter 14 and Meek in Chapter 19 discuss this in detail.] The scientists and other researchers observing Tony during an "operation" have often been heard to observe, "Tony seems to be in trance only from his shoulders down. He appears to be entirely unconscious of the movement being made by his hands." His invisible work appears to me as being of far more importance to the healing than anything which is visible. The criterion for successful healing is not the effect on the physical body but the changes brought about at the patient's etheric level of existence.

It is obvious to me that Tony can "see" the etheric body or the aura, because he can tell if other healers had touched a patient without his knowledge, and in fact he can give the other healer's name. Even though he treats as many as 120 patients per day during some periods, and could not be expected weeks or months later to remember a particular returning patient, Tony can always tell in an instant if he himself has previously worked on a patient.

Effectiveness Of The Healings

The more than twelve hundred patients whom I have accompanied to the Philippines were an unusual lot. Groups coming from Germany, Italy, Switzerland, Austria and occasionally from France, were almost entirely made up of patients who, for any one of many reasons had not been helped by the normal medical channels. Few patients are anxious to spend the large sums of money to travel to the other side of the world unless they have exhausted their hopes of getting satisfactory results at home. These patients suffered from the usual run of ailments: polyarthritis, diabetes, multiple sclerosis, tumors of all localizations, heart diseases of many types, allergies, stones of the kidney or gall bladder, spinal paralysis, cataract, glaucoma, ablatio retina, congenital diseases such as spastic children, paralysis after poliomyelitis, spinal dislocations, after effects of various accidental injuries, wounds which would not heal, after-effects of nuclear radiation, serious side-effects of previous medication, etc. Of course it was part of my responsibility to see that no patient would be allowed to make the trip if there appeared to be any serious danger to life from such an exhausting journey.

Due to a near fatal automobile crash in the Philippines earlier this year and the delay in returning to my normal work capability, it will be some time before I can hope to complete my records and analysis of the results of treatments of these 1200 patients. So just by the way of a very informal and admittedly inexact and incomplete statement of effectiveness, I would give the following:

> Two percent of the patients were healed instantly.
>
> Ten percent could be adjudged as healed in a medical way at the end of their ten-day or two-week stay in the Philippines.
>
> Thirty percent had at least partial success within the first month.
>
> Thirty percent felt better and some medical tests confirmed improvement in three to six months.
>
> Eighteen percent were patients on which no follow-up was possible.
>
> Ten percent seemed to have no benefit.

In this last group there were no doubt a few (as there are among patients everywhere) who no longer had a serious desire to become well. As all healers and physicians everywhere learn, a patient cannot be made to get well or to stay well if for any of many reasons he does not have such a desire.

No patient in my groups ever came home worse than when he went. No patient in my groups died while under the care of Tony. A few times I saw him refuse a patient in other groups, saying that he could do nothing.

I must say that I never saw a vertebral paralyzed patient completely dispense with use of a wheel chair. Myelitis patients showed limited improvement. Cancer in the last stages could not be stopped. Multiple sclerosis cases often showed considerable improvement.

In some cases where subsequent surgery was still indicated—for example the actual removal of kidney stones, and certain heart operations—the surgery took place with none of the complications which had been initially anticipated. The healing procedure was fast and without complications.

Of great significance was the fact that in many instances the patient got a whole new outlook on life in general and his illness in particular. The empathy of the healers, the understanding of other people's illnesses, and the group spirit all helped to improve the emotional well-being of many patients. Some patients still meet periodically in an effort to help each other.

It must also be observed that the psychological frame of mind of the patient who traveled to the Philippines was far different from that of the patient who goes just around the corner to see his physician. The former was expecting something extraordinary from the healer. Hence it is obvious that suggestion, autosuggestion, desire, expectation—call it what you will—was of great assistance to the healer. However, many of the more dramatic results were of a nature that cannot be explained by this one favorable factor.

Conclusions

It is not easy to find terms which give a neat and simple explanation for the many things involved in paranormal healing. Too much of it is outside our present level of science to be able to say what is going on. I feel that I have been very privileged to work in the field of paranormal healing research and to make use of my own psychic abilities.

The existence of phenomena involved in the work of the Philippine healers has been established beyond any doubt. Likewise it is beyond doubt that healers in the Philippines and in many other countries are capable of rendering service that is of great benefit to the lives of the individual patient.

People who have attempted to investigate "psychic surgery" in the Philippines from the standpoint of thinking it was similar to conventional medical surgery can be excused for not understanding what was actually involved. But if science is to make further headway in unraveling the mysteries of paranormal healing, it will first have to recognize that *there are non-physical levels to man,* levels involving *mind* and *spirit.*

Medical science would do well to find ways which recognize and utilize the abilities of both healers and psychics. In this connection, I have read that the American neurosurgeon C. Norman Shealy, M.D. has experimented with the diagnostic abilities of psychics in the U.S.A. It is reported that he found that good psychics can often come up very quickly with a diagnosis at less expense than for extensive present diagnostic techniques and often with a higher degree of accuracy. He looks forward to the day when the American medical establishment will be utilizing the services of as many as 40,000 medically trained psychic diagnosticians. Based on experience with my own patients, my own psychic diagnostic activities, and my observation of the diagnostic abilities of Tony Agpaoa and certain other very capable healers, I have every reason to believe Dr. Shealy's proposal is soundly based.

* * * * *

A Healing "Miracle"

[One of the best documented cases of the efficacy of the work of healers is to be found in the life of Sigrun Seutemann, author of the foregoing chapter.

Sigrun told in the opening pages of her chapter of the successful outcome of her initial trip to visit a healer in the Philippines. In the five years I have known her and collaborated with her on healing research, it has been obvious that the congenital heart defect which had made her life sheer misery for so long, was completely corrected. I have no friend nor acquaintance anywhere in the world who lives a more dynamic and action-packed life during 20 or more hours per day.

In January, 1975, while in the Philippines with a group of 50 patients from central Europe, she nearly lost her life in a motor crash. She was driving alone on the highway through the rice field area north of Manila when she swerved her car to miss a small child who darted out from the edge of the road. The resulting head-on collision with a large truck crushed the front half of her car to the extent that it was necessary to cut it apart in order to get her out of the wreckage. She was horribly mangled with what later was found to be 18 fractures. Her ankle was crushed. Her forehead from the eyebrows up into the hair was sliced into ribbons, and the entire skin which had been below the jaw, was now a flap folded down onto her chest. She was adjudged to be dying from loss of blood.

The accident happened almost in front of the home of one of my healer friends, José Mercado. He promptly proceeded to use his best efforts to keep Sigrun alive until they could get her out of the wreckage. She was finally removed to the local hospital where she was given 27 liters of blood and plasma expanders. Later, a three-hour ambulance trip brought her from Urdanata to Clark Airbase to get the necessary orthopedic skills. Upon completion of the examination she was told she had permanently lost the sight of one eye and that she could not expect to walk normally again.

By June, there had been so much improvement in the face that Dr. Kotthaus, a plastic surgeon from Essen, Germany, declared that his services were not needed. He had visited her in the Philippines after the accident, promising to rebuild her face when conditions were right. Now in June, the rebuilding was already well underway and he said there were obviously other energies working.

Ten months after the accident, while I was in Europe to confer with co-authors, I visited Sigrun in her office in Karlsruhe, Germany. While I sat watching her receive her patients, I could detect no limp whatsoever. When we finally got time to talk, I could see that only one scar remained under her chin where the great flap had been formed, and only one small scar was visible on the forehead near the right temple. She was her vibrant self, and had returned only a few days previously from taking another large group of patients to visit the healers in the Philippines. She had regained most of her vision.

From the time of the crash, numerous healers had focused their healing abilities on Sigrun. Their healing efforts, Sigrun's indomitable will and her unique psychic and spiritual understanding of her physical body's inherent recuperative capabilities all combine to stand as a monument to what can be accomplished by modern medical science, selfless and well-developed healers, and a patient who has the understanding and determination to surmount all obstacles.]

10

DECEPTION AND SLEIGHT-OF-HAND

> When I was hunting gurus in India, I came back enriched
> with one insight. It was: "Never ask whether 'that holy
> man' is a charlatan or really holy. Just ask to what extent
> he is a charlatan and to what extent holy. Never apply an
> all-or-nothing criterion." Showmanship comes in the mo-
> ment you get into the eye of the public. Exposed to the
> public eye of unlimited numbers of followers, you have to
> apply some showmanship. On bad days, when nothing
> works, you would be superhuman if you would not resort to
> 'corriger la fortune' by a few tricks.
>
> —Arthur Koestler[1]
>
> George W. Meek

THE BACKGROUND

This chapter responds to critics and skeptics, including the U.S. Government authorities, who have claimed that *all* aspects of "psychic
surgery" are fraudulent.

American, English, Philippine, German, Japanese and Swiss scientists, medical doctors, clinical psychologists, psychiatrists, hypno-
therapists, psychical researchers, and an expert in deception and
sleight-of-hand have pooled their on-the-spot findings over a three-
year period to present their findings on paranormal healing and
"psychic surgery".

A review of the history of healing in the Philippines reveals why
some of the practices have not been understood or accepted by Western
science, and why some of the present-day deceptive practices came
about. Our research has clearly established that most—perhaps even
all—Filipino healers who regularly treat *foreign* patients are both
saints and sinners.

Thereby hangs a story—certainly the most perplexing, frustrating,
time-consuming, thankless, and yet one of the most rewarding facets of
research into paranormal healing.

What *is* the truth about "psychic surgery" in the Philippines? Is it
100% fraud, a trap for tourist dollars as claimed so vehemently by some
investigators? Why are the healers so reluctant to permit specimens of

tissue and blood to be taken for pathological tests? Why do some specimens of tissue disappear from tightly closed glass bottles before tests can be made? Why does a blood sample taken from a patient in the presence of a healer sometimes test out as *non*-human blood? Do these questions arise only in regard to the Philippine healing activities? Can a supposedly spiritually-oriented healer be guilty of outright and willful deception and still have at least some success as a healer? While all of these questions cannot be answered in depth as of this time, the work done by the many scientists who collectively spent more than 120 weeks in on-the-spot studies in the Philippines will dispel at least some of the mystery.

The Genesis Of "Psychic Surgery"

The aborigines of the Philippines, the Aetas, over the centuries have received an infusion of peoples from the Polynesian Islands and from India. Discovery of the Philippines by Magellan in 1521 brought the first contact with the cultures of Europe. However, in many areas the beliefs and practices of these native peoples continued unchanged up to the time of the Spanish-American War in 1898. In large southern islands they carry on to this day, as any researcher can verify if he wants to brave the tribal and Indian-Filipino wars that currently prevail. In the rice field areas of north central Luzon such native beliefs and practices have continued through the first half of the twentieth century. They are still deeply embedded in the lives of all of the Filipino healers. It is significant that the majority of healers practicing today were born in this rice field area, within a circle sixty miles in diameter.

These native peoples, living in small, mostly open, one-room homes built of bamboo and palm fronds; having dirt floors, no covering on the window openings; no electricity or running water; surrounded by pigs, water buffalo, goats, chickens, and ducks; subjected almost yearly to the full force of the elements of tropical typhoons and torrential rains, are *totally immersed in nature*.

Witchcraft and white or black magic were, and still are, an important part of their belief system. One part of this belief relates to the idea that illness can be caused by an enemy using witchcraft to imbed some native object—fiber from a coconut, tobacco leaves, rope fiber, broken glass, etc.—into the patient's body. The patient goes to the native healer who then "operates" and seemingly pulls the "witchcraft item" from the patient's body. (As Dr. Hans Naegeli-Osjord explains in Chapter 8 these items usually have some symbolic function for the patient. Dr. Lyall Watson later in Chapter 20 discusses similar experiences with the natives in the Brazilian jungle.)

And here we must note that *each* of the Filipino healers is a *medium*, that is a person who serves as a connecting link and a go-between in the realm separating our day-to-day materialistic world from those levels of consciousness and being that seem to be quite different from the physical world as we presently know it. A definition from the viewpoint of the spirits themselves was given in 1925 through an entranced young German farm boy to the then Catholic priest Johannes Greber,[2] "The term medium means 'instrument'. Mediums are therefore human beings used by those of us in the spirit world as instruments to enable us to communicate with man."

The Filipino healers are in most cases what are called *natural* mediums, possessing such characteristics from early childhood. In addition, most of the healers were or are actively affiliated with the Union Espiritista Christiana de Filipinas, Inc., in which the development and enhancement of mediumship and its altered states of consciousness are given weekly emphasis.

After a century of study of mediumship by some of the sharpest minds in England, Brazil, U.S.A., France, and Germany, woefully little is still known about the functioning of mediumship. However, it is apparent that:

a. Paranormal phenomena such as "psychic surgery" with its materialization, dematerialization and apports can *only* be performed in the presence of a medium.
b. Mediumship capable of producing these specific phenomena is very rare.
c. Usually a rather simple, stress-free life and limited formal education facilitates becoming a "materialization medium".

We can also state the conviction that the more mediumistic and the more compassionate a person is, the more effective he becomes at paranormal healing.

Strange, unbelievable and ridiculous as such phenomena as materialization, dematerialization and apports may appear, there is a long and well-documented history of them. A good introduction to the subject is found in Nandor Fodor's *Encyclopedia of Psychic Science*.[3] A special bibliography of these phenomena can be found in Supplementary Bibliography A.

There was apparently no case of native healers actually "opening and closing" the body until shortly after World War II when Eleuterio L. Terte, Sr., a native healer who had rendered valuable aid to the American armed forces during the war, apparently developed abilities similar to those later observed in the work of Arigó in Brazil.

During the next ten years Terte is reported to have trained, in whole or in part, as many as fourteen of the approximately thirty healers who today treat foreign patients coming to the Philippines. Terte's teaching methods will be discussed in Chapter 16.

The first exposure of foreign patients to such "psychic surgery" seems to have taken place in the early fifties. By the time Henry Belk and Harold Sherman[4] visited the Philippines to initiate serious study of the healers in the mid-sixties there was already a considerable flow of foreign patients.

Some evidence exists that for Terte and for some of his pupils, "psychic surgery" became a mixture of actual opening of the body and the production of *apported* "witchcraft items". Later, in some cases, the apported native items were replaced by tissue and blood which may have been apported from a source nearby or far away. Whereas extracting a "witchcraft item" such as coconut fiber from the abdomen of a woman from Chicago, London, or Zurich would have been repulsive and non-productive psychologically, the appearance of *blood and tissue* was readily accommodated by the belief system of such a patient.

Some of the healers found this new development a bit disconcerting. Tony Agpaoa in recalling this period is quoted[5] in a purported "conversation" with his "protector" or guiding entity:

> "But let there be no blood," murmured Tony.
>
> "Without blood to show," came the 'voice', "even those completely healed will not believe.—Well, perhaps, not so *much* blood."
>
> "The sight and smell of it sickens me," said Tony.
>
> "It sickens me, too, but it is also *proof* that they might *believe.*"

As we delve into the subject of deception, we are more than ever certain of the validity of early accounts to the effect that the Filipino healers sometimes opened the body and sometimes materialized or apported "witchcraft items" or blood and tissue. The American psychologist, William James, who as president of *both* the American and British Psychical Research Societies spent many years studying fraudulent practices, had a valid point when he said in 1907:[6]

> ... to me it is dramatically impossible that the swindling should not have accreted around some originally genuine nucleus. If we look at human imposture as a historic phenomenon, we find it is always imitative. One swindler imitates a previous swindler, but the first swindler of that kind imitated someone who was honest.

Why Resort To Deception And Sleight-Of-Hand?

The native Filipino healers of ten to fifteen years ago, living in the primitive environment described earlier, were totally steeped in nature, and were about as stress-free as it is possible to be. They would interrupt their activity—often that of working in the rice or peanut fields—to ease the suffering of some of their neighbors who arrived on foot from the surrounding fields and small villages. Usually they received no pay. Sometimes they would get the equivalent of a few cents or a gift of some native food item.

Then things began to change! *Foreigners* started to show up in search of healing. These foreigners found that the healers were delighted with a gift of money, which was the merest fraction of what medical treatment would have cost them back home. The foreigners upon returning home showed films and extolled the "miracles" of healing.

In this situation some healers, quite understandably, became interested in getting ever more publicity so as to build up their own following—which in turn would mean more income and the ability to purchase motor bikes, cars, and better housing in which they would have electricity for air-conditioning and other appliances. Preoccupation with such pursuits just is not consonant with the detached, relaxed, meditative and stress-free existence, which is the atmosphere of the best mediumship.

Without almost *superb* mediumship it is not possible to produce materialization and apport phenomena such as they previously had done; let alone produce such paranormal phenomena as opening the body, removing diseased tissue, and then closing the body as they purportedly did at least on some occasions in bygone years, and as Arigó did in Brazil.

Our Philippine photo file does not contain any pictures of what we consider a major opening of the body cavity. It does contain photos of "operations" in which blood and tissue were apported or materialized; and others in which blood and tissue were produced by sleight-of-hand. One photo of the apported or materialized category is shown in photo section Fig. D1. This photo, taken in color by Sigrun Seutemann of Tony Agpaoa working on a foreign patient, shows a large flat piece of tissue which has been stretched over the surface. The fingers of each hand are merely pressed down into the soft area of the abdomen and have not penetrated into the body cavity. The upper arrow shows where the tissue overlies the surface of the abdomen. Just below the middle joint of Tony's right thumb a bump is beginning to form in the tissue membrane. During the following moments this bump grew in size and eventually Tony lifted off what appeared to be a tumor dripping with blood. This growth appeared while Tony's hands remained in precisely the position shown in this photo.

The paranormal actions involved in the just reported incident with Agpaoa, which took place in late 1972, cannot be produced day after day when the healer is under great stress, whether that stress comes from family life or from a flood of patients.

It took no gift of ESP on my part to write and circulate this statement on February 23, 1973:

1. In the next two to five years "comes the deluge". Many hundreds, perhaps thousands, of desperate patients . . . will arrive monthly from all over the world.
2. The healers presently available will be totally incapable of dealing adequately with this flood.
3. The disillusionment will be great!

Unfortunately, this condition has come to pass. Perhaps as many as 7,000 to 9,000 patients traveled to the Philippines in 1975. One healer was booked to handle sixty-five patients per month for six months from Australia; twenty patients per month from New Zealand; plus all of his other patients, both native and foreign. Sometimes there is a line of one hundred patients awaiting the services of a single healer. Patients arrive by the bus load.

And now books, magazines, radio and television are filled with accounts bewailing the "trickery". The Federal Trade Commission of the U.S. has, quite properly, taken steps to restrict the activities of unscrupulous tour companies in their flamboyant promotions. Whether the FTC is on equally sound ground in sending telegrams warning against such a move to each person known to be *planning* a trip to the Philippines for healing is open to question.

"Showmanship comes in the moment a healer . . . is exposed to the eyes of an unlimited number of followers," to paraphrase Koestler. Showmanship has come to the Philippine "psychic surgery" scene in a big way. Fortunately, there and in Brazil our research was timed, at least on rare occasions to witness the *actual* phenomenon.

A Practical Research Methodology

What is the relevance of mediumistic phenomena to paranormal healing? They seem to imply that matter—in this case the physical human body—is not at all the fixed reality that we have thought it to be. If it is something more than eight or nine gallons of water plus a few dollars worth of chemicals, perhaps the study of its other parameters might help in understanding what goes on between the healer and the patient at some *non-physical* level. In light of present scientific knowledge most scientists totally ignored the phenomena. But now several researchers are willing to lay their reputations on the line and say, "These phenomena *do* exist; we should investigate them; we should take a new look not only at medicine, religion and science, but at our whole concept of Man and his place in the cosmos."

As has been observed, it is impractical to study "psychic surgery" of a native Filipino healer in a scientific laboratory, either in the Philippines or in any other country. What brings about the difficulty is *mediumship*. The last 75 years of psychical research in England, Germany, Brazil, and the U.S.A. has taught that the paranormal phenomena a medium can execute—with the help of intelligences from those other planes of existence that present science does not acknowledge—must be studied in surroundings in which the medium is "at home". Hence, to be productive, any further research of the Filipino healer *must* be done in the Philippines and preferably within fifty miles of Pangasinan, Luzon. And, we hasten to add, even there the efforts will require great patience, and the researchers must be prepared for many frustrations.

First, an effort must be made by the researchers, perhaps over many months, to build up a very close rapport with the individual healer. The healer himself must become totally convinced that the investigators are sympathetic to the cause of paranormal healing and that the researchers have enough knowledge of mediumship and of the medium's connections with other states of consciousness and planes of being to be sympathetic to the idea that the phenomenon cannot always be produced "on demand". This same empathy must be established with each individual on the research team. Parapsychology research in the U.S.S.R. has clearly established just how critical this factor is in the production of the paranormal.

Second, the amount of "equipment" the scientists move into the healer's treatment room must be kept to a minimum. Primarily this should consist of a completely transparent "operating" table with transparent water basin, still and movie equipment (but no flood lights), and sealed packages of sterilized cotton.

Third, after the healer and *all* of the researchers have built up the necessary rapport and the whole procedure has been carefully discussed with and agreed to by the healer, the healer must agree to the positions to be occupied by the research team and the activity, if any, of each individual researcher.

We report here the first example of research conducted with the foregoing procedures. Since the team leader, over a period of three years, had made many trips to observe Josefina Sison she had built up confidence in him and agreed to work under the above conditions. In photo section Fig. C3 she is seen in friendly discussion with our research team in May, 1974. Psychiatrist Lee Sannella is leading an inquiry into Josefina's early training and experiences. The other members of the team join in the discussion. Josefina's brother and husband listen in and become familiar with each member of the research team and the plans for observing and photographing Josefina's work with any patients who on that day come to her seeking healing. The placement of all observers and equipment is shown in Fig. 4.

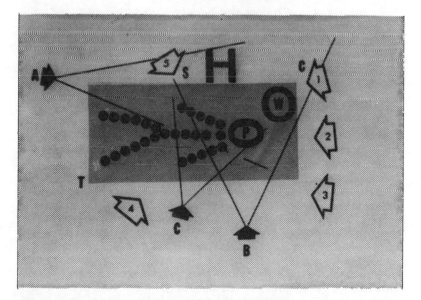

Fig. 4

The healer (H)—the key figure in the action—stands beside a patient (P) who is lying on a specially constructed transparent operating table (T) made of half-inch thick clear plexiglass. Movie cameras (16mm. with wide angle zoom lenses, electric drive, and 400 ft. magazines to permit uninterrupted filming of the entire sequence) are positioned at (A) and (B) to cover all action from two directions. Motorized still color camera (C) with adjustable intravelometer and 250 frame back is capable of taking photos as fast as two per second. Positions (1) through (5) are occupied by qualified observers. A transparent plastic basin (W) contains water for healer to wash hands as needed. Sterile cotton (c) is handed to the healer by observer in position (1) from sealed box purchased by observer in his home city. Specimens (S) are promptly handed by the healer to observer (5) who stores specimen in glass bottle with suitable preservative.

Two examples of experience with this arrangement will be reported. The observers making up this team were as follows:

Position	*Qualification*
1.	M.D. (Member of American College of Surgeons)
2.	M.D. (Psychiatrist and ophthalmologist on staff of large U.S. hosp.)
3.	M.D. (doctor of emergency medicine on staff of large U.S. hosp.)
4.	Bio-medical engineer (clairvoyant and student of occultism)
5.	Clinical psychologist (hypnotherapist and clairvoyant, a native of the Philippines who has studied the healers for many years.)
A.	Camera man (who is also a hypnotherapist.)
B.	Psychical researcher on his 4th trip to study work of Filipino healers.

CASE "A"—A native woman aged 45—third visit for treatment of cancer of the right breast. Patient claimed that previous visits had resulted in considerable improvement. First Josefina's fingers touched the skin at the base of the breast and "removed", *without making any incision,* the now blood-soaked cotton which she had inserted at this area during the patient's *prior* visit. Then Josefina took new cotton from the observer at (1) and proceeded to "stuff" it into the skin at the base of the breast. She repeated this procedure with additional pieces of cotton, taking them from the M.D. in position (1), and pushing them at the base of the breast. She was obviously not accumulating the cotton in her hand, nor was she otherwise disposing of it. (In this type of paranormal phenomena the healer seems to pass the cotton through the skin and into the body. It may be allowed to remain until the next visit, at which time it is removed, usually red with blood, or it may in a few moments be removed from the same or another area of the patient's body with little or no discoloration on the cotton.)

Josefina explained that what she was doing was to put the cotton which she had "blessed" (treated psychically) at the boundary between the healthy tissue and the diseased tissue, and that in due time the body would slough off the diseased tissue to the point where she could lift it off with her hand. She explained that this is basically the same thing she does with a brain tumor—that is, concentrate it into a more localized or accessible area where it can gradually be encapsulated so that eventually she or a regular surgeon can easily excise it.)

In this case there was no pathological sample generated. Our team had no Filipino medical doctor who could follow this case. It is obvious that there is an inherent weakness in any such investigations which do not have built-in plans for clinical follow-up. Such clinical follow-up will not be possible until members of the medical profession in the Philippines are willing to participate in such research and are permitted to do so.

CASE "B"—As I had been suffering from a slight urinary tract problem, it seemed like a good opportunity for some personal research with the transparent table and the other equipment and research personnel as shown in Fig. 4.

I climbed onto the table and fully exposed my abdomen. Josefina held her hands for inspection and then placed them to the left and slightly below my navel. Within seconds "blood" appeared under her fingers. (In the movie, this "blood" seemed thicker than was sometimes observed.) Soon the fingers of both hands were colored red and there was a small pool of "blood" formed by the depression in the skin where her hands were resting. She signaled for a piece of cotton which was given to her from the box of J & J sterile cotton I had purchased in my home town. Taking the cotton in one hand, while holding the other hand in place, she soaked up some of the "blood" and then threw the cotton into the waste basket. She returned the hand to its original position. From my line of sight—only sixteen inches from her hands—and looking horizontally across the surface of my abdomen, I could see the "blood" was still accumulating. She pressed in at one small spot so hard that I felt an intense localized pain. (It persisted for thirty minutes after the "operation".) After several seconds the pressure staunched the flow which seemed to come through the skin. Then with more cotton she cleaned up the remaining blood.

There was not the slightest chance that this "blood" was manufactured on the spot by fakery. I was just one of a long series of patients. Every motion of Josefina as she stood beside the transparent table had been under the closest scrutiny of the movie cameras and the medical doctors and scientists who were standing shoulder to shoulder with her and surrounding the patient on the table. As the patient, I had the advantage of having previously observed many hundreds of "operations" by 23 of the approximately 30 healers and had long since passed the "Gee-whiz" stage.

Later, while reviewing our movie film of other patients, we found another "operation" in which the camera angle was such that we could readily observe Josefina's difficulty in stopping the flow of "blood" *through* the patient's skin. Examining frame by frame where Josefina had generated "blood" just below the ear on the side of the patient's neck, it was observed that she needed to go back three times and press with the tips of two fingers before the flow was stopped. As soon as this was accomplished and the accumulated "blood" was wiped up, there was no opening visible in the pores of the skin.

But as the surgeon who stood beside Josefina during the above operation observed, "Even seeing is not believing." Our present science cannot accommodate the thought that liquid blood can be transported *through* the skin by an act of *focused consciousness*.

To add to the confusion as to just what is going on at the level of cells in the body and the molecules and atoms of the cotton, consider this incident: Tony Agpaoa and another healer were working on patients on adjacent beds. When Tony removed a piece of bloody cotton from a patient who had been "operated" on a week earlier by José Mercado, he said to the nearby healer, "You tell José that when he works on foreign patients he should not use local type cotton."

Obviously we have made just a small start in solving the many mysteries which relate to the paranormal healing scenes in the Philippines. The methodology presented here is costly in time and money but no other approach so far devised offers much hope of valid results.

Present Status Of Deception And Sleight-Of-Hand

In our initial news release regarding our studies in the Philippines in February, 1973, we carefully refrained from stating that the physical body was being opened. We saw that much painstaking study would be necessary to get to the bottom of the mixture of paranormal phenomena and sleight-of-hand which appeared to be present. As our studies proceeded we were sometimes appalled at the crudeness of the sleight-of-hand, as well as the fact that on one day a healer would resort to obvious deception in the "blood and guts" department (*See* photo section Fig. D2) and then turn around a few days later and produce valid paranormal phenomena. Working in a dimly lighted chapel packed with patients, the healer had a can of tissue parts sitting on a narrow wooden bench next to his knee. Standing on a raised area, a member of our research team took the flash photo at the left. A few moments later the photo at the right was taken, showing the "organ" after it had been "removed" and was being held up for all to see.

Yet, three days later *this same healer produced blood and tissue by paranormal means!*

However, as serious scientists working with paranormal phenomena have learned, the popular press as well as writers of scientific journals are all too prone to ridicule the researchers by saying, "They should have had a trained magician on their team." For a variety of reasons it was not practical during the major portion of our studies to tie up the services of an acknowledged master of deception and sleight-of-hand, day after day and month after month as our studies proceeded. However, as our studies of the Filipino healers neared their conclusion, Dr.

David Hoy accompanied me on a visit to some of the healers in February, 1975, for the express purpose of adding whatever insights he could contribute toward understanding the techniques used by these healers when resorting to deception and sleight-of-hand.

During the portion of the 5 days which Dr. Hoy spent observing the work of 5 of the roughly 30 healers, he encountered overwhelming evidence that four of those healers were using deception and sleight-of-hand to produce "tissue" and "blood".

REPORT FROM THE EXPERT OBSERVER (David Hoy)

Dear George:

By way of recollection and confirmation, our relationship began many months before our ultimate meeting in the Philippines in February, 1975, with the endorsement of me by authorities in the field of professional magic. Your purpose was to supplement your own studies by soliciting my opinion, as an expert in sleight-of-hand and staged deceptive techniques, as to the extent such practices were used (or could be observed) in so-called "psychic surgery".

My observations and conclusions are presented herewith:

First, my role as an observer was scrupulously limited to hand movements, the use of props and/or specially designed apparatus, the role of confederates and such other aspects of sleight-of-hand practice that are known to and used by professional stage magicians, illusionists, "mentalists", and the like. In this limited role, I suspended my own set of beliefs as to the "possibility" of paranormal healing practices. It was a difficult position to assume and maintain because the field of psychic phenomena is one of my basic interests and in recent years has become my major activity as a speaker, lecturer and author in the para-psychological field. As you might gather, I approached my assigned area with a certain ambivalence but what follows is confined entirely to those aspects of the healers' performances which are duplicable by many skilled magicians for the purpose of entertaining paid audiences.

I observed few consistent patterns of pre-treatment creation of an attitude on the part of the "patient" group, except that in several cases a religious emotional overlay was suggested. I subjected myself to the discipline of considering the religion-oriented trappings, dress, language of the "healers" and their assistants as simply representative of geographic and cultural mores and customs and of no moment in judging their effect on the "patient" group.

In general, the physical characteristics of the practitioners were typical of their geographic locales. In other words, elaborate costuming and/or stagecraft was not used to any significant degree. In stage magic, such psychological build-up and staging techniques are often a major part of the show and create an aura of receptivity among even very sophisticated audiences. In the case of the Philippine "healers", I felt subjectively that the audience (or patients) were already receptive to the performance of the "healers" by their physical conditions and emotional states as evidenced by their serious attitudes. In my opinion, the very presence of the majority of the people in attendance at the performances of the "healers" indicated a willingness to witness or experience "miracles", just as audiences at a magic performance indicate interest by paying an admission fee.

These, then, are the "psychic surgeons" whose performances I witnessed:

HEALER "B"—Critically, "B's" movements were skillful and indicated a high degree of graceful manual dexterity. Such grace is the mark of a sleight-of-hand artist who has practiced long and purposefully to misdirect the viewer's eyes away from one part of the field of action in order to use the other hand in unobserved actions.

One impression stands out: in each "operation" performed by "B" the patient experienced obvious pain. In one instance, "B" cauterized an obviously abcessed area in the lower jaw of a young girl. Apparently a tooth had been removed and infection had developed. He used a match stick wrapped in cotton and set aflame by one of his assistants, blowing the flame out just before reaching into the girl's mouth to apply the smoldering cotton to the abcess. This action was repeated four or five times and the patient reacted quite violently each time. In this instance at least, I couldn't help thinking that orthodox cauterization under local anesthesia and sterile conditions would have been much preferable from the standpoint of patient comfort.

Healer "B" prepared for another "operation" after reaching into his pocket for an unknown object in what I recognized as a classic magician's palming move. The patient, a male, was seated on a stool next to "B's" operating table and was told to bend forward to rest his head on the table. His physical problem was not clearly identified, but "B" apparently thought it was necessary to make an incision on the man's neck. "B" involved me in the procedure at this point by reaching for my right hand with his left, while at the same moment he touched the patient's neck briefly with his own right thumb. Then he guided my hand over the same area. Almost immediately a slight white line appeared on the man's neck and then began to ooze blood. This could have been accomplished by palming a sharp-edged object, perhaps a tiny razor blade, as I mentioned. It was a finely executed move, in any case, utilizing palming technique and misdirection at the moment just before using my hand to make the incision. A sleight-of-hand artist would describe it as a *cover move*.

When the two-inch wound had oozed a significant amount of blood, "B" placed a coin over the cut and placed a wad of cotton on the coin and set the cotton afire. Next, a small glass—like a whiskey shot glass—was inverted over the burning cotton. As oxygen was consumed, the flame of course went out and suction began to draw blood from the wound. "B" then stated that this "thick blood" was the cause of the man's pain and if not removed would cause the arteries to close and eventually prove fatal.

Here I analyzed that this particular treatment consisted of several skillfully executed moves: (1) palming an object beforehand (a razor blade?); (2) misdirecting my attention while making a slight incision with the palmed object; (3) using centuries-old technique to produce suction within the inverted glass and thus draw "thick blood"; and finally ascribing extremely serious consequences to the patient's health had the blood not been withdrawn.

My complete notes on the observation of "B" are largely repetitive of the above instances. My orthodox orientation was appalled at the crudity of the surroundings and the apparent lack of concern over obvious pain reactions by his patients. More to the point, however, as a sleight-of-hand artist myself, I was impressed by his deftness and willingness to perform closeup feats of misdirection and sense deception.

[To carefully examine both sides of the coin and weigh the evidence from both points of view, the reader is advised to consider these remarks as well as those of Dr. Stelter in Chapter 7 and of Lyall Watson in Chapter 20. Editor]

HEALER "T"—In my opinion "T" was very impressive in creating a receptive mood in his audience before treatment began. However, in action, his movements while performing "operations" were quite inept—a judgment in which you concurred, George, after seeing him crudely palm material which was later declared to have come from inside the body of one of his "patients". (*See* photo section.)

The mood preparation is enhanced by the air of religious solemnity in his rather impressive two-story building, the ground floor of which is given over to a church-like setup. His healing sessions were preceded on both visits I made to him, by sermons delivered in Tagalog, the native tongue, by an associate.

In the space provided for this informal report, I can only list the movements, props, physical surroundings, etc., that in my opinion would permit a skilled sleight-of-hand practitioner to produce objects and effects that are well-known to skilled magicians. "T" utilized many of them. For example, his pockets bulged suspiciously, to the eye of a magician; he moved in and out of the operating area, even going into adjacent rooms; he clumsily produced an object that had been secreted in his shoe top and placed it in a hidden position on a "patient's" body; his hand movements were characteristic of sleight-of-hand technique to cover deceptive moves behind his outspread hands. (Fig. C2—Photo section)

HEALER "J"—Here again, this female healer demonstrated consummate skill in rapid hand movements. She also surrounds herself with numerous assistants hovering or moving about, providing ample opportunity to pass material to her for use in producing her "miraculous" effects. Her specialty appears to be the supposed ability to implant balls or swabs of cotton within the body cavity of a "patient", later retrieving it with the implication that the cotton has purified the diseased or malfunctioning organ. Again, her truly amazing dexterity is, nevertheless, within the perimeters of orthodox magic and/or sleight-of-hand. [In our research of this healer described in this chapter, all of her "assistants" were replaced by a seven-man team of medical doctors, scientists and cameramen. Also the only material passed by this professional research team was sterile cotton which one of the M.D. members dispensed from a package he had brought from the U.S. Also the healer's hands were extended with fingers wide apart so that doctors and cameras could inspect both fronts and backs of her hands–Editor.]

OTHER HEALERS—As I indicated above, space does not permit a detailed account of the other two healers I observed "operating" or the two with whom I talked but did not see performing "operations". Healer "F", for example used classic misdirection to hide "sacred stones" between her legs before supposedly causing them to pass into the body of a patient. In your own alertness, George, you saw "F" hide the stones in the back pocket of her slacks.

In an unguarded moment, one healer, "P", distractedly and repeatedly thumb-palmed a cigarette lighter, almost as a reflex action. This is a common habit (or tic) among professional sleight-of-hand artists, but the best are careful never to display their mastery to the layman so openly.

In reviewing the transcription of notes tape-recorded during my sojourn among the healers of the Philippines, I cannot escape the fact that in every case I *did* witness techniques, moves and the use of suspect props that are reproducible by talented professional magicians. One may draw his own conclusions from the statement, of course, but I make it in the spirit of an objective investigator.

At the end of my short stay with you, you will recall, I was able to reproduce several of the *effects* with the very simplest materials which I procured from a Manila drugstore and an art supply store.

Inasmuch as I respect your own objectivity and demonstrated willingness to encourage your readers to enhance their understanding of unorthodox medicine by recommending respected reference books, I should like to add one of my own, *Sleight-of-Hand,* by Edwin T. Sachs (1946, Fleming Book Co., Berkeley Heights, N.J.) This is a basic reference book on sleight-of-hand feats and tricks with apparatus.

Finally, I feel I must emphasize that my area of observation was a limited one and that I spent only five days among the healers. I, like you and several of your colleagues in the production of this book, feel that paranormal phenomena are real and that orthodox science lags in acceptance, examination and evaluation of such phenomena. However, I am reporting what I saw in these instances without judgment of the validity of their abilities as healers.

David Hoy
Paducah, Ky.
Oct. 1, 1975

Pathological Tests

Investigators have been repeatedly mystified as to why Filipino healers are reluctant to give blood and tissue specimens which they had purportedly taken from a patient's body. This mystery is now largely solved by the representations in this chapter to the effect that the material might be:

A. Animal tissue and blood reconstituted from dried animal blood, in some form easily concealed and within reach of the healer, or

B. Animal tissue and blood apported from an unknown source, or

C. Human tissue actually removed from the patient, by
   a. opening and closing the body, or
   b. by dematerialization and rematerialization.

Another mystery may also be closer to solution—why have some specimens disappeared from tightly closed glass specimen bottles within hours or days, even when close surveillance was maintained? In case (B) we might speculate that since the apporting process involves the steps of dematerialization, transporting, and rematerialization, some molecular *instability* has been introduced in the apported matter. Whether the case reported by Dr. Lyall Watson (Chapter 20) fell into category (Ca) or (Cb) we have no way of knowing. And even if we did know, we would still have to admit that very little is known about the process itself.

To complicate the mysteries still further is a previously unmentioned fact that blood actually taken from a patient in a healer's presence undergoes chemical changes so extensive that it may test out as "non-human" blood. (Example: Lyall Watson's experience reported in Chapter 20 has been confirmed by other researchers.) The work by Miller and Reinhart (reported in Chapter 13) showing that the energies emanating from a healer change the hydrogen bonding in the water molecule may provide a clue as to how such a change is brought about in the blood specimens.

Detailed analysis of some 16mm. color film sequences indicates there may be still another factor contributing to the "blood" specimen mystery. In many cases it seems that the thin pale red liquid is being *drawn through* the skin of the patient. In a few film sequences it is observed that the healer has to actually put her finger over the spot where the liquid is issuing and press hard to stop the flow. In such cases the liquid looks more like blood. Immediate close-up inspection does not disclose any change in the surface of the skin.

Further pathological research in categories A, B and C will be difficult, since it is impractical to move a mediumistic Filipino healer into a well-equipped scientific laboratory and expect useful results in such surroundings, particularly if the research staff is composed at least in part, of skeptics.

Saints And Sinners

Before concluding this chapter dealing with one of the most important aspects of the research into the Philippine healing scene we must come back to the personal level—the Filipino healer as a human being. Suppose a healer is exhausted from trying to help far too many patients and finds his ability to dematerialize organs, tissue and blood and rematerialize them is nil at the moment. Is he a sinner if he fakes the organs, tissue and blood? Repeatedly, we encounter people who say, "Anyone once involved in misleading the public no longer deserves any consideration."

Yet it could be argued that this is not a valid viewpoint. Forrest J. Cioppa, M.D., discusses the "placebo effect" in which patients of orthodox medical doctors respond to treatment even though these patients had been given the equivalent of sugar pills. Are these doctors sinners for having fooled their patients? Dr. Cioppa says, "As I see it, the placebo effect is a simple non-toxic and oftentimes very effective method of stimulating the patient's own intricate healing process." Hans Naegeli-Osjord, M.D., also discusses the beneficial psychological aspects of such make-believe. (Chapter 8)

No less an authority than the American psychologist and long-time psychical researcher, Dr. William James, had a very personal experience with the "saint and sinner" problem. In an essay written in 1907 summing up his long association with psychical research in America and England, he tells why and how he obligingly manipulated a turtle's heart to make a demonstration in a lecture room in Harvard University produce the desired effect on the assembled students. He says:

> Fraud, conscious or unconscious seems ubiquitous throughout the range of physical phenomena of spiritism . . . . I have myself cheated shamelessly. . . . To this day the memory of this critical emergency has made me feel charitable towards all mediums who make phenomena come in one way when they won't come easily in another. On the principles of the Society for Psychical Research my conduct on that one occasion ought to discredit everything I ever do, everything, for example, I may write in this article—a manifestly unjust criticism.

William James on Psychical Research

However, this small and apparently temporary slip of Prof. James into the ranks of the "sinners"; the widespread current medical practice of issuing millions of placebos a month; and the "sometimes" use of simulated tissue and blood in "psychic surgery" pale into insignificance when compared to the deception perpetrated by an American surgeon. So violent, so partisan, and so devoid of calm judgment has become the debate about Philippine "psychic surgery" that this previously respected surgeon resorted to deliberate falsehoods in a book and in public talks. For example, after spending only a few days in the Philippines and visiting only a few healers, he wrote a very detailed "case history", telling how an American corporation president visited Tony Agpaoa in Manila after U.S. clinics had given a diagnosis of brain tumor. The surgeon-author is reported to have answered, "After all, I used a fictitious name and I will not tell you what person I actually had in mind." More specific details of the deceptive reporting of the Philippine healing scene by this surgeon-author will be found in other books. (*See* references [8] and [9] below.)

Ironically, as this chapter is being prepared, the local newspaper carried two news stories datelined Washington, D.C. which relate to the medical treatment of patients in the United States. The first story reports, ". . . unscrupulous American doctors . . . are performing operations without medical justification. Rep. John Moss (Dem., California), turned up evidence that $300,000,000 had been paid out in the U.S.A. for unnecessary surgeries." A few days later a story was headlined, "Some Doctors Reap Bonanza on Medicare Patients". This story told how one medical doctor had billed the government $415,156, and 207 medical doctors had billed the government an average of $130,000 for services rendered during the preceding twelve months to poor Medicaid patients. Even though it is presumed that such doctors and surgeons make up perhaps less than 1% of those practicing in the U.S.A., the problem of separating "saints" from "sinners" is obviously not confined to Filipino "psychic surgeons".

Our long association with many of the Filipino healers has shown that they are basically warm, generous, loving and compassionate human beings who are rendering a very valuable service to mankind. Like a respected medical doctor who dispenses placebos, and like no less a personage than William James, we find that they are saints *and* sinners. It is our hope, now that the whole situation has been brought out in the open, that the individual healers and any organizations to which they belong, will strive each day to *move away from the sinner category* by desisting from practices that bring them discredit and limit their remarkable ability as healers.

REFERENCES

1. Arthur Koestler, "The Perversity of Physics". In *Parapsychology Review,* Vol. 4, No. 3, May-June, 1973.
2. J. Greber, *Communication With The Spirit World* (New York: John Felsberg, 1932).
3. Nandor Fodor, *Encyclopaedia of Psychic Science* (London: Arthurs Press, 1933; New York: University Books, 1966), Articles on Apports, Materialisation.
4. Harold Sherman, *Wonder Healers of the Philippines* (London: Psychic Press, 1966; Los Angeles: De Vorss, 1974).
5. D. Thilis, *The Living Legend: Rev. Antonio Agpaoa* (Philippine Spiritual Church of Science, 1971).
6. William James, "The Final Impressions of a Psychical Researcher". In

William James on Psychical Research. Edited by Gardner Murphy and Robert O. Ballou. (London: Chatto and Windus, 1961).

7. John Godwin, *Super Psychic: The Incredible Hoy* (New York: Pocket Books, 1974).

8. Alfred Stelter, *Psi Healing* (New York: Bantam Books, 1976).

9. Jeffry Mishlove, *The Roots of Consciousness* (New York: Random House, 1975).

11

THE MEDICAL EFFECTIVENESS OF HEALING

Miracles do not happen in contradiction to nature, but only in contradiction to that which is known to us in nature.
—St. Augustine

Forrest J. Cioppa

The Big Question

Throughout history, man has continually sought new ways of preserving and restoring his health. Medical science has made tremendous advances in this regard. Our generation has witnessed the eradication of many dread diseases such as diphtheria and polio and even the transplantation of human hearts. Medical technology today is highly sophisticated and specialized; but in spite of this, we are unable to relieve the suffering of many patients.

Many of these patients continue to hope; others continue to search. There are patients who live with the hope that just around the corner there will be another technological medical breakthrough which will alleviate the problem from which they are suffering. Others look to the past and try a multitude of unorthodox remedies that have been handed down and endorsed by their fellow laymen—but not by the medical profession.

Among these controversial and sometimes miraculous remedies are a variety of healing techniques, many of which are described in this book.

The big question each potential patient asks before undertaking the time, expense, inconvenience and risk of ridicule that can be associated with seeking the services of a healer is, "Will it work for me?" Unfortunately there is no clear-cut answer to this very important question. Although orthodox medicine looks upon healing with a jaundiced eye, I know of no clinical studies proving or disproving the effectiveness of this medically significant phenomenon.

My own investigation of healing revolves around two trips to the

Philippines observing the phenomenon of "psychic surgery". As a Western-trained physician, I questioned the validity of the "surgery". Although the ritual was truly impressive, I was never convinced that the healer had actually penetrated a patient's body. Yet, each day I heard many testimonials from doctors, lawyers, ambassadors and other professional men and women who have the *means* to afford the best medical care in the Philippines, the *intelligence* to be skillful observers, and the *integrity* to be accurate reporters. Most of these people had nothing to gain by giving the testimonials. In fact, they run the risk of being considered "a little crazy" by their peers to whom the whole phenomenon makes absolutely no sense. The stories include cures in chronic peptic ulcers, well-established glaucoma, painful bone spurs, uncontrollable hypertension and even toxic goiter. On the other hand, while visiting the healing centers, I witnessed children suffering from asthma, who were still wheezing and gasping for air and appeared no better off after their healing. A simple injection of adrenalin, in most cases could have provided these children with almost instantaneous relief. In addition, I have heard reports from my medical colleagues in the Philippines of patients who believed that their cancer had been removed by the healer only to find on subsequent evaluation that the tumor continued to grow. This is an unfortunate circumstance for a patient whose tumor might be amenable to early diagnosis and treatment by modern medical techniques.

There is evidence that "psychic surgery" is effective and there is equally pressing evidence that it is not effective. One merely has to listen to whichever view suits his purposes or needs at the time to have his suspicions confirmed. "Psychic surgery", like orthodox medicine can, in fact, be both effective and ineffective. For example, penicillin is very good treatment for some infections but it does not cure peptic ulcers. Does this mean that penicillin should be discarded from medicine because it does not cure everything? Analogously, healing should not be discarded because it does not cure everything. Perhaps, after careful clinical consideration we will be able to identify more clearly those conditions in which healing is most effective. Then when choosing therapy for a patient, healing would be given as careful a consideration as drugs or surgery.

Power Of Suggestion

Healing is one of several alternative forms of medicine that interested me after graduating from medical school. Just before studying healing, I studied hypnosis and became aware of the power of suggestion and the influence of the mind over the body. The response of one of my patients to treatment by hypnosis was so impressive that I sought to publish a report of her case in one of our respected medical journals.[1] Briefly, the patient, at ten years of age, was diagnosed in at least two medical centers as having juvenile rheumatoid arthritis. She responded minimally to large doses of aspirin and physical therapy. Her ankles and knees were grossly swollen and she had to be wheeled around like an invalid. She was depressed and discouraged. After about three months of not responding to high doses of aspirin, her doctors reluctantly considered treating her with cortisone; but first they wanted to try hypnosis. The patient was wheeled into her second hypnosis session, still discouraged, depressed and unable to walk. Four hours after this session she rode her bicycle and was without pain for the first time in three months. The swelling of her knees and ankles subsided quickly and now, almost four years later she is a normal, healthy, happy teenager with no recurrence of her arthritis.

It is quite clear to me that one of man's greatest untapped natural resources is his own subconscious mind. It is regrettable that orthodox medicine does not put as much emphasis on exploring this resource as it does in developing new drugs and surgical procedures. In spite of the many examples of patients who have made remarkable recoveries by using the power of their own minds, orthodox medicine tends to discount this type of healing as *just* a placebo effect. However, there are those physicians in the profession who do recognize and write about the power of the mind. In November, 1971, a publication entitled, *Rational Drug Therapy,* printed an excellent article entitled, "The Placebo—A Poorly Understood and Neglected Therapeutic Agent", by Henry R. Bourne, M.D.[2] More recently the *Journal of the American Medical Association* published a commentary by two Boston physicians entitled, "The Placebo Effect, A Neglected Asset in the Care of Patients".[3] The authors, Dr. Benson and Dr. Epstein, summarize their concise but extremely well-documented commentary thusly:

COMMENT

In recent years, the placebo effect has been viewed with disdain due to the emphasis on controlled drug trials that test the efficacy of new drugs. Yet, if a placebo and the tested new medication both produce equally positive effects, is it justified simply to report the nonspecificity of the medication and then disregard both the medication and placebo? Since the beneficial effect is the desired result, should not the placebo effect be further investigated so that we might better explain its worthwhile consequences? For example, the physiology of the placebo effect remains a relatively unexplored area. There are substantiated, specific physiologic changes associated with the placebo effect that await further definition.

Patient and physician attitudes that create a sound doctor-patient relationship contribute to the production of the placebo effect. The placebo effect in most instances enhances the well-being of the patient, and thus is an essential aspect of medicine. The growing trend toward decreasing doctor-patient contact, for example, through the use of computer facilities to obtain histories, should be viewed critically. More emphasis on the potency of the placebo and its positive effects is needed. Research and instruction of efficient methods of establishing the appropriate doctor-patient relationship conducive to the placebo effect should be initiated. The placebo effect demands greater comprehension and must be allowed to survive if medicine is to provide optimal care for patients.

As I see it, *the placebo effect is a simple non-toxic, non-mutilating and oftentimes very effective method of stimulating and facilitating the patient's own intrinsic healing processes.*

The comments above are not meant to infer that all healing is a placebo effect. There have been some cases of distant healing reported in which a patient who was seriously ill made an unexpected recovery at precisely the time a group of people were praying for him without his awareness. I have no first-hand knowledge of such cases but believe it is possible. Until we develop some fine instruments to measure energy and energy transfer there will always be a question as to whether the healing process was stimulated by a powerful suggestive influence on the patient's own mind or by some actual transfer of energy from the healer to the patient.

Since I am more familiar with the realities of hypnosis and suggestion than I am with the realities of energy transfer, I would like to leave the latter topic to my colleagues who will discuss it elsewhere in this book. In focusing on some important techniques used to stimulate the patient's own healing mechanism, it is important to recognize that many of the patients who journey to the Philippines seeking relief from their suffering are in a frame of mind which is crucial to maximize their chances for recovery.

The majority of people making the long flight for "psychic surgery" have usually been through the therapeutic mill of orthodox medicine in their native land without any significant relief of their pain and suffering, hence they look to "psychic surgery" as their last hope of getting well. At times this motivation is aided and abetted by the ubiquitous fear of death. "Psychic surgery" is their last chance and they really want it to be successful.

The fact that they are willing to make this difficult journey, the commitment of time and money and the inconvenience of traveling to a totally unfamiliar foreign country, and the risk of being ridiculed by their family and friends for doing so, is clearly indicative of a potent motivation to get well. There will of course be exceptions. There are those people who go out of curiosity or just to keep friends and family happy, but in general, I think most of the patients who make the long flight to the Philippines are motivated to get well again.

Most of the patients traveling to the Philippines have heard the fantastic stories of friends and neighbors seriously ill for long periods of time who have been to the Philippines and undergone "psychic surgery" with remarkable success. In addition, these stories are illustrated by phenomenal home movies. So the patient travels to the Philippines with the expectation that he will be helped. If his friends had such miraculous results, he expects similar results in his own case and this expectation is important to his recovery.

The healer frequently will diagnose a patient in a most assured manner, leaving the patient to believe that he truly understands his case. In many instances these patients have been to the best clinics in the U.S. and returned with only a vague concept of what their problem really is. In other instances, the diagnosis is clinched but current accepted therapies offer little hope of a cure.

The healer sometimes will make positive diagnosis in a very confident manner either by a spiritual "X-ray" or by automatic writing. In the latter technique an entity on a higher plane presumably assists the healer in making an accurate diagnosis. At any rate, subconsciously the patient is assured that he or she has finally found someone who truly understands the problem—and has a solution.

The "operation" is usually performed in the presence of others who will be "operated" on the same day. They witness what appear to be tumors, blood clots and various forms of witchcraft being painlessly extracted from a patient's body in the dramatic setting of a bloody operative field.

This very impressive display assures the prospective patient that something truly miraculous is happening. The subconscious impact of one seeing the alleged tumor that has been plaguing him for so many years being removed from his body and discarded before his very eyes has a profound psychological effect, which undoubtedly can bring about physiological, metabolic, possibly even physical changes. I speculate that on the physical level these changes are probably mediated through the hypothalamus and the autonomic nervous system.

The combination of the motivation, fear, expectation, commitment and the visual effect of "psychic surgery" no doubt are sufficient to initiate an attitudinal change at a level sufficiently deep to bring about a remission or cure in many of the patients who have journeyed to the Philippines in serious hope of improving their health.

Psychosomatic Dis-ease

It is easy to see how under these conditions many patients will find a cure, especially those who are afflicted with a psychosomatic disease. That a patient's illness is psychosomatic, however, should not prompt us to dismiss it lightly since a good percentage of the medical problems that plague people are psychosomatic in nature.

A psychosomatic disease is a MIND-BODY disease. The mind is stimulated or stressed and the body reacts. The reaction of each person to emotional stress differs. Some people get migraine headaches and others diarrhea before, during, or immediately after a period of stress. In some people an emotionally upsetting experience leads to an elevated blood pressure or an increase in flow of stomach acids and ulcer symptoms. Migraine headaches, colitis, peptic ulcers, essential hypertension and asthma are only a few of the many psychosomatic diseases. The mind is clearly one factor involved in the precipitation of many common illnesses for which patients visit their doctors.

Unfortunately, orthodox medicine does not put as much stress on the treatment of psychosomatic disease as it does on the treatment of organic disease. This is regrettable because a great number of organic ailments are preceded by psychosomatic diseases. It is my belief that the longer any psychosomatic disease is allowed to progress, the more physical changes, however microscopic, take place and patterns may be set up which make it easier for the disease process to recur and progress to an organic disease.

Ideally, therapy should be aimed primarily at retarding or reversing the intrinsic disease process itself, and only secondarily at the results of that disease process. This approach to disease can be difficult because oftentimes it involves treating a patient on an emotional or even spiritual level.

If the psychosomatic disease could be successfully treated, its organic sequelae could be prevented.

The Chinese have a saying:

> The inferior doctor *treats* actual illness.
> The mediocre doctor *cures* imminent illness.
> The superior doctor *prevents* illness.

The comments above are not meant to belittle the amazing technical advances made in modern medicine. Rather, they are intended to point out the futility of separating the mind from the body in the treatment of disease.

Dangers To Be Considered

A discussion of the effectiveness of a drug or surgical procedure would not be complete without careful consideration of potential hazards. Until such time as proper studies on the efficacy and safety of "psychic surgery" are completed, treatment by a healer in the Philippines may be risky.

The dangers are as follows:

(1) *Precious time could be wasted* in the diagnosis and treatment of a problem that might easily be amenable to orthodox medical therapy.

For example a breast tumor, if discovered early enough, could very readily respond to modern medical techniques. Time wasted in detection, diagnosis and treatment of the tumor could result in metastatic spread of the diseased tissue.

A pain in the abdomen could represent an inflamed appendix which if treated promptly is a simple surgical procedure, but if allowed to progress and rupture, could take the life of the patient.

This is not to conclude that it would be impossible for a healer to cure a patient with appendicitis. However, the proven success rate is so high with conventional surgery that it would not be worth taking the risk to see if "psychic surgery" would be just as effective, unless, of course "psychic surgery" were the only method of therapy available at the time.

(2) *Infection might be transmitted* through the use of unsterile instruments. Until it can be unquestionably demonstrated that the small

skin incisions made by one of the healers does not involve the use of any physical instrument we must consider the possibility that a hidden razor blade may be used to make these small incisions. Thus, at this time, we cannot preclude the possibility of an already debilitated patient contracting a serious infection such as hepatitis from the use of an unsterile instrument.

(3) *Further damage might occur as a result of injudiciously applied pressure.*

If a patient suffered from a detached retina, pressure on the eye might cause serious progression of the problem. A patient with infectious mononucleosis and a fragile spleen might sustain a rupture if heavy pressure were applied over the left upper quadrant of his abdomen.

(4) *The long arduous journey* could further impair the health of already seriously debilitated patients.

(5) *The financial burden* imposed could greatly tax the already-dwindling monetary resources of a chronically ill patient.

The ultimate hazard of "psychic surgery" is its separation from orthodox medicine. The tragedy is that the medical profession is reluctant to discuss or investigate this phenomenon and the patient is fearful of discussing this topic with his physician at all. The result is that the patient in search of a ray of hope is forced to step outside of the protective confines of orthodox medicine and take the attendant risks.

At the present time anyone considering a trip to the Philippines for "psychic surgery" must weigh these risks against the uncertainty of a cure. Unfortunately, until serious study by competent, open-minded investigators is completed, the patient stands alone in making this decision.

It would be to everyone's benefit if the whole subject of psychic or paranormal healing could be discussed freely amongst the medical profession and patients could visit healers without fear of ridicule or losing contact with their personal physicians.

The ideal system would have the patients studied and an orthodox diagnosis made. If time were not of the essence, the patient would be allowed a trial of healing but always under the supervision of an understanding well-informed personal physician. In this way, the patient would be protected from obvious hazards such as infection and delayed diagnosis while at the same time giving healing a chance to spare him from possibly life-long commitment to drugs with concomitant side effects or to a traumatic surgical procedure.

The cardinal law of medicine is *primum non nocere*—"first, do no harm."

Physicians will be better able to abide by this law when both orthodox and unorthodox healing modalities are discussed openly and practiced freely under one protective roof.

Ethics Of "Psychic Surgery"

Before a new drug is offered to the public it is extensively tested for its safety and biological effectiveness. We have already considered the possible hazards of "psychic surgery" in the previous paragraphs but discussing its biological effectiveness is quite a bit more difficult if one applies the standards currently applied to the evaluation of new drugs. Carefully controlled double blind studies are performed to be assured that a patient's recovery is due to the intrinsic biological properties of the drug and not to the patient's expectations of the drug. However, as noted previously, I believe the patient's expectation plays a considerable role in stimulating his healing process. This could be considered a placebo effect and of little practical value to a hard-core scientific investigator. On the other hand, placebo effect or not, the patient does regain his health, which is of great practical value *to the patient*.

Even if further investigation proved the effectiveness of "psychic surgery" and paranormal healing to be based on a combination of the patient's motivation, expectation and the healer's proficiency in sleight-of-hand, would it be considered unethical thereby to "trick" a patient out of his disease?

A great number of diseases have been termed psychosomatic and for these orthodox medicine has very little to offer. In some instances if the psychosomatic problem is not arrested, surgical intervention may be necessary, as in the case of a bleeding peptic ulcer or severe ulcerative colitis.

Would it be unethical to "trick a patient out of his disease" when drugs and surgery have already failed to relieve his suffering or when the next step in management involves a life-long sentence to steroids or multiple debilitating surgical procedures?

The power of the subconscious mind to correct disease has barely been touched upon in orthodox medicine.

As I see it, the same basic rules of ethics should be applied to "psychic surgery" or healing in general, as is applied to orthodox medicine.

(1) That *no harm* should come to the patient either through *commission* or *omission*.

In the first instance, harm comes to the patient by something the healer does, such as the inappropriate application of pressure or the use of unsterile instruments. In the second, harm comes through not recognizing a problem such as pneumonia or appendicitis that can be easily corrected by orthodox medical techniques.

(2) *That one should not exploit the suffering of his fellow man.*

This rule should apply not only to physicians and healers but also to drug companies, surgical supply houses and tourist agencies associated with the healers.

Both of these rules should be assiduously applied to anyone who is involved in the treatment of patients who are ill.

If these two rules are complied with, "psychic surgery", or any other form of healing for that matter, should be considered as ethical as orthodox medicine.

The Bottom Line

Upon my return from the Philippines many of my colleagues confronted me with the question, "Well, does it work?" Rather than go into a long dissertation in the hospital corridor, I answered with a simple, "Maybe."

I have heard many stories of miraculous cures and there is no doubt that the dramatic display of "psychic surgery" is very impressive and capable of profound suggestive influences. It is my hope that the weight of the positive reports on healing and the increasing public interest will spur the medical profession to begin a long overdue, unbiased scientific appraisal of this fascinating and controversial therapeutic modality.

A casual study is of little value. For example, simply asking a patient what his diagnosis is can frequently result in error.

On one of my visits to a healing center, a gentleman told me he had been cured of glaucoma by one of the "psychic surgeons". When I asked him how he knew he had glaucoma, he replied that it was because he had blurred vision just like an aunt who had glaucoma. He himself had never been to a doctor for diagnosis of his condition. A woman told me she had a heart condition but did not know specifically what kind. When asked what medication she took she was able to describe two pills that she took, but had no knowledge of what they did for her.

In addition to an accurate, substantiated diagnosis of the disease being treated, the scientific investigation must also include a long-term follow-up study. The phenomenon of "feeling better" right after any treatment is well-known. The real test is *time*.

If it can be proven that a significant number of patients have improved or have been cured, we are still left with the question of *how*.

Is the healing process facilitated by the actual transfer of energy from the healer to the patient or is it facilitated by the powerful influence of the patient's own mind?

This is a very difficult distinction to make and perhaps in the last analysis it does not matter—*at least to the patient*. All healing ultimately occurs from within. The surgeon's knife, the internist's drugs do not heal the body. At best, they give the body's defense and homeostasis mechanism a chance to rally; at worst, they cause further stress and suppression of natural defense and homeostasis mechanisms. Perhaps "psychic surgery" and paranormal healing act in a similar manner, i.e. instead of a drug, it is energy transfer which arrests the disease process long enough to allow natural body defenses to get back on their feet.

On the other hand, perhaps "psychic surgery" and paranormal healing have no direct effect on the disease process specifically but rather act on the patient as a whole being. This influence may occur through suggestion, through energy transfer or through a combination of both suggestion and energy transfer. The net result is a restoration of "body balance" through the autonomic nervous system.

Ultimately all healing is self-healing. Ambrose Pare, a famous French surgeon of the 16th century recognized this when he wrote, after each operation, "I bandaged the wound—God healed it."

REFERENCES

1. Forrest J. Cioppa, and Alan B. Thal, "Rheumatoid Arthritis, Spontaneous Remission, and Hypnotherapy". In *JAMA*, 230:1388, 1974.
2. Henry R. Bourne, "The Placebo—A Poorly Understood and Neglected Therapeutic Agent". In *Rational Drug Therapy*, Vol. 5, No. 11, November, 1971.
3. Herbert Benson, and Mark D. Epstein, "The Placebo Effect: A Neglected Asset in the Care of Patients". In *JAMA*, 232:1225, 1975.

12

OBSERVATIONS

George W. Meek

The following observations on paranormal healing in the Philippines, basically those of the editor, are shared by many of the medical doctors, scientists, psychologists, psychiatrists, parapsychologists, clinical physiologists, and psychical researchers from five countries who have collaborated on the Philippine studies over the past several years. Some of us have made as many as five trips to the Philippines and, collectively, we have spent more than 120 weeks observing the work of the healers there.

1. Contrary to all publicity and contrary to what seems to take place in the many motion pictures you may have seen of Philippine healers at work, the physical body today is not opened in 95% + of the cases.

2. The red liquid and tissue which appear in "operations" on Western patients, and the so-called "witchcraft items" which appear in the case of native patients, fall primarily into two categories:

   A. They may be genuine apport or materialization phenomena, or

   B. They may be produced by deception or sleight-of-hand from a mixture of animal blood, and animal tissue or items from nature.

   (As of 1977, category B undoubtedly accounts for the overwhelming portion of the activities.)

3. The two categories just mentioned show clearly why there has been such total confusion in the results of pathological examination of the blood and tissue obtained from such "operations", and why the healers have often resisted attempts of researchers to obtain samples for pathological tests.

4. Regardless of the source of the "blood and guts" or witchcraft items, in any given "operation" the resulting powerful psychological impact is often highly beneficial to the patient.

5. Such healing as does take place in the patient's body results largely from energies emanating from or through the healer

which appear to stimulate or reactivate the cells in the patient's body.

6. Sometimes this rebuilding and reenergizing of cells, organs, and muscles of the patient's body can take place very quickly, say at hundreds of times the normal healing speed, sometimes it may occur over days, weeks, or months.

7. In addition to the completely valid but declining materialization and apport phenomena mentioned in item (2) above, other paranormal phenomena such as the following have been documented:

   A. "Psychic" or "spiritual" injections, which, although no needle is used, and the healer's hand may not come closer than two feet from the patient's body, can sometimes cause a feeling of sharp pain and produce a flow of blood (and even pierce four layers of plastic film concealed below the patient's clothing as described in Chapter 20).

   B. The making of a small opening in the skin without the use of instruments, an opening which will heal normally and leave no scar.

   C. The dematerialization and rematerialization of cotton and the apparent insertion into and the removal of such cotton from patient's body without any visible opening, and usually without physical discomfort. (This activity is also the subject of very frequent deception or sleight-of-hand.)

   D. The painless extraction of teeth, the healer using only his fingers and a gentle pull.

8. As to the relative effectiveness of the work of the healers, we make these points:

   A. No broadly based and carefully documented *clinical* reports have been prepared to date, and the very nature of the problems of organizing such research indicate it will be perhaps several years before such data will be available.

   B. In the absence of valid clinical data we offer these observations:

      a. Most of the patients who spend the money and effort to travel to the Philippines have already tried to get relief from their ailments through their own doctors and have not been successful for any one of several reasons. Some of the illnesses successfully treated by healers had previously been considered terminal.

      b. Once the patient is in the Philippines, possibilities for healing vary considerably from healer to healer, and may depend on whether or not the patient has access to the services of more than one healer. This is because of differing abilities of individual healers. (Example: One healer never works on hands or feet.)

      c. The chances for successful healing are increased if the work of the healer is complemented by lectures and counseling aimed at giving the patient a greater awareness of his own mind-body-spirit relationship. In such a case the patient learns the role which his thoughts and emotions played in making him sick in the first place, and how his thoughts and emotions can supplement and enhance the work of the healer.

  d. Some patients definitely *do* obtain the healing they seek. Many who do not obtain it, are better able to cope with the problems related to their illness.

  c. It would seem that the direct healer-to-patient relationship which prevails in the Philippines may produce substantially greater benefits and probably more lasting healing, than does a huge public healing service such as is sometimes conducted in the U.S.A. and in England,.

  C. While there is admittedly no solid evidence for such a contention, it would appear that the Filipino healers in general are unable to render substantial help to patients suffering from *mental or emotional* illness. (We encountered two such patients whose plight definitely *worsened* because of visits to the healers and participation in psychic development classes conducted by healers.)

 9. The attempt to explain scientifically HOW the healer accomplishes a successful result is extremely difficult. No complete explanation is possible at our present level of scientific knowledge. (In Chapter 19 we do our current best to outline an overall theory.)

10. Paranormal healing activities of the Filipino healers perform a very useful service toward alleviating mankind's suffering. The further development of these techniques (minus the deception and sleight-of-hand) should very definitely be encouraged and should never be ridiculed and discouraged.

Finally, there is an observation of paramount importance which applies to activities studied in the Philippines. Just as organized science refused to study materialization and apport phenomena when they were abundantly present in England and Brazil in the first quarter of this century science has, during the past two decades, failed to recognize and study the part these phenomena have played in the activities of the Philippine healers. Continued failure of science to face up to the full significance of these phenomena, (and the somewhat related "Geller effect") is delaying a fuller understanding of man's unique place in the cosmos and his potential for further self-realization. No "theory of the paranormal" that scientists may try to construct will be of any lasting value if it fails to accommodate materialization and apport phenomena—as well as discarnate entities, thoughtography, precognition, psychometry, and the "Geller effect".*

*So called after the Israeli psychic Uri Geller, the "Geller effect" is that phenomenon in which focused mind power of children in England, Japan and France modifies the crystalline structure of metal.

III

THE REALITY OF "HEALING ENERGIES"

Skeptics have long doubted the very existence of psychic, faith, and mental healing. Now serious scientific research in several countries has revealed the existence of energies that emanate from a person serving as a healer. Additional developments in the area of sophisticated electronic equipment add still more to our growing understanding of the natural forces that operate in and through the human body and are involved in the whole process of illness and health.

Every science requires a system of measurements. Previous scientific attempts to study healers and healing have immediately floundered because there did not seem to be any parameters susceptible of measurement.

Within only the last few years scientists have devised *instrumental* means for detecting the presence of energetic exchanges between the healer and the patient. With these breakthroughs it is now certain that rapid progress is possible in expanding our understanding of the exact nature of the healer-patient interaction. In a wider perspective, these developments begin at last to demonstrate the scientific reality of psychic, faith, and mental healing.

13

THE USE OF NON-HUMAN SENSORS

Jeanne P. Rindge

The paradigms of modern medicine have not stretched sufficiently to encompass the actuality of such healings as have been reported consistently through the centuries in all parts of the world—healing from the laying-on-of-hands, prayer, "spirit" agency, healings from a distance, any other "magic" (covering whatever is unacceptable or not yet understood).

The possibility that an unknown energy could be channeled through the hands or activated by the mind of one person so as to generate healing in another could not be countenanced. Although medical science still does not know exactly how healing takes place, it can be quite certain how it does not. In spite of this frigid medical atmosphere, unorthodox healings continue to be reported and, if anything, at an accelerating rate.

In spite of the fact that Paracelsus long ago recognized the power of suggestion in the cure of disease, a power used with remarkable skill by primitive shamans, medical orthodoxy did not legitimatize it until a century or more after the medically-rejected Mesmerists and hypnotists successfully practiced their hand passes. Now, the "power of suggestion"—or misdiagnosis—or spontaneous regression—or naivete, or hallucination, or outright fraud on the part of the investigator—or else some latent medical effect are the rugs under which unorthodox healings are swept.

When there has been argument, there has been more heat than light. In recent years, a few intrepid but fully qualified researchers, both within and without the medical profession, including authors of this book, determined to take a closer look.

To authenticate healings as paranormal—that is, outside accepted tenets of science—is more difficult than it might seem. An ill person is not a laboratory experiment with all variables but the desired one removed, nor can the exact situation be multiplied in sufficient numbers to obtain statistical results. Furthermore, the sick, at least in our society, seldom come to healers as virgin territory untouched by medical science (more often as a last resort). So long as there is one other lingering hypothesis, there is no incontrovertible proof.

Where proof seems obvious, only a few doctors have been willing to substantiate the evidence. Some, secretly sympathetic, feel blocked by Section 3 of the American Medical Association's Principles of Medical Ethics: "A physician should practice a method of healing founded on a scientific basis; and he should not voluntarily associate professionally with anyone who violates this principle." The stumbling block, of course, is the word *scientific*. Whether the "unscientific" practitioner is *successful* as a healer is, apparently, beside the point.

To a serious young biochemist from Montreal in the nineteen sixties, this was a challenge. A geriatrics researcher at McGill University's Allen Memorial Institute, Dr. Bernard Grad is a skilled scientist. He felt certain that the scientific method in properly controlled laboratory conditions could begin to find scientifically acceptable answers to the question of paranormal healing—if someone would make the effort. With carefully designed and painstakingly controlled research funded by the Parapsychological Foundation, he undertook the assignment. His significant results and rigorous approach have paved the way for other researchers and opened the minds of unnumbered antagonists.[1]

His question: *Does the healing method of laying-on-of-hands produce results through the "power of suggestion" or by some more objective means?* If there could be observable effects with small animals and plants, he reasoned, suggestion presumably could be ruled out.

He chose mice as his experimental target and, as subject, a retired Hungarian army colonel who had moved to Montreal. Colonel Oskar Estebany had discovered his healing ability during routine work with cavalry horses and later with people during the Hungarian Revolution when doctors were in short supply. A kindly man with courtly manners and military carriage, Colonel Estebany's one present desire was to heal. He also was curious as to what the research would show. In keeping with the code adhered to by most successful healers, he' charged no fee and made no personal claims for healing power. Healing comes, he says with limited English, "from up there", pointing heavenward. "I channel it."

Dr. Grad and staff spent weeks becoming accustomed to the mice, and accustoming them to research. This included "gentling" of the mice through handling and stroking, it having been found that nervous mice are not reliable experimental subjects. This done, and the inappropriate mice discarded, the staff removed like amounts of skin from the backs of the mice (under anesthesia); weighed them and then measured the wound sizes.

The forty-eight female mice were then divided into three groups; the first was treated by Col. Estebany in a cage resting on his left palm with his right hand held above the wire mesh—not touching the animals. The second group was cared for in identical ways but was not treated by the healer. The third group was given identical routine without treatment but was heated to the same degree as those heated slightly by the healer's hands. This was to test whether heat alone would accelerate wound healing.

The skin wounds were measured periodically up to 20 days and the rates of healing analyzed. The significant results are shown in Table I, and Figures 1 and 2, where the differences are obvious, visually as well as statistically. The wounds in the group treated by the healer are much smaller than are those in the control groups. The heated controls showed no additional speed of healing.

Table I

The effect of Mr. E's Field and of Heat on the Rate of Wound Healing in CF₁ Female Mice: Weight (Mg.) of Paper Projections of Wounds

Treatment	On day of wounding	One day after wounding	Eleven days after wounding	Fourteen days after wounding
MTR (Control)	7.547*±.211**	7.705±.493	3.194±.363	2.043±.379
STTR (Mr. E)	8.051±.234	7.394±.393	1.322±.326	.562±.146
HTR (Heated)	7.711±.284	7.299±.437	3.575±.396	2.323±.442

*Mean.
**Standard error.

Fig. 1

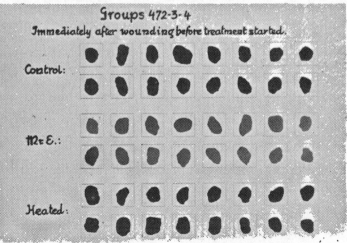

Fig. 1. Graphic representation of surface area of the wound of each of the mice immediately after the wounds were made and before treatment was started. It is obvious that there are no real differences in wound surface area between the three groups despite some variation from mouse to mouse.

Fig. 2

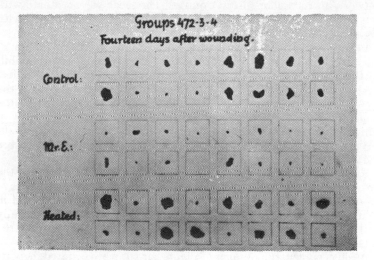

Fig. 2. Graphic representation of surface area of the wound of each of the mice fourteen days after wounds were made. Obviously, the wounds in the mice treated by Mr. E are smaller than those of the other two groups, statistical analysis showing that the differences are significant beyond the .001 level. It is also obvious that there is no significant difference between the control group and the heated group.

This experiment was repeated with the cooperation of Drs. Remi J. Cadoret and G. I. Paul at the University of Manitoba under strict double blind conditions to rule out any possible unconscious manipulation or psychokinetic effect on the part of the investigators. Three hundred mice were used. An added control in this experiment was a group treated by persons not claiming healing ability.

Results again showed that the rate of wound healing was significantly faster in the group treated by Col. Estebany than in the control groups. Some agency beside "suggestions" was responsible for the healing.

Search for a more rapid method than the five-week wound healing stint, plus the desire to discover how widely in the biological realm this effect could be observed, led to a series of experiments with barley seeds. Dr Grad found in preliminary studies that there were certain optimal conditions under which the experiments should be conducted: 1) Seeds should be studied while implanted in the soil. 2) Some inhibitions (dis-easing) along with otherwise optimal growing conditions should be arranged. This was done by watering the seeds initially with a one per cent sodium chloride solution to make them "ill". This was followed by several days of drying and subsequent watering with tap water at suitable intervals. 3) The third remarkable discovery was that significant differences in growth rate could be obtained without the need for Col. Estebany to treat the plants directly with his hands. It was enough for him to treat only the saline solution by holding the bottle between his hands for fifteen minutes! The seeds were watered with this treated solution only once. Thereafter they were watered with regular tap water which was not treated by the healer.

In early experiments, the saline was contained in open beakers; in later experiments, in sealed glass bottles. This eliminated the possibility that sweat or breath or any other known physical factor could affect the solution. Whatever the effective agent, it was able to penetrate the glass jar and to be transferred through the saline solution to the implanted seeds. Elaborate double blind precautions were used in which a different person handled each part of the experiment without any one person being aware, until the experiment was over, which were the treated and which the untreated pots.

Following the watering with treated saline (and for controls, the untreated saline) the numbered seed pots were heated for 48 hours in an oven kept at 38-40°C. The pots were then randomly arranged in columns in an appropriate location and all were watered periodically with 25 ml. of untreated water. Col. Estebany did not come near the pots.

As days passed, the number of plants per pot were counted, heights measured and yield calculated. The experiments were terminated after 12 to 15 days, with each of the six experiments analyzed separately. There were significantly more plants and plant yield or else more height in the plants in the treated pots. Once again, it was evident that some factor—hardly attributable to suggestion, unconscious manipulation, or outright fraud (as study of the original data will show)—was at work on these seedlings. The data do not tell us what this force may be.

An interesting sequel to these experiments does tell us something about some conditions under which the "force" is operative—or suppressed. Dr. Grad had heard frequent reports that healers believed it essential to be in a tranquil frame of mind (in many cases prayerful) before healing power could be activated successfully. For some unknown reason, mice treated by medical students used as controls in the former wound-healing experiment healed more slowly than the non-treated controls.

It occurred to Dr. Grad that really disturbed patients might significantly inhibit the healing process. He prepared an experiment in which the agents were a 26-year-old depressive neurotic woman, a 37-year-old man with psychotic depression (both hospitalized) and a psychiatrically normal J. B. who had a "green thumb". Each agent "treated" sealed bottles of saline, prepared by Baxter Laboratories, Ltd., for 30 minutes. The experiments with barley seeds then continued as before.

J. B., the normal agent, provided consistently greater stimulation to plant growth than did the other two persons or the untreated controls. Although not claiming to be a healer, J. B. had reported feeling a "flow" of "something" down his arms when attempting to treat an ill member of his family. He concentrated upon inducing this sense of flow while treating the saline.

The results with the psychotic man, as hypothesized, were below those of the controls. This indicated an inhibition of plant growth (or of healing of the damaged seeds). His attitude while holding the bottle was anxious, agitated and depressed.

The results with the depressive-neurotic woman, were better than with the untreated controls. It so happened that, when she was told the nature of the experiment, her mood brightened and she cradled the bottles as one would an infant.

Results suggest that one's immediate rather than long-term state of mind is the one that counts. (This was borne out later in Dr. Justa Smith's experiments). They also suggest that some kind of unknown energy may be activated or inhibited by a far wider spectrum of humanity than has been suspected.

What, in fact, actually happens when a mother immediately and instinctively places her hand over a child's hurt or a feverish brow? What else may be activated during the hospital patient's longed-for nightly massage? Where the power of suggestion is acceptedly utilized, as in psychotherapy, what additional influence, helpful or detrimental may be quietly taking place? What else is involved in the successful "bedside manner"?

Is the practitioner's mind-set and emotional state of far greater importance than we have realized? Can his or her "personal set," or gestalt actually wield a force or energy? How much, Dr. Grad asked himself, does this unknown factor relate to the well-known "placebo effect"? Haas, Fink and Hartfelder (*Pharmacology Service Center Bulletin,* Vol. 2, July, 1963) reported that 40.6% of 14,177 patients with various ills obtained relief from placebo—sugar pills. The effect is sufficiently powerful in some cases to *reverse the normal pharmacological effect* of certain drugs. Is the belief system of the patient wielding an unknown energy upon himself?

Of equal interest is the case in which a doctor, running a series of experiments with a severe asthmatic, found that a new drug was helpful and the placebo not. The only problem was that the drug company, without the doctor's knowledge had substituted placebo for the active drug. Hence, the positive effect on this patient evidently was due to the doctor's—and not the patient's belief that the placebo was the agent! (J. S. Bell, *Applied Therapeutics,* Vol. 6, 1964) Was the *doctor* activating an energy or force which was not in the placebo? Does the personal bias of different investigators "energetically" influence the experiment in ways which may explain different results under identical experimental procedures?

Dr. Grad now hypothesizes that there may be some common denominator in success or failure from the laying-on-of-hands, psychotherapy and the placebo effect. This common denominator may be an *energy,* self-activated in the patient through suggestion, or channeled externally through the agency of the practitioner. Further light on this all-important hypothesis is of extreme importance to the healing professions. [*See* Chapter 19.]

Dr. Robert N. Miller of Atlanta, Georgia is another scientist concerned with the need for scientific rigor in the search for this illusive energy, if there is such. An industrial research scientist with a Ph.D. in chemical engineering, he holds four patents and is the author of numerous scientific papers relating to metallurgy, high polymers, fluid flow and heat transfer—his fields of research. He, too, was interested to know if there were an energy which could affect the rate of plant growth. He designed his first plant experiments in 1967.

To measure growth, Dr. Miller connected a rotary electro-mechanical transducer to a strip chart recorder (an arrangement first used by Dr. H. H. Kleuter of the U.S. Dept. of Agriculture). With a lever attached to the tip of a growing plant, the instrument can measure its growth rate with an accuracy of a thousandth of an inch an hour.

After considerable experimentation, Dr. Miller chose ordinary rye grass because of its sturdy, rapid growing nature with new growth importantly occurring at the bottom of the blades (beans, for instance, grow from the top).

His volunteer agents for "energizing" the plants were veteran healers Ambrose and Olga Worrall whose healing work is reported in *The Gift of Healing* and *Explore Your Psychic World* as well as in many magazines and newspaper articles. Individual medical doctors have sanctioned their work. [*See* Chapter 2.] Ambrose, a retired aircraft engineer with the Martin Company of Baltimore, was no stranger to scientific research; Olga, who calls herself a "housewife" is a motherly, no-nonsense advocate of the healing power.

The Worralls agreed to cooperate in a distant prayer experiment from their Baltimore home, 600 miles from Atlanta. Before the experiment began, the growth rate of a blade of rye grass had stabilized at 6.25 thousandths of an inch per hour. The Worralls were asked to hold the seedling in their prayers at their usual 9 p.m. prayer time on January 4. Until then, the strip chart recorder had traced a straight line with a slope representing the stable growth rate. Exactly at 9 p.m. the trace began to deviate upward and by morning the growth rate was 52.5 thousandths of an inch per hour, an increase of 840%! It gradually decreased but did not fall back to the original rate. During the period, the lab door was kept locked and there were no other known physical variables which could have influenced the plant. The results indicate that Ambrose and Olga Worrall by visualizing the grass filled with light and energy, caused an eight-fold increase in its growth rate from a distance of 600 miles.

Not content, Dr. Miller searched for additional means of identifying the existence of an illusive energy which conventional instruments fail to register. Cloud chambers have been used by physicists to make visible the (also illusive) high energy nuclear particles. Could suspected energy from a healer be detected in like manner?

Dr. Miller chose the Atomic Laboratories' Model 71850 cloud

chamber which consists of a cylindrical glass chamber seven inches in diameter and five in height with a sheet aluminum bottom and a viewing glass across the top. The chamber floor is covered with a ¼ inch layer of methyl alcohol, and the entire unit is placed upon a flat block of dry ice. Vapor is formed when molecules of the liquid alcohol evaporate upon contact with the closed volume of air. The dry ice causes a misty condensation which permits a visual trail of ionized molecules to form as a charged particle passes through.

Could energy from a healer manifest similarly? Mrs. Worrall, nearby on a speaking engagement, agreed to experiment. Placing her hands at the side of the chamber without touching the glass, she mentally "treated" the contents as she would a patient. A wave pattern developed in the mist, paralleling her hands. When she shifted the position of her hands 90 degrees the waves also shifted to right angles of their former motion. Similar results were obtained in experiments with the well-known psychic Ingo Swann and two other subjects.

The experiment was twice repeated with Mrs. Worrall concentrating from her Baltimore home 600 miles away. There were similar results. A camera picked up the pulsating waves in the mist which required eight minutes to subside following the test. Members of the research team, although nearby, were unable to influence the mist. The research is reported in the July, 1974 issue of *Science of Mind*.

Were long "discredited" data being verified? The 18th Century Mesmerists claimed to direct healing "fluid" into ailing bodies. Soon after that, Reichenbach's "somnambules" in Germany reported clairvoyantly to "see" energy flowing from not only healing hands but also from all bodies and from magnets as well. Reichenbach named the energy "od".[2] In this country Wilhelm Reich was hounded to his grave for aggressively championing his "orgone energy" which not only could heal, he and his followers said, but also could be stored in appropriate containers. In England, the de la Warrs[3] recently faced lawsuits for claiming to heal at a distance through the agency of a "useless" instrument, and for photographing with an unorthodox camera, water (among other things) which, when blessed, radiated energy in a different manner from ordinary water—according to the resulting photographs. All such claims are scientific heresy. But are they, in fact, calling attention to some different order of reality or to an unknown, possibly omnipresent, energy too subtle for present instruments to detect?

For several years, Dr. Shafica Karagulla, a neuropsychiatrist in California, having forfeited a prestigious conventional career because of nagging questions as to the nature of reality, has been quietly monitoring the responses of present-day clairvoyants who "diagnose" the physical condition of patients from the energy emanations which the clairvoyants "see" around the patients' bodies—diagnoses which concur remarkably with her own medical data. Her book, *Breakthrough to Creativity* (De Vorss, 1967), describes her early researches. Across the country in New York City, another medical doctor, John

Pierrakos[4] is checking his own medical diagnoses with what he, clairvoyantly, is beginning to see—"layers" of energy which seem to correspond to physical, emotional and mental aspects of the patient, shot through with colored flares corresponding to physical imbalances or disease. These reports are significantly similar to ancient Eastern teachings of "energy bodies" said to interpenetrate and extend beyond the physical body which is said to be the "condensation" of the pre-existing body or force field.

In forty years of quiet research at Yale Medical College, the late Harold Saxton Burr[5] discovered what he called a "life field" of unknown extension into space, surrounding all living things. None of this has shaken the scientific establishment's present assumptions.

Some physicists and parapsychologists and others *were* shaken, however, when Sheila Ostrander and Lynn Schroeder (*Psychic Discoveries Behind the Iron Curtain,* Prentice-Hall, 1970) having charmed secrets from Russian scientists of high repute, returned home with their psychic Sputnik—reports of a "bio-plasmic energy body" whose thought-activated forces can move objects without touch, can heal, hypnotize telepathically at a distance of at least 1,000 miles, which can be stored in "psychotronic generators", and whose colored flares can be photographed with a high frequency spark generator.

High frequency photographs (called "Kirlian" for the Russian originators) and high frequency controversy broke out all over the United States and have yet to be satisfactorily resolved. Are these multicolored emanations, showing spectacularly on Polaroid film, electrical artifacts as some believe? Are they physical effects? Are they subtle "auric" energies of Eastern and occult literature and clairvoyant observations as other researchers claim? Much hangs on the ultimate answers. Dr. Thelma Moss[6] of U.C.L.A. and Dr. Wililam Tiller at Stanford University are among the scientists actively engaged in this controversy.

Is this the same energy which activated Dr. Miller's cloud chamber? If healing energy could be thus identified, Dr. Miller hypothesized, and also its strength quantitatively measured, then healing centers about the country would have tools for accelerating the training of healers through feedback as to their progress.

With this in mind and armed with an Ernest Holmes Foundation grant, Miller found after scores of tests that cupric chloride solutions are reliable indicators of energies, providing all variables are carefully controlled. His research disclosed that solutions treated by Mrs. Worrall as well as control specimens initially crystallize in a green color. After two days at room temperature and 50% relative humidity, the control specimen is still green but the treated one has turned a beautiful turquoise blue. Why the difference?

Dr. Miller suspected changes in the properties of the water as the cause. His tests showed that the most significant differences are found in surface tension and infrared absorption. Using a Fisher Model 20 Du Nouy Type Tensiometer to measure the water's surface tension, experiments revealed that a maximum amount of energy is transferred into the water when a healer takes two $1/16$ inch diameter stainless steel rods, grasps an end of each in each hand, and places the other ends into the water for three minutes. Surface tension of water thus exposed to energy from a healer's hands is substantially reduced.

Further experiments showed that magnets also reduced water surface tension and turned cupric chloride crystals blue.

Additional tests were conducted to determine the effects of water treated by a magnet and water treated by a healer upon the growth of rye grass, both compared to controls. After eight days, the average height of control blades was 2.8 inches; for healer treated, 2.9 inches; and from magnets, 3.6 inches.

Mrs. Worrall, however, had treated the healer-specimen water 30 days prior to the test. Subsequent tests showed that both healer treated and magnet treated water give up the additional energy to the surrounding environment within 24 hours. (The energy can be withdrawn in a few minutes by swirling the water in a stainless steel beaker, Dr. Miller found.) Further analysis by Dr. Edward Brame of Wilmington, Delaware showed that normal water is 100% hydrogen bonded, whereas the healer-treated water is only 97.04% hydrogen bonded.

The pioneering work of Dr. Robert Miller and his associates in establishing the reality of healing energies being transferred from the healer to the patient is summarized[8] at the time this chapter is written, as follows:

1. An energy associated with healing does exist and it can be measured with suitable instruments.

2. Water which has been treated by a healer or a magnet changes the color of crystal solution and thus gives visual indication of the presence of the healing energy.

3. Water treated by a healer or a magnet changes surface tension, hydrogen bonding, and electrical properties of water.

4. A healer is most effective when in an alpha relaxed state of consciousness.

Ambrose Worrall, who died in 1972, called the energy from a healer's hands "para-electric" because of its similarity to the action of electricity which flows from a high potential source to a person or object at lower potential.

Dr. Miller recommends that the unit quantity of "paraelectricity" be called a "Worrall" and be defined as the energy required to reduce surface tension of 100 milliliters of distilled water from its normal state (72.75 dynes/cm at 20° C.) by 10 dynes/cm as the result of a three-minute exposure.

For the benefit of the scientists reading this book who might not have otherwise seen the details of any of these tests, this one example may be of interest.

PROCEDURE FOR MEASURING HEALING ENERGY

Pour exactly 100 ml of freshly distilled water into a glass Petri dish. Allow the water to reach room temperature, then measure the initial surface tension with a Du Nuoy type tensiometer. Take the average of three readings.

Obtain two pieces of stainless steel wire 1/8" in diameter and 8" long. Rinse the wires with distilled water and allow them to dry. Hold one wire between the thumb and forefinger of each hand with a firm pressure and then immerse the ends of the wires to a depth of 1" into the distilled water in the Petri dish. Keep the wires immersed for exactly five minutes. Do not transfer the water *to another container, as this will permit a transfer of energy and cause erroneous results. Measure the surface tension of the energized water with the tensiometer, taking the average of three readings.*

Use the following formula to calculate the Worralls of paraelectricity absorbed by the water:

Worralls of
energy absorbed

$$= \frac{(Initial\ surface\ tension) - (Final\ surface\ tension)}{10}$$

Reproducible results with paraelectricity experiments require strict control of all variables involved. Because this energy is absorbed and conducted by various materials in unpredictable ways, the use of glass containers is mandatory, since plastic beakers will cause a variation in results.

The above formula, according to Dr. Miller, can be used to measure an individual's vital energy. He suggests that this energy may be synonymous with the "life force" (chi) of the ancient Chinese, the "prana" of the Yogi, Reichenbach's "odic force", and the "orgone energy" of Wilhelm Reich. It may also relate to the "life field" of Dr. Burr.

It is significant to note that orthopedic surgeon Robert O. Becker of Syracuse, N.Y. has been speeding up bone grafts and enhancing tissue regeneration by the use of electricity. In measuring electrical potential on all parts of the skin, Dr. Becker found that the potentials are organized into an electrical field, represented by lines of force (he recognizes the similarity to the acupuncture "meridian" theory), that roughly parallels the nervous system.

Those versed in Eastern thought will recognize the similarity to the hypothesis of the "nadis"—interlocking lines of force said to make up an "etheric" or "energy body" which pre-exists the physical, interpenetrates it, and which externalizes in the nervous system. Harold Saxton Burr's delicate voltmeter picked up the potential of the nervous system of a salamander in the "life field" of the egg before the egg had been fertilized—thus indicating pre-existence of the field.

We are challenged to discover possible relationships between these various hypotheses and actual life processes, including healing.

Dr. Miller also hypothesized that plants may be used as sensors to detect energies associated with healing. Controversy still rages over the possibility that plants respond to human thought as claimed by polygraph expert Cleve Backster as reported in publications such as *The Secret Life of Plants* (Thompkins and Bird, Harper & Row, 1973).

In preliminary tests, Miller attached a galvanic skin response electrode to a philodendron plant leaf. Leads were connected through an amplifier to a strip chart recorder. Electrical responses were elicited in the plant and recorded as rapidly increased oscillations (compared with previous base line recordings) whenever experimenters discussed possible damage to the plant. Dr. Miller concluded that the plant was capable of reacting to human thought.

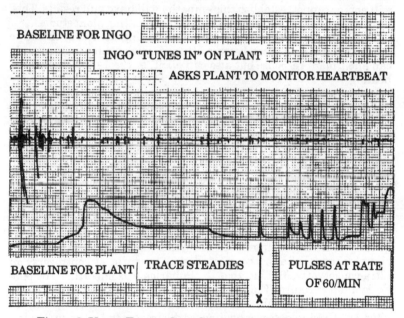

BASELINE FOR INGO

INGO "TUNES IN" ON PLANT

ASKS PLANT TO MONITOR HEARTBEAT

BASELINE FOR PLANT | TRACE STEADIES | PULSES AT RATE OF 60/MIN

X

Figure 3. Upper Trace—Ingo Swann's Brain Waves; Lower Trace—Plant Registers Series of Rhythmic Pulses (Chart Speed — 12in/min)

Next, Ingo Swann, a frequent experimental subject, was hooked up to a brain wave monitoring device which would record his brain wave changes on a strip chart recorder simultaneously with any electrical changes with the plant. (*See* Fig. 3) When Mr. Swann mentally (with no electrical connections to the plant) directed the plant to monitor his heart beats, an immediate change appeared in the plant. Response traces, shifting from a relatively steady base line to a pulsed rate corresponding to 60 beats per minute. Swann's brain wave recordings altered at exactly the moment he gave a mental directive to the plant. Before giving this directive, he mentally attuned himself to the plant.

This and other experiments by Dr. Miller lead him to believe that there is a fertile field for further research in the use of plants as thought and energy sensors.

However far-fetched such conclusions may be, they are corroborated by others such as IBM's brilliant research scientist, Marcel Vogel, winner of many awards for discoveries in the sophisticated fields of optics, magnetics and liquid crystal systems. After years of private research on plant-human relationships, he is convinced that plants are highly sensitive instruments for recording human emotional states. He has discovered that there also can be generated a remarkable energy exchange between plants and humans who are in tune with the plant (the "green thumb syndrome"?) He has found that experimenters who will not (or cannot) establish this empathy will have null results. This, he believes, explains the many failures in replicating plant studies.

Vogel hypothesized a Life Force surrounding all living things to which certain persons can become attuned. Such attunement not only can elicit plant response but also can elicit, or create the climate for, healing.

In the spring of 1967, a highly skeptical woman scientist entered the picture. Dr. M. Justa Smith, a Franciscan nun, was at that time chairman of the Natural Science Department at a private college, Rosary Hill, in Buffalo, N.Y. She was invited to an evening program shared with Dr. Bernard Grad and Dr. Andrija Puharich, a pioneering medical research scientist who had been investigating paranormal healings in various parts of the world. The evening of lectures was sponsored by the newly-formed Human Dimensions Institute at the college.

This was a return engagement for Dr. Puharich. At an earlier lecture, his descriptions of fantastic healings—such as those of the medically untrained Brazilian Arigó who nightly healed hundreds, frequently using major surgical procedures without ensuing pain, shock or unfortunate aftermath—created such a storm of controversy in ultra-conservative Buffalo, that Dr. Puharich was importuned by public demand to return. The sponsoring Institute, in an effort to include possibly more acceptable—at least more understandable—data, invited Dr. Grad to describe his impeccable research on the same platform.

Dr. Smith (Sister Justa), stunned by the reports of Puharich and Grad, determined to make her own investigation. Biochemist and enzymologist, she had received her doctorate (Smith, 1963) for original research on the effects of magnetic fields upon enzyme activity. Enzymes are the catalysts of the metabolic system. Any healing, or diseasing, first must activate the enzyme system. If, she reasoned, magnetic fields could increase the activity of the digestive enzyme trypsin—which in her research they did—and if ultra-violet light could decrease the activity—which in her research it did—then what effect upon the same enzyme could be had from the laying-on-of-hands, if any? She determined to find out.

Sister Justa and her half million dollar laboratory were well equipped to make the test. The Human Dimensions Institute forthwith designated Dr. Smith its Director of Research and obtained modest grants from the Shanti and the Parapsychological Foundations to underwrite a study on the effects of laying-on-of-hands upon enzyme activity. Col. Estebany, the healer used in the Grad research, was invited to Buffalo for a month's intensive research.

Dr. Smith proposed, initially, to compare the effects of the laying-on of Col. Estebany's hands upon the enzyme trypsin (purchased from the Worthington Biochemical Corporation) with magnetic field effects upon the same enzyme, as well as upon controls.

To do this, she prepared solutions of trypsin in a chromogenic substrate (BAPA) which were then divided into four glass vials or aliquoits. One was treated by Col. Estebany who simply placed his hands around the stoppered flask for a maximum of 75 minutes. A second was exposed to ultraviolet light at the most damaging wave length for protein (Dr. Grad has suggested that the enzyme be made "ill" in order to show more evidence of healing). A third aliquot was exposed to a high magnetic field (8,000-13,000 gauss) for hourly increments to three hours. The fourth aliquoit, untreated, was the control. From each of these, three millimeter portions were pipetted out at stated intervals and tested for activity in a Bausch and Lomb VOM 5 Spectrophotometer. The results were averaged for each process and then compared.

Results of the month-long study (Details in *Human Dimensions Professional Paper*, No. 2)[7] indicated that energy or force from Col. Estebany's hands activated the enzymes both quantitatively and qualitatively comparable to the activity created by a magnetic field of 8,000 to 13,000 gauss. This is a very significant activity considering that we live in a magnetic field of about 0.5 gauss. Effects on the injured enzymes (exposed to ultraviolet light) were essentially the same. There were no enhanced activities in the controls, nor with subsequent experiments with randomly chosen persons acting as agents.

During this first experimental period, a young medical doctor offered the use of his office and his own services in testing 24 human volunteers with assorted complaints. Following his medical screening, the patients were treated by Col. Estebany by the laying-on-of-hands. Of the group, twenty-one reported improvement. Two were recommended by the doctor for psychiatric treatment.

Unfortunately, due possibly to severe peer pressure upon the doctor, plus lack of time, the doctor did not write up a report on this experiment so we have no authentic record. One young patient, paralyzed on one side without improvement after long medical care at leading medical centers, recovered completely after several months of periodic follow-up visits to Col. Estebany in Montreal.

Another young Buffalo patient was hospitalized and was clinically at the point of death from a long-standing intestinal ailment. On supplication by her mother, her doctor gave permission for Col. Estebany to see the girl. She was given two treatments by the healer who simply held his hands above her abdomen, morning and early afternoon, for 15 minutes. A massive release of infectious material immediately ensued. She was released from the hospital within a few days. No statement was made available by her own doctor who did not witness the treatment. Dr. Smith and this writer were present during the treatment and the aftermath.

An interesting sequel to Sister Justa's first experiment happened months later. The first experiment had been conducted under optimum conditions for the healer. At the time of the second series, he was under intense emotional strain due to a family situation. There were no significant results in this experiment. This seemed to bear out Dr. Grad's hypothesis and the belief of most healers that healing can take place only when the healer is in a mental and emotional state of stable tranquility.

The results of the first test indicate that some kind of energy was channeled by Col. Estebany's hands sufficient to activate enzymes to a significant degree. Was this, however, "healing" energy? Dr. Smith believes that increased activation of the digestive enzyme is in the direction of improved health due to improved digestive metabolism. It would hardly seem possible to claim that the enzyme, isolated in its aliquoit, could be amenable to "suggestion". It seems apparent that some other force is at work, possibly the same as, or similar to, that activated by the other experiments. As in Dr. Grad's experiment, activation seems to be susceptible to the mental or emotional state of the agent.

As a next step, Dr. Smith questioned whether a healer necessarily would increase the action of all enzymes, or in fact, would this necessarily indicate healing action? She accordingly undertook some research with very different enzyme systems and with three other psychic sensitives who believed they had healing ability.

The sensitives were asked to "treat" the enzyme NAD (nicotinomide-adenine dinucleotide) which assists in the metabolic production of ATP (adenosive tri phosphate) an energy releasing compound. The body tissues contain NADase, another enzyme which breaks up NAD into its components. In illness, the proper balance of NAD may well be upset.

When NAD was treated in the same way as in the trypsin experiment, the results were a decrease in activity. Dr. Smith suggests that this would appear to play a positive role in healing as it would leave NAD intact to perform in ATP formation.

The enzyme research (much more extensive than can be reported here) indicates that a healer's ability does not affect all enzymes in the same way, although the present amount of data suggests that the kind of effect may be in the direction of improving health.

Whatever the energy is that is channeled by a healer's hands, it is not, according to Dr. Smith, in the electromagnetic spectrum. It is interesting to note, however, the similarity of reactions with *magnetic* effects both in the Smith and the Miller researches. Many questions about healing energy in general await answering.

Nurses, intimately involved with "touching" are showing interest in this research. Dolores Krieger, Ph.D., professor of nursing at New York University, had the opportunity to observe Estebany's ministrations for several weeks each summer at a temporary healing clinic. She was impressed by the numbers of persons whose health improved, including some given up by medical science.

Motivated by the Grad/Smith experiments, she searched the literature for further light. "Prana", she read in Eastern accounts, is the all-pervasive vital energy abundant in healthy persons but deficient in the ill. It was said to be intrinsic in the oxygen molecule. Perhaps, it occurred to Dr. Krieger, research on hemoglobin (the oxygen-carrying pigment of the red blood cells) would be helpful. Hemoglobin also is similar to chlorophyll, which was increased in Grad's barley experiments and is involved in several enzyme systems.

Dr. Krieger subsequently conducted three experiments. She hypothesized that the mean hemoglobin values of experimental groups tested by the laying-on-of-hands would exceed their before-treatment hemoglobin values and that those of the control (untested) groups would show no significant difference. In the first experiment with 19 ill experimental patients and 9 ill controls with Col. Estebany as healer, her hypothesis was confirmed at the .01 level of confidence *(Human Dimensions,* Autumn, 1972). In the second experiment with much more rigorous controls over the research design, with 46 and 29 ill persons, the confirmation was at the .001 level. *(Psychoenergetic Systems,* Vol. 3, No. 3, 1974)

Her developing subjective observations as she predicted and taught therapeutic touch was that healing is a natural potential for any person with a sincere motivation to heal, plus a fairly healthy (energetic) body. With this in mind, Dr. Krieger designed her third test for 32 registered nurses (out of 75 who volunteered). These she had screened through use of Shostrom's self-actualization tests for strong motivation. She found 64 patients willing to participate. Sixteen of the nurses who had been taught therapeutic touch by Dr. Krieger used it during routine care; 18 used routine care only. Her original hypothesis of hemoglobin change was born out at the .001 level with no significant difference in the controls. Dr. Krieger is continuing to teach touch to nursing classes.

These and other researches are straws in the wind. There is a crying need for replications and for new, creative research design. Dedicated researchers cannot continue indefinitely with meager or no supportive funds—the case to date. Researches, wherever conducted, need to be correlated, new hypotheses drawn, and the information made available to the growing number of churches and centers where healing efforts are taking place.

In our scientific zeal to isolate specifics, it also is important to recognize the probability that in healing, we are not, as so long assumed, dealing with a linear activity alone, what is done to whom, but with a larger, encompassing gestalt of physical, emotional, mental and spiritual relationships which can be activated in many ways, of which the hands of the healer may be one. Unless the individual, as center of his own gestalt, is inspired to take responsibility for his own well-being—on all levels—any healing techniques may be shortlived. Real healing, therefore, must become "wholing" hence, holy, if it is to be long-lasting and worthy of mankind's unfolding potentials.

REFERENCES

1. Bernard Grad, "An Unorthodox Method of Treatment of Wound Healing in Mice". In *International Journal of Parapsychology*, Vol. 3, Spring, 1961.

2. Baron Von Reichenbach, *Lectures on Od and Magnetism* (London: Hitchinson, 1952).

3. Langston Day, and George De La Warr, collaborators, *Matter in the Making* (London: Vincent Stuart, 1966).

4. John Pierrakos, *The Energy Field in Man and Nature* (New York: Institute of Bioenergetic Analysis, 1971).

5. Harold Saxton Burr, *Blueprint for Immortality: The Electrical Patterns of Life* (London: Spearman, 1972).

6. Thelma Moss, *The Probability of the Impossibility* (Los Angeles, Tarcher, 1974).

7. Sister Justa Smith, "Paranormal Effects on Enzyme Activity". Professional Paper No. 2 in *Human Dimensions,* Vol. 1, No. 2, 1972.

8. Robert Miller, "Detecting and Measuring Healing Energies". Lecture at Harold Sherman Body/Mind/Spirit Workshop, July, 1976.
————, "Research into Healing Energies". In *Science of Mind Bulletin,* Vol. 49, No. 1, January, 1962.

14

PHYSIOLOGICAL MEASUREMENTS AND NEW INSTRUMENTATION

From personal studies among the healers in the Philippines and tests conducted with Filipino healers in his laboratory in Tokyo, Motoyama presents evidence of energy exchanges between the healer and patient that affect the physiological functioning of each. These studies, plus the insights gained by many years of actual experience with acupuncture and with the physiological studies of yogis, have led to the development of equipment capable of detecting energies flowing from the chakras and the acupuncture meridians.

This electronic instrumentation would seem to have potential for *diagnosing* illness and disease, *as well as* for adjusting the energy balance in the patient's body in ways that will assist in *restoring health*.

The theories on which these devices are based supply insights which are of assistance in efforts to build an overall theory of paranormal healing.

Hiroshi Motoyama

I have visited the Philippines on three different occasions in order to observe "psychic operations" and do research into their validity, the first time being in 1966. On these occasions I was able to observe many different healers at work: Tony Agpaoa, Virgilio Gutierrez, Blanche, Terte, Mercado, and others. Also on several occasions, healers have visited my laboratory in Tokyo to go through a number of tests.

My personal opinion regarding the "psychic operations" is that some of these are valid although they are very difficult to verify from the Western medical viewpoint.

The psi-energy used in performing them is very different from the usual physical energy worked with in Western medical operations. However, laboratory investigations in my laboratory of various blood specimens, tumors, and cancerous tissue removed from a patient during an "operation", have confirmed that such specimens truly belonged to the patient undergoing the "operation". I had these specimens checked in various university and hospital laboratories, and thus from these results we must say that the "operations" are true, even though there are admittedly some fakes, too. (*See* Chapter 10) The mechanism is not completely clear and as mentioned above, difficult to ascertain by existing methods.

In this short chapter I will tell of one type of test I have made with healers in my laboratory and then discuss briefly new instrumentation I have devised for establishing the reality and nature of subtle energies flowing to and from the chakras of yoga and the meridian points of acupuncture.

Physiological Tests

I devised a special A-P (agent-percipient) test to verify the existence of PK. Our institute in Tokyo is a three-story building and on the second and third floors I have two rooms *shielded by lead to isolate them from physical energy coming from outside.* In one room I placed the agent (sender of power) and in the other room the percipient (receiver) and had them lie on their backs. We attached various physiological testing equipment to them such as EEG (electroencephalograph), ECG (electrocardiograph), plethysmograph (a device to measure the situation of the heart and circulatory functions), a GSR (galvanic skin resistance) recorder showing the function of the sympathetic nerves, and a device for measuring respiration, etc. Neither the agent nor the percipient was told anything about the test procedure beforehand.

In the first test, I had them just lie quietly for a period of time and recorded their respective physiological processes. Shown in Fig. 1 is the data of the percipient (K.M.) during this quiet period. The top line of the chart is the plethysmogram, the second line the respiration, and the bottom line the GSR. Notice that the plethysmogram and respiration are very regular and constant, as is the GSR which is very flat.

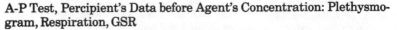

A-P Test, Percipient's Data before Agent's Concentration: Plethysmogram, Respiration, GSR

Fig. 1

Next the sender began to concentrate on the percipient and send power to her, and the results were very interesting. (Fig. 2) Notice that the plethysmogram and respiration have become very irregular and unstable. Change in GSR is only slight. This change in the plethysmogram and respiration of the percipient, effected by the concentration of the agent (a person of great PK ability), shows the existence of PK power. Since this power was able to act through lead shielding we may say that it is not of a *physical* nature.

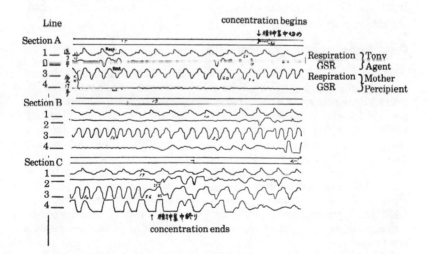

A-P Test, Percipient's Data during Agent's Concentration: Plethysmogram, Respiration, GSR

Fig. 2

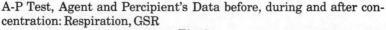

A-P Test, Agent and Percipient's Data before, during and after concentration: Respiration, GSR

Fig. 3

I did a similar test using Tony Agpaoa, a psychic healer from the Philippines as the agent and my mother, K. Motoyama, as the percipient. Fig. 3 shows data for the agent and percipient before, during and after Tony's concentration directed to my mother. The first and third lines show the respiration, and the second and fourth the GSR. Notice that before concentration in Tony's case, the respiration is rather rapid and the GSR line somewhat fluctuating, while my mother's breathing is slow and her GSR line flat.

Next, with the beginning of concentration, Tony's (the sender's) breathing slows down and becomes very regular and his GSR line flattens out. On the other hand the percipient's speeds up and becomes irregular, and the GSR line begins to fluctuate.

Finally, several minutes later, the sender is asked to stop concentration. Notice how great the amplitude of my mother's GSR had become during Tony's concentration directed to her. However, with the termination of concentration, her respiration begins to slow down as before the period of concentration, and her GSR gradually flattens out, while Tony's rate of respiration increases and his GSR begins to fluctuate again.

I believe the above experiments show beyond a doubt the existence of PK and that this PK energy is not of a physical nature. A more detailed description of these experiments can be found in my monograph, *The Non-Physical in the Correlation between Mind and Body*. (This publication and others of mine subsequently referred to are published by the Institute for Religious Psychology, 4-7-11 Inokashira, Mitak-Shi, Tokyo 181, Japan.)

Psychoenergetic Phenomena

Through more than twenty years of yoga practice and the study of parapsychology, I have found that such paranormal phenomena as PK and ESP are caused by a higher dimensional energy, which tentatively we call psi-energy. Also through my research into the chakras and nadis of yoga and the meridians of acupuncture, I have found that this psi-energy is ejected from the chakra and the points on the acupuncture meridians. The chakras are the centers of the subtle energy system which is called, according to the yoga doctrine, the "Linga Sharira" or the "subtle body" (also referred to as the bioplasmic body). Through the chakras, *prana,* a higher dimensional vital energy force, is received from the universe and converted into a kind of physical energy. Through this energy, psi-phenomena are produced. Below are listed a few examples.

In the Soviet Union, scientists have carried out a number of experiments with persons having strong PK ability. One such person, a Mrs. Miharavich, can effect the levitation of a ping-pong ball through her PK power. In such a feat she sends her power to the ball through the tips of her fingers or the palms of her hands, and charges the ball with a high static voltage. She can then levitate the ball or move it to the right or left if she or anyone else passes a hand over the ball in the direction of the desired movement. This is due to the fact that the ball has been greatly charged by energy emanating from Mrs. Miharavich.

Another example of PK phenomena, is that of "psychic operations" such as those carried out in the Philippines. One psychic healer whom I observed in depth, Mr. Blance from Manila, can make an incision on the body by waving his finger 30 to 40 centimeters above the area to be incised. Our tests ruled out sleight-of-hand. The incision made by Mr. Blance is unlike that made by a knife or razor blade. Rather it resembles more the incision made by a laser in modern surgery. It is about ½ millimeter in depth, 2-3 millimeters in width, and 3-4 centimeters in length. (A knife or razor blade incision is less than 1 millimeter in width). Through this small incision the healer can remove infected tissue or tumors, and after the "operation" the incision still remains but it will heal in several days without suppuration. The healers themselves call this energy which makes the incision and prevents suppuration, "electro-magnetic power".

The above, then, are two examples of PK power. However, we don't know the exact mechanism or the essential nature of the psi-energy involved. According to some of my "agent-percipient" tests to investigate the correlation between mind and body this energy seems to be of a non-physical nature. (Refer to *The Non-Physical in the Correlation between Mind and Body*) This psi-energy also appears to be the energy flowing through the meridians and/or that energy directly received through the chakras. I also believe that this psi-energy is what is called *prana* and *Ki* in ancient yoga and acupuncture texts, respectively.

If a yogi awakens his chakras through years of concentration, then the chakras become more active than in the case of the usual person, and can receive a higher dimensional energy (prana) from the universe. This prana is in turn converted into physical or nervous energy and sent to the spinal nervous system, especially the central spinal tube, where it seems to be stocked or stored, as in a pond or lake, for future use. This prana is also distributed throughout the body, to each tissue and internal organ, through the meridians. If a chakra is thus awakened, a person can control the receiving and ejecting of energy through the chakra by *mental concentration*. This energy ejected from the chakra is very strong and can make a great change in an electro-magnetic field in terms of frequency and potential. (*See* Fig. 4)

Development And Operation Of The "Chakra Machine"

To measure the effect of such energy ejected from a chakra on an electro-magnetic field, I constructed a special machine which I call the "Chakra Machine". This consists of an electrode box placed inside a lead-shielded room—somewhat resembling a telephone booth (*See* photo section Fig. E1)—with two copper electrodes on the top and bottom (floor to ceiling) and a sliding square panel with electrodes attached on all four sides—left, right, front, and back. These are free to

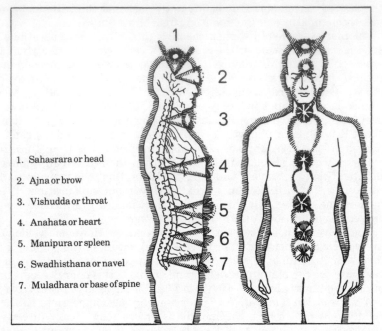

1. Sahasrara or head

2. Ajna or brow

3. Vishudda or throat

4. Anahata or heart

5. Manipura or spleen

6. Swadhisthana or navel

7. Muladhara or base of spine

Fig. 4

traverse up and down the frame structure so as to be positioned at any
part of a person's body.

An electro-magnetic field is set up between the electrodes, and as the
subject stands inside the box without any electrodes directly touching
his body (30-40 cm from the body), any energy ejected from the body can
be detected as a change in this electro-magnetic field. Placed inside the
lead-shielded room with the above-mentioned electrode frame is a
special pre-amplifier designed by me with an impedance of near in-
finity which allows even the most subtle energy ejection to be picked up
and recorded. The pre-amplifier in turn sends the measurement information to various amplifiers, analyzer, and computers outside the
lead-shielded room, where the data are recorded on a highly sensitive
chart recorder. (*See* photo section Fig. E-1.)

A person with an awakened chakra can to some extent control the
ejection of energy from his body at will, and the nature of this energy in
a psychic person, in terms of frequency and voltage, is somewhat
different from that in the normal (non-psychic) person. This energy, in
addition to being ejected from the chakra directly, can also be ejected
from the body through the palms of the hand or from those points on the
tips of the fingers and toes, called "seiketsu" points (*See* Fig. 5), where
the meridians of acupuncture begin and end. "Sieketsu" ("sei" = well of
spring, "ketsu" = point) means the "spring" or "well" points from which
energy can flow out of or into the body.

Seiketsu of each meridian

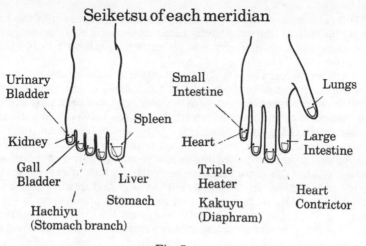

Urinary Bladder

Small Intestine

Lungs

Spleen

Kidney

Heart

Large Intestine

Gall Bladder

Liver

Triple Heater

Stomach

Kakuyu (Diaphram)

Heart Contrictor

Hachiyu (Stomach branch)

Fig. 5

Apparatus For Measuring The Functions Of The Meridians And The Corresponding Internal Organs

Through many years of research into acupuncture, I have found that the situation or function of energy flowing throughout the meridians can be known by measuring the electrical resistance, capacitance, and potential (or the reverse potential to a charged potential) at the "seiketsu" point of each meridian. I therefore designed a machine, called the AMI which can diagnose the functions of the meridians and the corresponding internal organs through measuring skin current values on the "seiketsu" meridian points. It consists of an electrode box, computer interface, and calculation computer and data print-out machine as shown in photo section Fig. E3 (left to right).

To operate the machine, first special electrodes of my own design are covered with anti-polarization paste and attached to the 28 "seiketsu" points on the tips of the fingers and toes. Next, 3 volts DC are charged through the electrodes and the machine measures skin current values at the "seiketsu" points just before, during, and after the body reacts to the charged voltage. This reaction of the body to a charged voltage, an action of the homeostatic function, we call "reaction-polarization", and by measuring the skin current before, during, and after the above reaction—reaction-polarization—we can diagnose the function of the meridians and the corresponding internal organs. That is, if the skin current values before, during, and after polarization (the reaction) are less than a criterion which has been determined at a certain meridian seiketsu point, we can assume that the function of the meridian, and sometimes its corresponding organ, is underactive. In addition, if the skin current values are more than a certain statistically significant criterion, we may assume that the function of the meridian, etc. is overactive. The supporting data are confirmed on the basis of over

2,000 subjects tested. This machine is unique because it is the only machine to date that can exactly measure so fast a reaction as that of reaction-polarization, a very fast phenomenon, taking 1 to 10 microseconds.

Through measuring over 2,000 subjects with this machine and comparing their data with the results of other medical examinations and with their professed subjective symptoms, we have been able to draw up criteria of normality and abnormality for the values obtained before polarization (BP), after polarization (AP), and polarization (P). Thus there is an upper and lower limit for normality—a value appearing above the upper limit indicating excessive energy in the meridian, and a value below the lower criterion indicating a lack of energy or vital force in the meridian. This information is stored in a computer and after a patient's raw data are measured, it is fed into the computer for standardization (%) and is calculated against the criteria for normality. This done, the computerized data are run out on roller paper and are subsequently cut and pasted on a data sheet. The values exceeding or less than the criteria for normality are printed out in red. This permits a very rapid visual check of departures from normality.

The data sheet has value for the right (Ri, R%) and left (Li, L%) branches of each meridian for BP, AP, and P, and also for the difference (D%) between the left and right branches for AP, BP, and P.

Generally BP tells us about the long-term constitutional state of the body, the degree of metabolization. Viewed from the electrical standpoint, it tells us about the capacitance of tissue cells. P is a reverse, or reaction, potential generated in the body against the stimulus given from outside, and it is affected by weather and climatic conditions. AP tells about temporary functions of the body, and resistance of tissue.

By making a diagnosis from the data, one is able to know the functional situation of each meridian and the whole body. That is, *one is able to know disease tendencies before an organic disease actually manifests*. Thus, this machine can be used for *preventive* medicine by informing the patient what steps he must take to prevent his coming down with disease. Many of us are of the opinion that this is the direction medicine must take in the future.

This book is primarily about healers and the overall subject of paranormal healing. Hence this is not the place to go into great detail about the scientific aspects of these two pieces of equipment. Such information can be found in my work, *How to Measure and Diagnose the Functions of the Meridians and the Corresponding Internal Organs* and *The Ejection of Energy from the Chakra of Yoga and Meridian Points of Acupuncture.*

However, what is of great importance for the subject of paranormal healing is that no great progress in solving its mysteries has been possible within the framework of traditional Western medicine. Only by developing instrumentation which permits us to make a start at studying the *energy flow* in the acupuncture meridians and the chakras of *both* healer and patient, can we expect to make much headway in developing our understanding of the modus operandi of paranormal healing.

If the flow of energy is stopped in a meridian, then at the point of stoppage, subjective symptoms (pain, etc.) are likely to appear, as well as skin rash or an increase of skin temperature. From such a point also, a strong energy will be ejected. If this condition continues for a long time, then one will experience nervous pain, skeletal muscular pain, rheumatism and organic disease. If we can remove the excessive energy from that point and correct the blockage so that energy can flow smoothly again, then the disease or the subjective symptoms, pain, etc. will disappear.

In observing the work of the Filipino healers both in the Philippines and in my laboratory, I have seen many times that the healers use their fingers and hands to send energy to those parts of the patient's body lacking energy, or extract energy from those parts suffering an excess. Five or ten minutes after this is done, the person's pain disappears. Also in the case of causing a ball to levitate, the psychic person sends energy through her hands and fingertips to change the energy field around the ball. Although we do not as yet know the exact mechanism by which a higher energy is converted into physical energy to produce paranormal phenomena, I believe we can say that many of the PK phenomena in healing are caused by psi-energy ejected directly from the healer's chakra, and the seiketsu points at the tips of the healer's fingers and toes. The tests carried out with my chakra machine and AMI are adding support for this hypothesis.

REFERENCES

Hiroshi Motoyama, *The Non-Physical in the Correlation between Mind and Body* (Tokyo: Institute of Religious Psychology).

————, "ESP Chakra, and the Autonomic Nerves". In *Religious Psychology Journal,* Tokyo, 1966.

————, *Chakra Nadi of Yoga and Meridians: Points of Acupuncture* (Tokyo: Institute of Religious Psychology, 1972).

————, "How to Develop Paranormal Abilities (Kundalini Yoga)". In *Tokyo Sports Newspaper,* 1974.

————, "Do Meridians Exist and What Are They Like?" In *Journal of Religion and Parapsychology,* (Tokyo) No. 1, 1975.

————, *How to Measure and Diagnose the Functions of Meridians and the Corresponding Internal Organs* (Tokyo: Institute of Religious Psychology, 1974).

————, "The Mechanism by Which Psi-Ability Manifests Itself". In *Impact of Science on Society,* Vol. XXIV, No. 4, (UNESCO) 1974.

IV

THE PRACTICE AND PROBLEMS
OF TEACHING HEALING

15

TEACHING CANCER PATIENTS
TO ACCELERATE THEIR HEALING

The role of the mind in health as well as in illness is
dramatically revealed in recent research with terminal
cancer patients. The achievements related in this chapter
add an entirely new dimension to self healing.

George W. Meek

A study of what were said to be the 70 greatest inventions or scientific
advances in the first 75 years of this century revealed that the great
majority were made by individuals who were not directly connected
with industrial or scientific organizations. We soon may find we have a
parallel in the field of cancer research.

Throughout the world billions of dollars have been channeled into
scientific research organizations, both governmental and private. By
any yardstick results to date are disappointingly meager. Could it be
that science has been looking in the wrong direction?

It is possible that from the vantage point at the close of this century it
will be concluded that five individual cancer researchers, working
alone and outside the establishments in England, the U.S.A., and
Japan, looked in other directions and made outstanding contributions
toward overcoming the scourge of cancer. Here are brief accounts of
research carried on by these men—and its significance:

Lawrence LeShan, Ph.D. and Gotthard Booth, M.D., New York

Psychologist LeShan working in the late 1950s and the '60s carried
on meticulous studies on the psychosomatic illnesses of terminally ill
patients.[1] At about the same time, psychiatrist Booth also became
deeply involved in such studies, particularly in regard to cancer cases.
Gradually both of them reached the personal conclusions that there
was, first, a close correlation between the emotional patterns of the
cancer patients and the site of the cancer—breast, anus, cervix of the

womb, lung, throat, etc.—and second, that most of the cancer patients had encountered a personal crisis that was somewhat more than they could cope with in view of their particular emotional resources.[2]

It is important that their pioneering served to stimulate others to push this research into new ground and devise new techniques for helping cancer patients to assemble and utilize their own mental and emotional resources to help in throwing off the cancerous growth.

O. Carl Simonton, M.D., Ft. Worth

In 1969, while serving his three-year residency in radiation therapy at the University of Oregon Medical Center, Simonton began to speculate on the role that the patient's mental and emotional processes might have played in the original development of the cancer. His search through the literature brought him into contact with the work of LeShan and Booth. Upon accepting his first assignment as Chief of Radiation Therapy at Travis Air Force Base, California, he decided to start his own research. His work over the past four years has been reported.[3, 4] Simonton first worked alone and later was assisted by his wife, a psychologist. Together they evolved a technique which supplements radiation therapy by using individual and group therapy which seems to reverse the patient's negative thinking. In part this involves getting the patient to visualize the affected organ in the act of throwing off the cancerous growth.

The work of Simonton, now in practice with Oncology Associates, 1413 Eighth Ave., Fort Worth, Texas, 76104, has now been picked up and confirmed by other researchers. Similar assistance is now being given to cancer patients in the following centers as of late 1976:

Gerald Jampolsky, M.D.
  Center for Attitudinal Healing
  21 Main St.
  Tiburon, Cal., 94929

Center for the Healing Arts
  11081 Missouri Ave.
  Los Angeles, Cal. 90025

Charles Garfield, M.D.
  Univ. of Calif. Medical School
  San Francisco, Cal.

Robert G. Gilley
  Dayspring
  Charlotte, N. Car.

Dr. Masaharu Tanaguchi, Japan

A few years before Booth and LeShan began their studies on the psychosomatic aspects of cancer, Dr. Tanaguchi of Tokyo was helping terminal patients to throw off their cancer and continue to live productive and cancer-free lives. His book[5] describes the work he has done with cancer patients over many years in different cities of Japan.

Dr. Tanaguchi accomplished his results through a completely spiritual approach which has resulted in his now being accepted as one of the spiritual leaders of Japan. Through his lectures, books, and magazine articles he reaches millions of people each year. His message is simple, direct, and changes lives as well as disease-ridden bodies.

What makes the work of Tanaguchi so interesting is that he uses *none* of the visualization techniques of a Simonton, Jampolsky, Garfield, or Gilley. He uses no autogenic training technique as such. Moreover, he uses no bio-feedback techniques. What he does use is a meditational and prayer technique which, of course, has been fitted into a spiritual belief system that is readily acceptable to the average Japanese man or woman who is seeking healing. This system, utilizing Shinto beliefs, would not be readily transferable to any other culture without drastic revisions. However, anyone who has studied the details of the program devised by Dr. Simonton could only conclude that Dr. Tanaguchi's methods produce the same dramatic and highly desirable results of helping cancer patients to heal themselves.

Harry Edwards, Great Britain

Harry Edwards, one of the world's most effective and best-loved healers, is referred to in Chapters 2 and 4. For more than 25 years he was of great assistance to cancer patients in the British Isles and to those he encountered on his travels to Africa, Australia, and Europe. Many years ago he became convinced that "Spiritual Healing", as practiced by himself and fellow members of the National Federation of Spiritual Healers, had a message that should be taken seriously by those in the British medical establishment. His message was that Britain was needlessly wasting vast sums of money on largely nonproductive cancer research, and that medical researchers should at least look with an open mind at what was being accomplished by the healers of the Federation.

His message was ignored and in fact, derided for many years. Finally, in April, 1972, Dr. Gotthard Booth was invited to be the principal speaker before the Federation, assembled for their annual meeting in the Free Trade Hall, Manchester, England. Dr. Booth's address was entitled "The Prevention and Cure of Cancer". Dr. Booth's research and conclusions closely paralleled everything Edwards had been saying for many years. The fortunate outcome of this meeting was that a research program was then established by the N.F.S.H. (*See* detailed reference in Chapter 4). Now, as this is being written in late 1976, the initial research findings have been as valuable for saving lives and reducing human suffering in the British Isles as has the work of Simonton in the U.S.A. and Tanaguchi in Japan.

And just what is the significance of the work of Booth, LeShan, Simonton, Tanaguchi, and Edwards? Leaving aside all psychiatric, psychological, and medical terminology, it is just this:

For the first time there exists irrefutable proof that even in the case of far-advanced cancerous situations, the patient's own psychosomatic process in a positive mode can be utilized to restore the healthy condition which that same process in a negative mode was previously destroying.

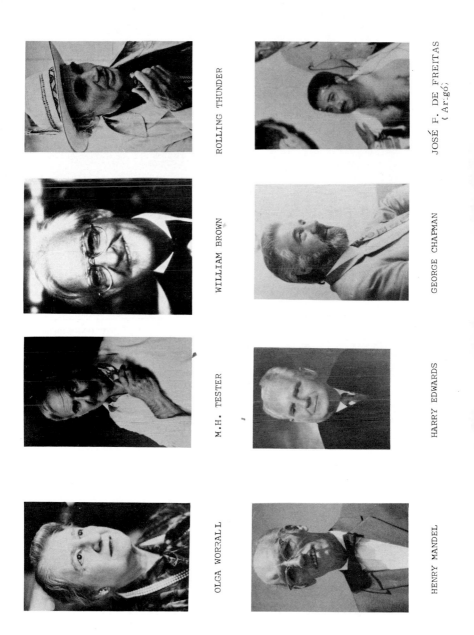

ROLLING THUNDER

JOSÉ F. DE FREITAS
(Ar-gó;

WILLIAM BROWN

GEORGE CHAPMAN

M.H. TESTER

HARRY EDWARDS

OLGA WORRALL

HENRY MANDEL

(Chapter 2)

Felisa Macanas

Romy Bugarin

Tony Agpaoa

José Mercado

Josefina Sison

Marcelo Jainer

(Chapter 6)

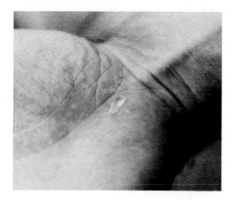

Figure C 1)
(Chapter 6)

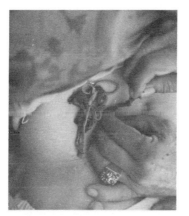

Figure C 2
(Chapter 10)

Figure C 3
(Chapter 10)

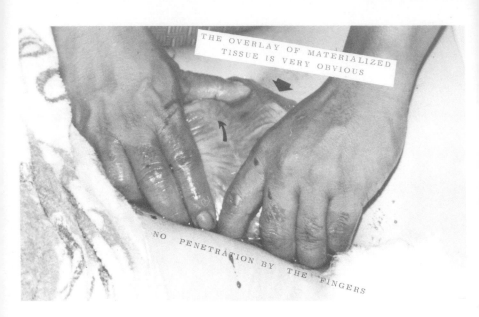

Figure D 1
(Chapter 10)

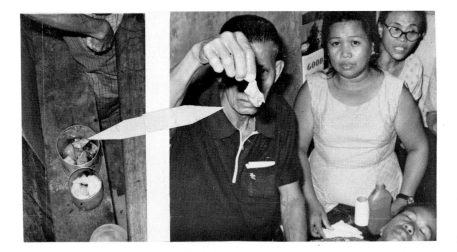

Figure D 2
(Chapter 10)

Figure E 1
(Chapter 14)

Figure E 2
(Chapter 14)

Figure E 3
(Chapter 14)

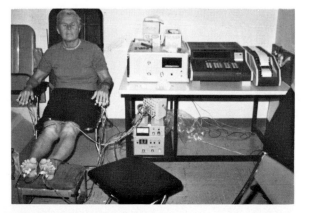

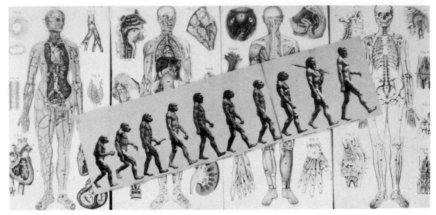

Figure F 1
(Chapter 19)

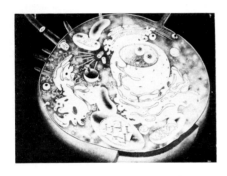

Figure F 2
(Chapter 19)

Figure F 3
(Chapter 19)

Figure F 4
(Chapter 19)

Figure G 1
(Chapter 19)

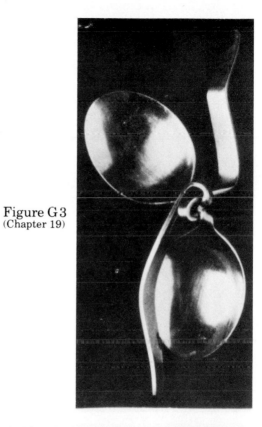

Figure G 3
(Chapter 19)

Figure G 2
(Chapter 19)

Figure H1
(Chapter 19)

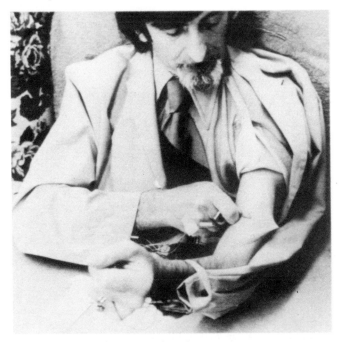

Figure H2
(Chapter 19)

To use still less scientific language, the conclusion is:

It is entirely possible for the patient to utilize his own thoughts and emotional processes to rid himself of cancer.

The chief functions of this short chapter have been to alert the reader to the existence of such assistance and to give him a better basis for understanding the concepts which he will encounter in Chapter 19, "Toward a General Theory of Healing".

REFERENCES

1. Lawrence LeShan, *You Can Fight For Your Life* (Philadelphia, Pa.: J. B. Lippincott, 1977).

2. Gotthard Booth, "The Psychosomatic Relationship in Cancer". In *ACTA Medica Psychosomatics,* Roma, 1967, pp. 598-601.

⸻, "General and Organ-Specific Relationships in Cancer". In *Ann, N.Y. Acad. Sci.,* Vol. 164 (2), 1969, pp. 368-577.

⸻, "Irrational Complications of the Cancer Problem". In *American Journal of Psychoanalysis,* Vol. 25, 1965, pp. 41-44.

⸻, "The Cancer Patient and the Minister". In *Pastoral Psychology,* Vol. 17, February, 1966, pp. 15-24.

⸻, "Krebs und Tuberkulose im Rorschachschen Formdeuteversuch" (Cancer and Tuberculosis in the Rorschach Test). In *Ztschr. F. Psychosomatische Medizin,* Vol. 10, 1964, pp. 176-188.

⸻, "The Prevention and Cure of Cancer". A talk before the National Federation of Spiritual Healers, Eng., April 20, 1972.

⸻, et al., "Psychsomatic Aspects of Evolution". In *Psychosomatic Aspects of Neoplastic Diseases* (London: Pitman and Philadelphia, Lippincott, 1964).

3. Jean Shinoda Bolen, "Meditation and Psychotherapy in the Treatment of Cancer". In *Psychic,* July-August, 1973.

4. O. Carl Simonton, "The Role of Mind in Cancer Therapy". A talk before the Academy of Parapsychology and Medicine, September, 1972.

5. Masaharu Tanaguchi, *The Role of Mind in Cancer* (Gardena, CA.: Seicho-No-le, 1965).

16

TEACHING PEOPLE TO BECOME HEALERS

George W. Meek

Considering how very little we understand of what takes place between the healer and the patient and what is responsible for healing in the patient's body, perhaps it seems a bit ridiculous to even raise the questions, "Can people be taught to be healers? What would they be taught and why? Is there any historical record of classes being held for the purpose of teaching people to become healers?"

As the authors of this book traveled the world researching the subject of healers and healing, the above list of questions grew:

- Why and how did YOU become a healer?
- Did someone teach you?
- Do you think it is practical to organize classes to teach people to become healers?
- Of what should a curriculum consist?
- How long a training period is required to become really proficient?
- Can all people be taught the art or must a person have s specific "gift"?
- What part do age and sex play?
- Does a good education help or hinder?
- What part, if any, does a person's religious belief play in his becoming proficient at healing?
- Can a completely non-religious person become a good healer?

As the years wore on and we met more and more healers in different countries and cultures, answers to these and many more questions began to develop. While still far from having all the information we would like in some areas, it is the purpose of this chapter to share with you our research findings to date.

Early Efforts

Teaching people to become healers is as old as recorded history. Four to six thousand years ago the so-called Mystery School of Egypt included instruction on healing. The priests were custodians of the collected lore and passed it on to initiates. As Jeanne Rindge reported in the opening chapter of this book, in most of the intervening centuries there have been a few men in each tribe and nation who have been the custodians of knowledge, which was imparted to one person, or at most to a very few individuals, who had the responsibility for carrying on the healing practices.

There are, however, very few chapters in recorded history where classes were formed and conducted with the specific object of magnifying the abilities of the teacher. Shining out through the pages of history like a beacon light is, of course, that exception reported in the Christian Bible—the teaching of disciples by the Nazarene. Rather detailed accounts are given of his efforts with his first "class" of 12 men. The accounts of his training of 70 men are very scanty but there is the indication that his "curriculum" was similar for both classes. (Bibliography C)

During most of the twenty centuries since, teaching efforts were confined largely to the individual tribal medicine man, shaman, witch doctor and priest. These usually followed the established practice of selecting one, two, or three individuals and then spending from a few years to as long as twenty years in the instruction in and practice of such healing art as that individual teacher possessed.

Not until we come to the present-day do we encounter serious efforts to organize "classes" and develop a teaching curriculum with the avowed purpose of teaching the students to become healers. During the past six years in which the authors of this book have traveled the world researching the subject of healing, we have encountered four serious efforts to organize classes of persons who have the wish to serve as healers. Each is in a different country and each follows practices and belief systems of its own culture.

We will now take a brief look at each of these efforts but in general will refrain from observations or editorial comments on any specific aspect of the instruction, the pupils, the curriculum, the relative effectiveness of the work of the student after his "graduation," or the potentials for expanding the usefulness of the individual effort in these or other countries of the world. We will reserve comments on these subjects until later in this chapter.

The Philippines

The present-day work of some 30 healers in the Philippines had its beginning in the teaching abilities of Emanuel Terte. Shortly after World War II, in which he participated as a guerrilla with the Americans, Terte developed the rare ability to make surgical interventions—penetrations of the body cavity with his bare hands. His fame quickly spread through the rice fields in northern Luzon and young people asked him to give them training as healers. Working largely on a one-to-one basis he trained perhaps a third of those healers who are currently working. Initially he worked under the banner of the

Union Espiritista Christiana de Filipinas, a loose organization of very small and very poor native spiritualist churches where the only language was and is Tagalog. He later broke away over policy clashes, and while the Union churches still conduct classes in mediumship and healing, I present here a summary of Terte's original training procedure. The reader will of course observe that all of the basic principles involved come strictly out of the Sermon on the Mount.

Terte stresses that a *sincere desire* is the first qualification. Then every night before bed the student should read Psalm 119. The student should learn by heart all of the healing references in John, chapters 15, 16, and 17. The student should learn to practice the humility of Jesus. While the student can take an occasional drink of alcohol for social purposes, "frequent drinking will spoil the power."

Terte thinks that prayer is extremely important but does not feel that it is necessary for most students to spend days or weeks in isolated meditation.

After a student has spent a few months memorizing the Biblical references, meditating, and dedicating himself to the principle outlined, Terte will pick out a patient who has come to him for treatment and allow the student to practice. The student is instructed to spend from 30 to 60 minutes in prayer and meditation. Then Terte turns the patient over to him for 5 to 10 minutes and observes. (Terte is a highly developed medium and uses his psychic abilities to observe the student-patient interaction in detail.)

Terte says that he teaches the student that the healing activities break down into these categories of treatment or action:

> Prayers—where the healer merely utters a heartfelt prayer for the patient.
>
> Divine—here he apparently has in mind divine intervention.
>
> Magnetic—where the healer uses some of his own magnetic force for healing.
>
> Absent—where he teaches the student to use mental telepathy.
>
> Blessing—involving movement of hand over the patient's head.
>
> Psychic Surgery—Terte taught pupils to open the body.

Terte assures each student that if he applies himself he can be certain that he will gradually be attuned to his own spirit protector (guide) and be able to get instructions on both diagnosis and treatment. Moreover, as in Terte's own case, he will gradually have help from *more* than one protector, as it is believed each one has a certain field of expertise. Thus several protectors are of help in handling the wide range of ailments an individual healer will encounter. (*See* Appendix B, "The Role of Discarnate Entities".)

We have presented the barest outline of what is done in the Philippines to teach people to develop their inborn healing abilities. How this relates to training in three other countries can be gleaned from what follows.

Great Britain

During the 25 years that the very modest events just described were transpiring in the Philippines, the British Isles witnessed a growth in the teaching and practice of healing which in sheer numbers of students, the numbers of cooperating hospitals, and the numbers of patients treated annually, is almost beyond belief. The story itself of the more than 3,000 healers, the more than 1,500 cooperating hospitals and the present rate of a million patients per year was detailed in Chapter 4. Here we will confine our comments to the teaching phase of the work of the National Federation of Spiritual Healers.

This growth has been possible directly as the result of efforts started by Harry Edwards to develop training courses in spiritual healing. The basic courses are covered in three manuals:

> Theory and Practice of Spirit Healing
> Absent Healing
> The Science of Spirit Healing
> (The availability and the present cost of the printed material for these courses may be obtained by writing to The National Federation of Spiritual Healers, Short Acres, Church Hill, Loughton, Essex, England.)

Later in this chapter a tabular comparison is presented showing the content of the courses in all four countries being discussed.

Brazil

During the same 25-year-period Brazil witnessed an even more dramatic development of activities in teaching people to become healers. In Brazil, the growth came from members of the Spiritist churches which, incidentally, have no connection with the Spiritualist churches in England.

One of the most important ethnic groups in Brazil has been the Africans, originally transported to Brazil as slaves. These people brought with them the belief systems of the African tribes and their descendants readily accepted the teaching of Alan Kardek, a Frenchman who wrote books on mediums and the spirit world.

Although Brazil is 90% Catholic, at least 10,000,000 Brazilians look to Spiritism for most of their guidance on things relating to physical and mental health. This is even more surprising in view of the fact that the federal government, the Catholic Church, and the medical establishment have all shown their disapproval of the healing activities of the Spiritists.

But as has been observed, it is hard to argue with success. On my several trips to Brazil, I have been particularly interested in following the activities of a large Spiritist Healing Center in downtown Sao Paulo. This center is open to the public and no charge is made for any services. When I visited there in April, 1976, these statistics applied:

Patients in the previous 12 months	482,000
Healers on the staff	1,520

Healers in attendance at one time	35
Hours per healer (each of 2 days per week)	2
Students in the training course	240
Length of training program (years)	3

This remarkable activity—which is helping almost half a million patients per year in just one Spiritist healing center—is possible, in part, because of the successful development of teaching programs to train the Spiritist mediums who then become the healers. For several years this training program has been under the direction of

Carmen and Jarbas Marinho
Rua Luis Dib Zogaib 420
(05613 Morumbi) Sao Paulo, Brazil

Unlike the programs in the other countries, the São Paulo program provides some elementary training for the patients. I feel that this is one of the big factors that has resulted in the word-of-mouth recommendations from satisfied patients and the tremendous patient flow to this healing center. As a visitor to this center during several years, I have observed a significant refinement of the patient processing procedure. From the patient's very first visit he is given an insight into the part which his thoughts and emotions played in triggering the present ailment.

As soon as the personal history forms are filled out, patients in groups of about fifty, regardless of what is wrong with them, are given a friendly and informal discourse on at least some of the psychosomatic aspects of ill health. They are also given information on the reality of their own individual spirit and its relationship to the all-prevading Spirit which is beyond the world of appearances in which they are of necessity immersed.

Following this indoctrination, the patients are then assigned to the healing room where five healers work in a very concentrated fashion with each patient for only three to five minutes.

A personal interview with each patient follows, the data are entered on the records and an appointment is made for the next visit.

On the next visit the patient (as a part of a group) gets another discourse on the inter-relationship of mind-spirit-body, and the parts that stressful situations, thoughts, and emotions have played in his current malfunction. Again there is a personal interview which may then result in special personal counselling or assignment to healers noted for their special effectiveness with certain diseases.

Through the São Paulo centers, through centers in other Brazilian cities, and through a few small hospitals which they maintain with staffs of psychiatrists, medical doctors, dentists, and nurses of Spiritist persuasion, the Spiritists of Brazil are rendering a great service in personal and public health.

United States

In general, medical groups in the United States have been far behind those elsewhere in recognizing, and then beginning to work in collaboration with persons who have psychic or spiritual healing gifts. This, of course, is the reason behind our carrying on so much of our research on these matters outside of the U.S.A. Fortunately this situation is at least starting to change. Now we can come home and carry on meaningful research.

One man who has done much to bring about the change in the healing-healer environment in the U.S.A. is psychologist Lawrence LeShan, whose earlier pioneering work in researching the psychosomatic aspects of terminal cancer patients is reported in the preceding chapter. He was the first in the U.S. to plan and conduct research aimed at teaching people to become healers.

I have been interested in LeShan's work with healers since its inception, having myself been a member of one of his earliest experimental training classes. Hence it was interesting to me as I traveled to many countries to observe the similarities and differences between LeShan's approach and, for example, that of a South African witch doctor; or a relatively uneducated native Filipino in the rice field area of Luzon; or a well-educated former professional man in London who followed the concepts of the British Spiritualists; or Brazilian healers of Spiritist persuasion whose educational level varies from practically no schooling to that of graduates of medical schools.

LeShan, being the meticulous researcher that he is, has been slow to publish any results on these past five years of his efforts to teach persons to become healers. Hence, it would be premature to make a disclosure of his techniques or his underlying principles. I can, however, state that he is trying to develop healers with absolutely no reference to the two factors that tie the Philippine, British, and Brazilian programs together, namely, the concept that help is available to the healer for both diagnosis and treatment from individual intelligences in the world of spirit; and the concept that man himself is first and foremost a spiritual being temporarily occupying a physical body. Only the years ahead will reveal just how well the achievements of healers trained by LeShan compare with those of healers trained in the other countries.

The only other effort at teaching healing in the U.S.A. at this date, was mentioned in chapter 13, the work of Dolores Krieger in teaching nurses to develop psychic healing abilities. One of the most significant aspects of this research was the utilization of an *objective* test that made a scientific measure of change in a physiological index (hemoglobin). Ultimately this type of scientific measurement combined with other techniques mentioned in that chapter will enable us to cut through all of the subjective and anecdotal reports we have today.

Comparison Of The Above Teaching Programs

Since space does not permit presenting each of these four teaching efforts in detail, I will utilize my familiarity with the programs to offer the following analysis:

The healer training program:	Philippines	Great Britain	Brazil	U.S.A. (LeShan)
1. Teaches anatomy	No	*	*	No
2. Encourages the healer to make positive verbal comments	*	*	*	No
3. Places emphasis on the emotions of love and compassion	*	*	*	*
4. Encourages the healer to consider himself a "channel" for healing	*	*	*	*
5. Is permissive with respect to the healer's accepting remuneration	*	*	No	No
6. Recommends physical contact of the healer's hands with the patient in certain cases	*	*	*	No
7. Recommends the use of so-called "magnetic passes"	*	*	*	No
8. Specifically encourages the student to develop clairvoyance and clairaudience	*	*	*	No
9. Is tailored to the student's personal religion and belief system	*	*	*	*
10. Teaches meditational and attunement techniques	*	*	*	*
11. Teaches the patient to solicit help from spirit entities for both diagnostic and healing purposes	*	*	*	No
12. Recommends counseling by the healer to help the patient understand the body-mind-spirit-health-illness concepts	*	*	*	No
13. Stresses that the healer must encourage the patient to consult a medical doctor if one is available	*	*	*	*
14. Encourages medical doctors to work in partnership with healers	*	*	*	*

Effectiveness Of The Teaching Programs

It is virtually impossible to arrive at an accurate conclusion regarding the relative effectiveness of these programs. Good before-and-after clinical records are nonexistent in most cases handled by healers. The fact that the patient's doctor may have given him the wrong diagnosis or that the patient misunderstood the diagnosis adds complications. The patient's own attitude toward treatment is a paramount factor—as are family or business stress-producing situations which can quickly *reimpose* the dysfunction. The list of such pertinent factors is indeed long.

If the list were already not long enough, we must mention another complication, which alone would prohibit any meaningful evaluation. I refer to the so-called placebo effect. Forrest J. Cioppa, M.D., (Chapter 11) in discussing the effectiveness of the healing work in the Philippines, covers in detail this crucial factor. When one considers that in the healer, the patient has probably for the first time found someone who has the sincere desire to listen to his troubles and who emanates love and compassion, it becomes obvious that the patient has received something even more valuable than a sugar-coated pill. In addition, if we fully understand that something more than 70% of the patients going to any healer—or medical doctor—have an ailment which was triggered initially by some mental or emotional thought pattern, we can understand even better the tremendous importance of the "placebo" which the patient receives from a good healer. Unfortunately this situation has not been recognized even by people who should know better. I have heard a psychologist—of all people!—say with some pride that such and such a healer-training program has resulted in 50% of the patients receiving help. The psychologist well knows the literature on placebo research but fails to recognize that in the work of the healer there are factors which are at least as powerful as in the case where 70% of the men receiving colored distilled water (which they were told was a fine new treatment for a urinary condition) were cured or reported some benefit!

I bring up this crucial matter of placebo effect NOT to belittle the subject of psychic, faith or mental healing. Far from it. The important thing is to identify this factor, study it and then fit it into its proper place in developing an overall theory of healing. This is precisely what we have done in Chapter 19. When we see the "how and why" of all healing, then we will see why every healer-training program should be redesigned to *enhance* the placebo effect.

When the present equipment and techniques are fully developed for measuring changes in hemoglobin, copper salts, the surface tension of water, the hydrogen bonds, etc., we will at least be ready to start an evaluation of the effectiveness of these teaching programs. But not until still more sophisticated technology such as a full color moving picture type aura scanner is invented, will we be able to evaluate, refine, and greatly improve the teaching techniques.

Summary

The significance of the information generated by the research presented here is that the accomplishments of a well-trained healer are not figments of the imagination of the patient. More than two million people per year (as mentioned in the reports on healing in Brazil, England, the Philippines, the U.S.A. and elsewhere) are obtaining benefits that they cannot otherwise afford under the present high costs for medical treatment, or that, for any one of several reasons, they did not obtain from the medical establishment. Many hundreds of millions of people throughout the world who are without even minimal medical care could benefit from the introduction of healer-training programs in their respective countries. Even in the countries that have the finest medical facilities and well-trained medical specialists, the work load of the doctor prevents his spending enough time with the patient to treat him as a human being and learn enough about the personal family or business situation that triggered the dysfunction. The failure to uncover these factors and bring them to the attention of the patient results in a perpetuation of the illness-producing factors.

Readily available and well-trained healers *would* have the time and capability for this activity. Their love, compassion, and sympathetic understanding would supplement the doctor's services and help the patient to achieve and them *maintain* his mental and emotional stasis.

17

HEALING YOURSELF AND EXTENDING YOUR USEFUL LIFE SPAN

George W. Meek

In the Bible we are advised that to enter the Kingdom of Heaven, one must become as a little child. Healing, particularly healing oneself, is very similar. So in this chapter we will drop our effort to be *reasonably* scientific, or not *too* pseudo-scientific and will try to keep it simple.

But as there are many paths to God, so there may be several paths which lead to an understanding of self-healing. For example, if you want to do it the intellectual way, you can study the following chapters on *theory*. If you read those chapters enough times the sheer strength of your intellect might take you a considerable way up the mountain. Please recall that in earlier chapters dealing with specific healers, one important observation was that education or intellect is *not* a requirement for becoming a good healer of others. The same is true with respect to healing ourselves. Having little or no education is not a barrier, in fact, it is often a great advantage. It is in this sense we must "become as little children" and set aside much of the misinformation we have picked up as we climbed up the ladder of intellectual attainment.

As previously indicated, this book is based on research initially intended to investigate the healers and their work. As we progressed in these studies, however, an unexpected and immensely valuable dividend developed—an understanding of the *means* by which a patient could avoid getting ill in the first place.

In studying the healer-patient relationship it became necessary to look far more critically at WHY the patient had developed the illness that brought him to the healer. The traditional concepts of germs, bacteria, virus, and infections—and even that catch-all "psychosomatic"—just did not seem adequate to cover the complete spectrum of illness and disease.

Gradually, as more was learned about the complex and many-level interaction between the healer and his patient, it appeared that in the majority of cases, including many cases of cancer and most heart ailments, the PATIENT HAD BROUGHT THE ILLNESS ON HERSELF OR HIMSELF. Moreover, even if the healer were totally successful in restoring the patient to health, the old ailment might reappear or the patient might succumb to a totally different illness.

The theoretical basis of patient-caused illness is admittedly complex, (Chapter 19) but fortunately, a person need not understand even the bare elements of theories and hypotheses expounded in that chapter to avoid much illness. Consider this simple analogy. A wealthy man is teaching his teenage daughter to drive his $35,000 Rolls Royce. The girl need not know anything about the decades of superb engineering embodied in the smoothly working cam shafts, valve-lifters, connecting rods, pistons, alternator, electric ignition, and the carburetor, fuel, water, and electrical systems. Now, in comparison to the Rolls Royce, the human body and its levels of mind are infinitely more complex. Yet the individual who wants to remain in good health needs little knowledge of the function of the gall bladder, liver, lungs, heart, reproductive organs, intestines, stomach, brain, etc., its blood, lymph and nervous systems, or its chakras, nadis, and acupuncture meridians. In learning to drive the Rolls Royce, all one needs to do is to follow specific instructions. You soon learn not to step on the accelerator pedal when you should be stepping on the brake. So each of us can avoid the increasingly expensive trips to the medical doctors, psychiatrists, and hospitals if we will but learn and apply what are basically some very simple and easy-to-understand routines.

Any person who is free of congenital or hereditary defects, has not been subject to damaging radiation, has not taken excessive amounts of alcohol or other drugs, who partakes of a nourishing diet, and who really *wants* to enjoy good health, *can do so*. Each person, without use of any medication, can avoid as many as 4 out of 5 minor illnesses (coughs, colds, flu, headache, some allergies, asthma, etc.) and major illnesses (including many types of cancer, non-malignant cysts and tumors, many types of heart trouble, stomach and intestinal disorders mental and emotional breakdowns, etc.) by following instructions which are as easily understood as learning how to drive.

However, therein lies a problem. The instructions may appear to be so simple that a worldly-wise or intellectually arrogant adult may think that is just *too* simple to work; that it is nothing more than self-hypnosis; that it is beneath their dignity to even try it. Here we present three separate pathways by which one can save the money, aches, pains, and heartaches mentioned in the preceding paragraph. (1) You can take the simple, in this case "pictorial approach". (2) You can exercise your mental facilities more fully by learning the "A.B.C.'s of Metascience". (3) If neither of these fits your intellectual pattern, then you can get semi-scientific about it and ponder all of the ramifications of Chapter 19.

Pathway #1 To Better Health And A Longer Life— The Pictorial Approach

To start we must learn that neither sex, nor race, nor color, nor organized religion, creed, or dogma have anything to do with learning to be a healer of oneself or of others. Realize that for countless centuries enlightened men and women in Buddhism, Confucianism, Judaism, Christianity and other religions and all races have been known for their healing touch.

The first step on the climb up the ladder to *any* meaningful achievement is "desire". If you WANT to heal yourself or anyone else there must first be a desire at both the conscious and unconscious level. It does no good to say with the conscious mind "I want to be healed" if, buried deep in the subconscious, there are thoughts and emotions that make the illness more desirable than wholeness. We have seen cancer patients completely healed by the healers in the Philippines, the U.S., Brazil and England only to see them succumb within months or a few years to some other ailment simply because they had found illness, with its greatly reduced responsibilities, more desirable than facing up to the problems of daily living.

How does one go about acquiring the necessary level of "desire"? Volumes have been written to help one increase will-power, but if you are as weak-willed as I am, that first step up the ladder is a forbidding one. A much more comfortable but equally workable concept is to substitute "want power" for "will power." If you can visualize what it is that you really *want,* in this case good health, and decide that, after considering all of the alternatives, that is what you *really* want, then you are well on your way in your search for healing!

Next, as a part of the *visualizing* process, try to create in your mind's eye an image of yourself WHOLE! HEALTHY! VIBRANT! See yourself full of life and completely freed of the ache, pain, disease, or illness in question. The words "focus", "one-point", and "concentrate" are frequently used in describing what one must do to add vitality to the image. Over thousands of years men in all parts of the world have developed techniques to facilitate this focusing and concentration. These techniques are frequently labeled meditation, attunement, at-one-ment. Over the centuries books have been written outlining various techniques and in recent years these subjects have been made available to any interested reader. [1, 2]

Practically all of the time-proven meditation techniques have had the purpose of helping the individual increase his attunement to the dynamic universal and cosmic forces in which he lives and moves and has his being. It matters not whether you refer to your communicant as Heavenly Father, God, the Great Spirit, Cosmic Consciousness, or any other term which is pleasing to you.

Any person starting out on the somewhat uncertain and seemingly unsubstantial path of meditation and attunement finds that he must pay a price for being allowed to travel on that particular toll road. The currency required is simple faith.

As the student continues to follow the path of meditation, attunement, and at-one-ment he accumulates experiences that enable him to discern that the road actually is beginning to climb upward and that occasionally he comes to a turn or viewing point that permits him the *belief* that he has made progress. After further, sometimes weary and tortuous sections the road of experience brings him to a vast tableland where he suddenly "knows" that he is on the right path leading to understanding and wisdom. His speech and his actions are such that his contemporaries can sense the change in his whole attitude toward life.

Having arrived at this stage of "knowing", he is aware that his previous thought and emotional patterns of greed, jealousy, avarice, fear, hate, envy, and anger are totally non-productive and lead to ill health, discomfort, pain, sickness, and anguish in body, mind and spirit. He then realizes what the great religious leaders had in mind when they taught that such thoughts and emotions should be replaced with the thoughts and emotions of love, compassion, fellow-feeling, kindness, devotion, harmony and unselfishness. A life built on these thoughts and emotions is surprisingly free from illness, both physical and mental.

Chapter 19 on "Theory" gives some indication as to how the billions of individual cells in the human body can be affected for better or for worse by the *thoughts* and *emotions* at the various levels of the mind. The non-scientific reader may find it much easier to create visual images or thought pictures conducive to his good health by taking a lesson from the wise men and healers in the Polynesian civilization and in the civilization of the American Indian. For centuries Polynesians, particularly the wise men in Hawaii, had a highly workable knowledge of the three levels of the human mind. The religious philosophy system of the Hawaiians was loosely referred to as Huna, *Ka*huna literally meaning "keeper of the secret". Fig. 1 shows a totem pole indicating the

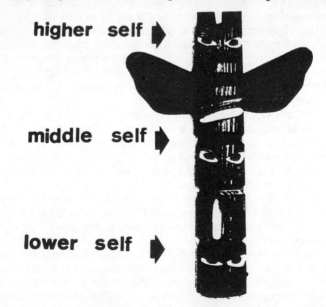

Fig. 1

similar understanding enjoyed by the medicine men among the American Plains Indian tribes. Thus hundreds of years before the birth of Freud these men, responsible for the health of the Hawaiians and the American Indians, daily utilized the concept of lower self, middle self, and higher self. These terms have found their *approximate* counterparts in other systems of terminology as indicated in the following table. They all work!

subconscious	instinctive	lower self
conscious	intellectual	middle self
superconscious	spiritual	higher self

A Kahuna who was bringing about an instantaneous healing of a broken bone, or a modern-day American Indian medicine man such as Rolling Thunder are, in effect, following the diagram in Fig. 1. In each case the middle self (the conscious mind) was collaborating with the lower self (subconscious mind) to bring about a beneficial change at the level of the individual cells of the physical body of the patient. At the same time and through a separate set of disciplines, the middle self of the Kahuna and the Indian was in communication with his higher self (his superconscious) to bring about the desired change of the mental and spiritual levels of the patient. Should the reader want to go further in understanding these processes he will find helpful the books by Max Freedom Long.[3] It is amazingly easy for *your* middle self to carry on communication with the lower self and the higher self. Actually you have been doing this all of the time without realizing it and that is why you had better begin *now* to be more careful of your thoughts and emotions if you want your physical body to be a picture of good health.

Science has helped us greatly in recent years to understand the importance of proper relaxation and sleep in maintaining good health and overcoming disease and illness. The amount of relaxation and sleep needed varies widely between individuals. It is assumed that readers of this volume are fully acquainted with the effect of proper diet and personal hygiene on health. Any person who had enough "want" power to start out on the road toward personal health and who has made any substantial progress toward the "knowing" stage, has learned not to stuff himself with such vast quantities of "junk" foods that his body must build new capillaries to service great gobs of fat. By the same token he will have learned the importance of good personal hygiene.

In treating problems in your *physical body,* firm instructions must be given by your middle self (conscious mind) to your lower self (subconscious mind). Do not attempt to tell the lower self *how* to do the job. It has at its disposal the knowledge of eons of time! It knows far more about your physical body than is in all of the medical libraries of the world. Just kindly, but firmly tell it the job to be done and to get on with it without further delay! And do not feel foolish or self-conscious during your very private daily meditation and devotion period to talk *out loud.* Your lower self is most effectively impressed by short, simple verbal commands.

Admittedly, for most of us intellectually arrogant adults, it takes some time to develop this relationship between these two levels of mind. That is the sole purpose of the focusing, the concentrating, the devotions, the meditation, the at-one-ment.

When you have a mental, emotional, or spiritual problem that needs your personal attention, the channel of communication is from your middle self to your higher self. It is also helpful in this connection to first solicit the help of the lower self when you decide to "go upstairs" to contact your higher self.

Your higher self is a wise old intelligence who is on good speaking terms with a lot of other wise old intelligences. In fact, the American Plains Indians felt it was most presumptuous to try to talk to God or The Great Spirit with just the conscious mind. That is why the Indians so wisely used the emblem of wings. The wings symbolized that the middle self depended on the higher self to carry its thoughts upward for communication with God.

Now you still may be thinking that the mind and brain are two terms referring to the same object. You may say, "Obviously these concepts of the Hawaiians and American Plains Indians are just quaint figures of speech." We feel that such a view is no longer tenable for reasons we will develop later in this book. For the time being, just try to keep an open mind with respect to the message—the brain is NOT the mind(s).

When a person progresses up to the level of understanding just described, he is somewhat surprised that his level of consciousness seems to impel him to be thankful. Do not misunderstand. This is *not* a case of *having* to give thanks in order to get a reward. Far from it! Rather, there is an abiding peace, a one-ness with nature, with the cosmos, which is almost indescribably wonderful. A feeling of being at home in the universe. A feeling of being an intimate and essential part of all that is, a part of the all-wise Creator in whom "we live and move and have our being."

To summarize the basic steps in the process:

1. Earnestly desire *health*. Concentrate on it. Visualize it.

2. Attune yourself to the source of *Power*.

3. Watch your rest, diet, and hygiene.

4. Channel your thoughts and emotions to love, compassion, equanimity, quietness, and confidence.

Does it really work? Does this simple regimen help to ward off illness and disease. Of course it works. It has worked for thousands of years. It worked for the Nazarene. He taught his disciples that it worked. He said that *you* can do it, too. He also said to his disciples, "Greater things than these can you do."

"But," you say, "get specific. What did it ever do for you, Meek?" In answer I give you these examples:

ITEM I—My right foot swelled and became very painful. The shoe lace could not be tied. The instep became badly discolored and the rest of the foot became bright red. After several days, I became worried. Finally, one evening I said to my wife, "I guess I will have to go to the doctor in the morning. This is really getting serious." Her reply was to the effect that, "Oh, come on. You have been traveling all over the world studying healers. Why don't you do the job yourself?" With a challenge such as that, what alternatives did I have?

Before retiring, I took the badly swollen and discolored foot into my hands and gave it a "treatment". By this I mean that I went step by step through the procedure just outlined: I began with an intense "wanting" the healing to happen, focusing all of my being on this objective by use of a meditation and attunement technique which fits my belief system. I then continued step by step as I have just set forth.

The next morning on awakening I stood up, putting the full weight on the foot. No pain. Taking the foot in my hands for a close look, I saw that all of the inflammation was gone and only a slight yellowish coloring remained.

ITEM II —While traveling in northern U.S.A. I developed difficulty in breathing and was forced to interrupt my business trip to see a doctor. After examining my chest, he picked up the phone to report to the hospital, "I have a patient with a bad case of pneumonia. I'm sending him right over by taxi. He will need a room for two weeks." After I was installed in the oxygen and humidity tent, it suddenly struck me that in 3 days I was due to be 1,200 miles from that bed to meet a foreign client who was already en route and there was no way of contacting him to tell him to stay at home.

Here again I followed the step by step procedure outlined on the preceding pages, with an addition. I gave thanks for the wonderful facilities available in the hospital, for the kindness of my doctor and nurses and for the years they had spent in training to be able to help me. I welcomed whatever antibiotics they gave me and advised my lower self to use these most effectively and promptly.

Within 62 hours I had improved to a point that the astonished doctor signed a slip permitting me to get my clothes and be discharged. I caught a jet to fly the 1,200 miles and was on hand to meet my visitor when he came off his plane.

ITEM III—I developed a painful build-up in the heel pad of my right foot—usually referred to as a heel spur. My family physician said he could help the matter by a cortisone injection, and my orthopedic doctor friend said he could operate. The physician said there would be recurrence within six months, requiring further injection. I declined and wore a thick plastic pad and a stiff molded plastic cup under the heel. In spite of this protection, the pain was severe.

On my next trip to the Philippines I asked a healer to take care of it. He replied, "I do not work on hands or feet." Another healer said, "I will have to consult my protector tonight and will tell you tomorrow if we can help you." The answer was negative. I asked another healer to do the job. He made two "operations". No results. I used still another healer with no beneficial results.

Then I started with a group on a two-month trip across southern Asia. By the time we reached Singapore the discomfort was so annoying that as a last resort, I took on the job myself. Reasoning that in my own research with plants, I had found I could influence their rate of growth and blooming, it seemed logical I could take care of a small calcium deposit. I applied myself for 30 minutes. That day my wife and I walked perhaps 6 or 7 miles around the fascinating harbor area of Singapore. I wore heavy leather English walking shoes from which I had left out the thick sponge pad and the plastic heel cup. There was almost no pain. That was three years ago. I have had no need to go to a healer or to a doctor or to treat myself further for this ailment.

ITEM IV—In 1968, I developed excruciating pains in my spinal column and several joints. Jack Warnock, M.D. diagnosed the trouble as gout. He prescribed Zyloprim to quickly bring the uric acid level down to an acceptable level and Benamid on a continuing daily schedule to maintain the desired level of uric acid. After six months I rebelled at the prospect of taking this medication for the remainder of my life and put into practice some of the material given in the preceding pages. Except for one short period of high uric acid level in 1972 when I had a particularly strenuous foreign travel schedule it has remained at the desired level, as proven by a complete blood analysis once or twice a year. I have taken no drugs for this condition for the past seven years.

None of the above is from the standpoint of saying, "What a great self-healer am I." Far from it! Most of you readers can do far better. After all I was already 60 years old when I started my really intensive studies of paranormal healing. I had acquired a lifetime of knowledge that acted as a barrier to the step of "becoming as a little child."

It seems to me that this is the right place to report a remarkable self-healing incident relating to another of our co-authors. On March 23, 1977, Dr. David Hoy (*See* Chapter 10) arrived home on a late evening flight from Cincinnati, having been on a three-week lecture tour. Almost as soon as he prepared for bed, he was stricken with a massive coronary. His wife, Shirley, with a strength born of necessity, somehow managed to get the nearly 300-pound Hoy down a long flight of stairs, out to their car, and rushed him to the Emergency Room of Paducah's Western Baptist Hospital. In the first shocking hours, David was in tremendous pain and, of course, anxious. He was placed in Intensive Care in the Cardiac Care Unit. During the next two days, Hoy suffered a second attack. The outlook was not good and his doctor felt that David's case was extremely serious and required specialized equipment which they did not have. He was, therefore, transferred to the Special Cardiac Care Unit of St. Thomas Hospital in Nashville, Tennessee and placed under the care of cardiologist, Dr. W. Barton Campbell.

After treating him for the pain (which was considerable) they were also able to keep him under constant surveillance with electronic scanners which told of any minute difference in the heart's activity.

Waiting for his condition to stabilize, the cardiologist carefully and graphically explained to Hoy that his heart attack was much like an explosion in his right coronary artery. They would have to know the precise location to see if they could repair the damage with a surgical arterial by-pass. If the infarction were far enough from the heart so that there would be enough undamaged artery, then they would attach the by-pass; otherwise—well, they just didn't know.

By April 1, they decided Hoy was in stable enough condition for the catheterization and cineangiography. This procedure allows them to pass a catheter up the leg, completely through the trunk of the body and into the heart, all the while being able to watch it on a screen, so as to locate the exact position of the occlusion.

You cannot imagine the surprise that those in the operating room experienced when they saw that in the intervening three days David Hoy had created his own arterial by-pass which was functioning perfectly! Now, it is not unusual for the body to do this in smaller veins or over a longer period of time; but in this case it was something akin to a miracle. One of those present flatly stated that it was.

By Sunday, April 3, Hoy was sitting up in bed where, with his considerable psychic ability, he had already made up his own version of a "pong" game with the sophisticated electronic equipment to which he was attached. He said he had no difficulty making one of the red lights go "on" and ring the nurses' station, but it took a bit more biocontrol to get all three lights to light up simultaneously.

This is truly an exciting case of a healer healing himself. As his doctor told him, "David, when I have a heart attack, I want it to be just like yours." I agree.

As we observed, there are several roads that can be followed in developing our paranormal healing abilities. So in case some readers find that neither the very simple "pictorial" pathway #1 described above, nor the more complex pathway #3 as related in Chapter 19 on theory of healing, fits his or her psychological bent, we introduce:

Pathway #2—A Middle-Of-The-Road Approach

This one we call the "A.B.C's of Metascience". In a series of 21 short and succinct statements, we will set forth an overall view of the nature of man's mind, body, and spirit and the possible relationship of these aspects of man to the Universe. This is indeed conceptualization on a cosmic scale! The postulates show that our universe and the cosmos are far different from what our five senses have taught us since childhood. Only by expanding our awareness of these nonsensory parameters of the universe can scientists begin to understand the modus operandi of paranormal activities. These postulates rely heavily on the modeling of Prof. William A. Tiller, Itzhak Bentov, and Stanley R. Dean, M.D. as presented in my book, *From Enigma to Science* (Samuel Weiser).[5]

THE A.B.C's OF METASCIENCE,* 1976

A

Everything in this universe, and probably in other universes, is *vibratory* in nature.

B

The human being consists of several (possibly as many as seven or more) *vibrational* systems.

C

The physical or material body, composed as it is of just certain of the elements of the periodic table, is in the LOWEST RANGE of the vibrational frequencies spanned by man's several vibrational systems.

D

Man's conscious, subconscious, and superconscious minds; his memory; and the portions referred to as soul or spirit, may each involve a separate but intermingling energy field or system of vibrational nature, each with its own frequency range. (It seems to be a good speculation that one or more of these vibrational systems involves a type or types of energy as of now unknown, and/or outside our present concept of the electromagnetic spectrum.)

E

The formation of the physical body, its repair and maintenance, and the replenishment of its cells, appears to be the result of the operation of the energy field system of the next higher level of vibration. This vibrational "body" has been called the etheric or the bioplasmic.

F

Most of the energy systems of the human being which vibrate at frequencies higher than those of the physical body, continue to survive the death and disintegration of the physical body.

---

*This term is used in the sense given in Webster's 3rd New International, "underlying, transcending, beyond all . . . individual branches of science . . . designating new but related disciplines such as can deal critically with nature, structure or behavior . . ." of science.

G

Thought is a form of energy; it has universal "field" properties which, like gravitational and magnetic fields and the L-fields of all living things, are amenable to scientific research.

H

Thought fields (T-fields) can interact, traverse space and penetrate matter more or less simultaneously, instantaneously, and with little or no attenuation.

I

Thought fields can be permanently attached to or recorded in the energy fields of physical matter.

J

Thought fields of one person can intermingle with the thought fields (or energy systems) of another person and physically interact with resulting out-pictured physical results in the physical body(-ies).

K

Thought fields are eternal; they make up a portion of what Jung called the "collective unconscious".

L

There is good reason to believe that those energy fields of an individual which survive so-called death move on to other planes of existence. ("In my Father's House are many mansions.")

M

Entities on the immediately higher planes can and do communicate with persons still in their physical bodies on the earth plane of matter, provided the vibrational frequency of the field making up the subconscious of the person can be raised slightly and/or the vibrational rate of the entity can be lowered sufficiently.

N

This attunement mentioned in (M) has been accomplished frequently in all ages by means of prayer, meditation, and concentration. The information, knowledge, enlightenment, and guidance coming through such exchanges has been a major source of wisdom and growth of human consciousness throughout the ages. (Feedback on a Cosmic scale!)

O

Human beings who, because of training and/or some chemical or other deviation in their physical makeup, are unusually sensitive to such vibrational interchanges may, by faculties we call clairvoyance and clairaudience, receive visual and auditory impressions.

P

The more skilled or adept of such human beings have been called witches, saints, prophets, seers, and mystics in the past, and are usually referred to as adepts, mediums, sensitives, and gurus in this century.

Q

While it is difficult to even speculate with any degree of assurance today, intuition indicates that in the centuries ahead we will prove the existence of the spiritual "field" postulated in the modeling of Tiller, Bentov and Dean, and may very well find that its full development and perfection is man's chief evolutionary goal.

R

In ultimate reality, we are each "spirit", a form of cosmic energy which has been in existence for eons in the past and will continue for eons into the future—in this universe and in all other universes.

S

That portion of this universal sea of energy which is *you,* is, in this instant of what we call time, occupying your physical body, hence the *real* you is not the cloak of dense matter you call your physical body but rather the eternal spirit *essence* which guides and directs the body you *temporarily* occupy. You can and should be the *master* of the body, just as you are master of your automobile, typewriter or any other physical mechanism of which you are the temporary owner.

The person who has reached the level of mental and spiritual evolution and attunement mentioned in (S) *can enjoy superb health* and physical well-being himself; can

avoid most major and minor illnesses for the remainder of
his life span on planet earth; and can, if he wishes, serve as
a *channel for the healing of other persons.*

T

The L-fields pioneered by Burr and Northrup; the T-fields pioneered by
Vasiliev and his team; the multilevel vibrational fields or bodies postulated by Tiller; and the energy exchange levels postulated by Bentov,
when further explored and understood in the decades ahead, will go far
toward explaining the nature of all ESP and paranormal activities.

U

Any person now alive on planet earth who is willing to follow the
Biblical injunction to "seek, knock, and ask" with sufficiently strong
motivation, open-mindedness, and study can:

a. Attune to sources of wisdom and enlightenment capable of bringing
    inner peace, happiness, and lasting satisfaction with life, and
b. Look forward with trust and confidence to his or her survival of
    bodily death, and *know* the certainty of eternal life.

Of course we readily acknowledge that this material has existed for a
long time in many different cultures in different parts of the world. The
important thing is that many health professionals are coming to believe that the *choice* between health and long life on the one hand or
pain, sickness, and disease on the other hand *is up to each individual
person.* It is *not* a "will of the gods", fate, bad luck, or any other excuse or
"cop-out" in current use.

Alvin Toffler[4] estimates that man, as we currently know him, has
been around for approximately eight hundred generations. In time,
hopefully as short as *two* generations, it is conceivable that individual
man can learn to accept the responsibility for avoiding many illnesses
and prolonging his useful life span.

If the majority of individuals achieve this level of understanding, the
whole nature of public and private health care systems would be dras-
tically changed for the better. Gone would be the ages-old idea that
most illness results from "outside" causes and that only the intervention of the drug-dispensing medical practitioner could restore the
individual to health. Gone would be the constantly mushrooming costs
for more and more grandiose facilities for physical and mental health
care.

Two thousand years ago man was admonished to heal himself in
body, mind and spirit. Now, with man's rapidly expanding insights into
the far reaches of human consciousness, enlightened individuals are
challenged to see just how far each can move toward that worthy goal.

REFERENCES

1. Lawrence LeShan, *How to Meditate* (New York: Little Brown, 1974).
2. Deborah Rozman, *Meditation for Children* (San Francisco: Celestial Arts, 1976).
3. Max Freedom Long, *The Secret Science Behind Miracles* (Santa Monica, CA.: De Vorss, 1950).

   _____, *The Secret Science at Work* (Santa Monica, CA.: De Vorss, 1950).

   _____, *Self Suggestion and the Huna Theory* (Santa Monica, CA.: De Vorss, 1958).
4. Alvin Toffler, *Future Shock* (New York: Random House, 1970).
5. George W. Meek, *From Enigma to Science* (New York: Samuel Weiser, 1973).

V

AN EVOLVING THEORY OF
THE HEALING PROCESS

Research into the work of the healers, the patients, and the healing process itself leads into a study of the nature of man. It becomes apparent that no one science or no combination of sciences has assembled a theory capable of accommodating all of the phenomena observed and verified.

The recent explosion of information in many sciences, combined with the specific research findings of the authors, now makes it possible to start to assemble the first outline of a comprehensive theory of the healing process. The theory to be presented here, inadequate as time will prove it to be, at least has the advantage of encompassing practically all of the observed phenomena—even that "sticky" problem of spirits or discarnate entities.

Since today's scientific materialism and allopathic medicine have been unable to provide a theoretical framework for understanding the many aspects of paranormal healing discussed in the foregoing chapters, it is hoped that this section will stimulate thought and discussion in medical and scientific circles. Neither chapter is complete in itself, but each reinforces the other.

18

THEORETICAL MODELING ON
THE FUNCTIONING OF MAN

*We have to remember that what we observe is not
nature itself but nature exposed to our method of
questioning.*

—Werner Heisenberg

William A. Tiller

Up to the present, medicine, biology, and agriculture have viewed
living organisms as operating via the following sequence of reactions:

$$\leftarrow \text{function} \xleftrightarrow{\rightarrow} \text{structure} \xleftrightarrow{\rightarrow} \text{chemistry} \xleftrightarrow{\rightarrow} \begin{array}{c} \text{electromagnetic} \\ \text{energies} \end{array} \quad (1)$$

Thus, flaws in the function area were traced to structural defects in the
system that arose out of certain chemical imbalances. The rectification
procedure was usually via an adjustment of the chemical environment
with more and more sophisticated chemical complexes being utilized to
trigger the organism's defenses and repair mechanisms. The dilemma
that arises is that both the organism and its threatening invaders
adapt to the new chemical complex becoming progressively less sensitive to it and so the escalation of potency must continue.

One very deleterious aspect to this procedure is that the unnatural
chemical content of the organism increases and begins to influence
other levels of functioning of the organism than the one being corrected. This effect is particularly serious in the agricultural area where
the method of application of the chemicals is via the soil so that as
chemical equilibration develops between the plants and the soil, perco-
lation of water through the soil spreads the chemicals over a large area
and the whole ecosystem begins to suffer from chemical pollution. In
addition, there is some question concerning the long-term effects on
other organisms associated with the intake of these chemicals residing
in the plants. Clearly, mankind must find a better way of under-

standing and dealing with flaws of function in living organisms. The electromagnetic energies, in the forms of X-rays, diathermy, etc., have been primarily utilized to modify the density and flexibility of the living structure. These methodologies have some well-proven benefits but also deleterious side effects as well.

In searching out alternative procedures for influencing the well-being of living organisms, one must first question the validity of completeness of equation 1. Are there other effective physical, as distinct from chemical, techniques or modifying organismic functioning? Are there potential techniques for doing likewise in the domain of what would be called "nonphysical energies"? We know that osteopaths have had considerable success with human functioning using physical techniques and for the last two hundred years there have been serious reports of various types of nonphysical effects which suggest to the naivete of equation 1.

Incorporating the author's multidimensional mode of substance, it is proposed that equation 1 should be replaced by

$$\text{function} \overset{\leftarrow}{\to} \text{structure} \overset{\leftarrow}{\to} \text{chemistry} \overset{\leftarrow}{\to} \begin{array}{c}\text{(positive}\\\text{space-time)}\\\text{energies}\end{array} \overset{\leftarrow}{\to}$$

$$\begin{array}{c}\text{(negative}\\\text{space-time)}\\\text{energies}\end{array} \overset{\leftarrow}{\to} \text{Mind} \overset{\leftarrow}{\to} \text{Spirit} \overset{\leftarrow}{\to} \text{Divine} \quad (2)$$

Here, positive space-time and negative space-time stand for the physical and the etheric*, respectively, and have been denoted with this new labeling to illustrate their conjugate nature as well as the algebraic sign of their respective mass and energy states.

In support of these new reaction components, a large number of observations have been made which deserve brief mention: (a) Under hypnosis, the human body has been found to exhibit remarkable feats of strength and endurance attesting to the mind/structure link. (b) In Aikido, Zen or Yoga disciplines, we see the conscious link between mind, structure and function, probably via the intermediary links. (c) In modern psychotherapy, we see chemical treatments influencing mental states and mental treatments influencing chemical states. (d) In neuropsychiatry, we see that small electric currents between certain specific points in the brain give rise to the same behavioral changes as observed with certain chemical intakes. Becker has shown that small DC electric currents ($1\ \mu\mu A/mm^2$ to $1000\ \mu\mu A/mm^2$) cause cell regeneration, tissue repair and fracture rehealing, whereas DC currents greater than $10,000\ \mu\mu A/mm^2$ cause cell degeneration, thus supporting the positive space-time energy/chemistry/structure link. (f) Present-day U.S. osteopathic studies of kinesiology show a direct influence of specific minerals or chemicals held in the hand giving credence to the negative space-time energy/function linkage.

---

*The term "etheric" as used here is synonymous with "bioplasmic" as used by Meek in the following chapter and by Stelter in Chapter 7.

(g) Studies of acupuncture show that the application of energy at certain specific exterior body points causes changes in the structure and function of corresponding specific body organs giving support to the energy/function link. (h) Studies of the influence of prayer on the growth of plants such as noted in Findhorn and other projects support the Mind/structure link. (i) Studies in the alteration of enzyme activity (trypsin) by placing solutions in magnetic fields and between the palms of a "healer" show the linkage between positive space-time energies and function plus negative space-time energies and function. (j) Absent healing studies show that space and time are no barrier to the Mind/structure and function linkage. (k) Studies of radionics indicate the ability to broadcast energy of a nonphysical nature that nourishes certain specific organisms while being anathema to other specific invading organisms. The foregoing list could be made much longer; however, the point seems to have been made that there is wide support in human experience for the general soundness of equation 2. This book dramatically and substantially supports such a view.

We may liken conventional scientific understanding of the universe to the visible tip of an iceberg. We have come to know that exposed tip very well; however, like the iceberg, most of Nature is still hidden from us. History contains references to, and speculation on, many aspects of the hidden iceberg and very recent psychoenergetic research suggests some fascinating possibilities.

(a) From experiments on telepathy, psychokinesis, manual healers and traveling clairvoyance, we seem to be dealing with *new energy fields* completely different from those known to us via conventional science.

(b) The universe seems to organize and radiate information in *other dimensions* than just the physical space-time frame with which we are familiar. From experiments on PK, radionics, materialization-dematerialization, etc., the cause-effect relationships seem to follow a different path of "field line" than we have been used to dealing with in the conventional space-time frame of reference.

(c) At some level of the universe, we are *all interconnected* to each other and to other things on this planet. We see this in the Soviet telepathy experiments with rabbits and in the Backster experiments with plants, eggs and assemblies of living cells (yogurt, blood, etc.).

(d) *Time, space and mass are deformable;* i.e., they are not as immutable and confining as we have tended to think. Experiments on precognition, out-of-the-body traveling, materialization and dematerialization, etc., point to this.

(e) With our physical sensory systems, we *cannot perceive reality.* From modern information theory, we deduce that we cannot know reality but can only gain some information about reality. We settle for a set of consistency relationships. Slater's experiments on the "upside-down" glasses strongly support this view.

(f) Finally, a *biological transformation* seems to be taking place in man at this point in time. From personal experiential feelings and from those of others, from observations of the rapid rise of endocrine gland dysfunction (hypoglycemia, etc.) in humans plus from observations of the manifesting instability of the human sector of our planet, new energies appear to be circulating in man that, on the one hand, cause internal tensions and subliminal fears and, on the other hand, cause manifestation of psychic experiences and abilities.

Mankind seems to be voyaging into a new world of perception and does not yet have reliable tools to cope with this new apparent environment. Just as most of the key ideas, upon which our presently accepted science is based, were known to the Greeks and lay fallow for almost 2,000 years before development, most of the key ideas upon which this new science will be based seem to have been known to the Eastern cultures for even longer. Now seems to be the time for transforming these ideas into an accepted science!

From the foregoing, we can gain the idea that man is a multidimensional Being, functioning on many different levels of Nature simultaneously. He is mostly unaware of these levels of self and cannot grasp the visualization that he has an extended energy structure that interconnects and integrates his Beingness with seemingly separate localizations of Beingness. We are so chained to our view of reality as perceived with the five physical senses that we are unable to give credence to our true nature. We must come to realize the potential of man as expressed by equation 2 and to recognize that, if man's energy structure is perturbed at any one of the indicated levels, ripples of effect flow out in all directions to produce corresponding perturbations at all of the other levels. However, the magnitude of the effect and the time of manifestation of the effect at another level will depend upon things like the intensity of the original signal, the conductivity of the medium of the original signal, and the degree of coherence of wave structures at the boundaries between levels.

As an example to illustrate the point, consider Fig. 1 and the author's model that all of space-time is imbedded in a non-space/non-time reference frame so that events at this level form the potential for wave propagation changes in space-time. Here, we represent an event occurring at the level of Mind at our origin of time. The wave patterns representative of that event (thought) impinge upon negative space-time and propagate in this medium to produce the required wave coincidence at time t_1 later, which represents the event manifestation at that level.

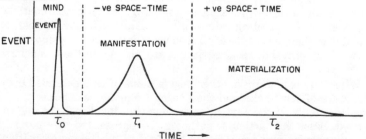

Fig. 1. Illustration of cause-effect relationship in the universe.

These waves, in turn, stimulate corresponding wave motion in the medium of positive space-time, which flow at a slower rate but produce an eventual coincidence at a later time t_2, which represents the event materialization as perceived by the five physical senses. If we had well-developed senses at the negative space-time level, we would have had precognitive awareness of the event at a time t_2-t_1 before its materialization at the physical level. Thus, what we call the future coexists with the present but at a different level of substance of the universe. Perhaps the most important point to be emphasized in this example is that the original thought was the event at the mind level serving as *cause* to eventually produce the materialized event or *effect* at the physical level.

The foregoing leads quite naturally to a perspective on healing; i.e., that pathology can develop at a number of levels and that healing is needed at all of them to restore the system to a state of harmony. The initial pathology begins at the level of Mind and propagates effects to both the negative space-time and the positive space-time levels. We then perceive what we call disease or malfunction at these levels and try to remove the effects by a variety of healing techniques.

The best healing mode is to help the individual remove the pathology at the *cause* level and bring about the correction by a return to "right thinking." The next best healing mode is to effect repair of the structure at the negative space-time level. The next best level of healing is that which medicine practices today wherein they effect repair of the structure at the positive space-time level. Since the energy structures at these different levels are coupled, repair at a lower level will still produce some feedback modification of energy structure at a higher level. However, if harmony is not restored at the higher level, then a force will continue to exist for pathological development in the energy structure at a lower level. Of course, this force is basically like a thermodynamic potential to produce change so that the effects may be manifested or materialized in very different forms depending upon what alterations have already been made to the energy structures of the positive and negative space-time frames. The closest analogy to this can be found in the field of "phase equilibria" of materials. If you heat a complex alloy containing a number of chemical constituents to a high temperature so that it melts, then by cooling it again you produce a thermodynamic driving force for a phase change; i.e., to one of several possible solid forms. By making very slight but specific modifications to the chemistry or cooling rate or other variables in the process, it is possible to change the type of solid phase that initially develops and the crystalline form that results without any change in the basic driving force.

When one is healing another, use is made of this extended energy structure of self to channel the needed frequency components of the needed energy at the particular dimensional level into the one to be healed. Since the particular pathology is represented by a particular energy pattern and all patterns are formed by the superposition of waves, then a pattern can be altered or completely eradicated by the input of the appropriate wave components at the appropriate intensity level. To do this effectively, a number of conditions need to be satisfied: (1) one must be able to generate or tap the needed wave components of the requisite type, (2) one must be able to tap these wave components from his extended energy structure at the specifically needed ratios of relative intensities, (3) one needs to tap the requisite correction energy pattern at a high overall intensity so that the healing needed is of short duration, (4) one needs to be sharply attuned to the one to be healed so that these energy components can be brought into their extended energy structure without scattering losses and (5) one needs to have the confidence of the one to be healed so that he doesn't mentally distort or undo the healer's efforts because of fears or doubts. By considering these conditions, we may begin to see a rationale for the play of illusion in paranormal (or normal) healing and for the cooperative alignment of life forms at nonphysical levels of the universe to provide the requisite energy balancing.

To understand how this is possible and to gain an appreciation for the implications of such healing events, let us consider the necessary structure of an electrical system designed to deliver electrical energy to a load over a broad frequency range with a specific intensity distribution of frequencies. The individual components in the system will be resonators having a restricted band width of frequencies and restricted output intensity. Thus, to obtain the required frequency range, a number of different kinds of resonators would need to be coupled in series. To obtain the required output intensity distribution, many resonators of the same kind will need to be coupled in parallel. Finally, in order for this energy to reach the load, the supply must be properly coupled or impedance matched to the load. Such a situation is illustrated in Fig. 2.

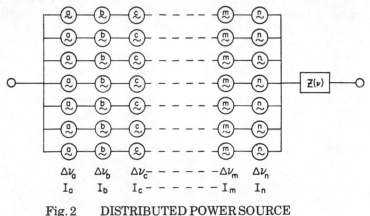

Fig. 2   DISTRIBUTED POWER SOURCE

Fig. 2. Illustration of a composite healing power supply providing broad band and high intensity characteristics.

The same type of situation must obtain when we are using biological resonators in the healing mode. The implication is that the extended energy structure of the healer must include a number of different biological resonators functioning on basically different but overlapping frequency bands integrated into a functioning energy system. Further, as the healer expands his consciousness to resonate over a larger frequency range and builds himself to transmit energy at higher intensities, the more effective will he become as a healing channel.

In the framework of this author's model, man appears as a Being whose primary level of existence is at the *non*-space, *non*-time levels of the universe and who has placed himself in a space-time *vehicle of consciousness* for the purpose of growing in awareness of the True Self and of generating coherence in the True Self. Our perception mechanisms at the space-time vehicle level lock us into a very narrowly restricted view of reality and the Self. Disharmony created by the ego at the deeper levels of self, materializes as error or disease in the space-time vehicle as an indicator that error has been created at a primary level.

Self-healing or healing by another involves energy coordination at a variety of levels and teaches us that the sensory apparatus of the space-time vehicle perceives only the "World of Appearances" and has no knowledge of Reality. It teaches us that the space-time vehicle is not Life but only a simulator of Life whose only role is as a teaching tool. With our *thoughts and attitudes, we continuously reprogram the simulator from the Mind level of the multidimensional universe* and continuously generate our individual and collective futures by such behavior.*

Our chief problem associated with accepting the truth about paranormal healing is that it appears to grossly violate our "World Picture", our view of reality—and yet none of us is capable of perceiving Reality at our normal levels of consciousness. Without some degree of personal experiential awareness of these "other" energies, it is indeed difficult to readily accept the contents of this book. For such readers, I would advise self-constraint with respect to habit attitudes, patience and as much openmindedness as possible. Having had the privilege of reading the manuscript of this book, it is my opinion that it offers both valuable knowledge and perspective of the unfolding revolution of human consciousness presently fracturing the shackles of self-bondage to outdated ideas and forms.

---

*Prof. Tiller's concept is embodied in Fig. AA of the chapter which follows.

19

TOWARD A GENERAL THEORY OF HEALING

The final conclusion is that we know very little, and yet it is astonishing that we know so much, and still more astonishing that so little knowledge can give us so much power.
— Bertrand Russell

George W. Meek

Never did a quotation epitomize the position of an author more precisely than does this one from Russell. In the two years it has taken to write and rewrite this chapter, we were constantly reminded of how little we know of this subject. But we are astonished that we actually know enough about the theory of psychic, faith, and mental healing to find we can daily perform what in bygone centuries would have been considered "miracles".

We are even more astonished to find that the "very little we know" has enabled us to construct a theoretical framework which does much more than just "explain" paranormal healing. It seems that for the first time we may have a basis for beginning to understand the modus operandi underlying most, if not all, so-called psychic phenomena—clairvoyance, clairaudience, mental telepathy, psychometry, and out-of-the-body or astral travel.

If this all sounds a bit presumptuous, we hasten to explain that what we present in these few pages must be regarded as a *starting point* for further research. Considering the complexity of the subject—a subject that has challenged man since the beginning of time—it is certain that this initial statement will require many deletions, revisions, and expansions in the years ahead.

In our studies we were benefited enormously by many who have attempted to construct theories which relate to the nature of man. Valuable stimulation has come from many sources:

Andrade of São Paulo, Brazil with his Biological Organizing Model related to a 4-dimensional world, (private correspondence)

Bentov[1] and Bohm who postulated the idea of a 4-dimensional hologram,

Todeschini, Pulitzer, and (Michael) Watson with their newest (unpublished) theories which postulate a fourth state of water (beyond ice, liquid, and vapor) as an up-to-date replacement for the ether theory,

Puharich[2] for his Psi matter theory,

Eisenbud[3] who has done some very useful theorizing under the heading of *The Mind Matter Interface,*

Broad[4] in his *The Mind and Its Place in Nature,*

Ashby[5] in his *In Search of a Theory to Explain the Psychic Realm,*

LeShan's *Toward a General Theory of the Paranormal,* and *The Medium, the Mystic and the Physicist,*[6]

Thouless and Weisner[7] for combined biochemical and psychological insights into the healing process,

Watson, (Lyall) in private correspondence and in *Supernature,*[8]

Fitzherbert[9] for useful insights into the role of hypnosis in healing,

Karagulla,[10] who for many persons stimulated interest in the energy fields of man,

White[11] for his *Frontiers of Consciousness,*

Mishlove[12] for his *Roots of Consciousness,*

Musès and Young[13] for their *Consciousness and Reality,*

And many other researchers who in the last ten years have contributed helpful insights into the nature of man.

The goal of expanding the work of the healers and making such services available to hundreds of millions of people in the decades ahead, can be converted to reality only by constructing, testing, reworking, and refining our theoretical understanding of the nature of the healing process. The sole objective of this chapter is to make the first step in that direction.

If you choose to dismiss what follows as pseudo-science or science fiction, that is your right. One should observe, however, that science fiction of just a few decades ago has now been far outstripped by subsequent scientific advances. Let us use as a starting point the conceptualizations which follow, and then work to perfect the theoretical framework in the years ahead.

Basic Considerations

Out of my own research findings and those of my co-authors, and from our study of the literature in many fields, I have arbitrarily isolated information that I consider of key importance. The full significance of these points and their interrelationships will become apparent in due course.

1. Self-Healing

A healer does NOT do the healing. It is accomplished by his *reinforcing or supplementing the patient's own extraordinary capability of self-healing*. Each of the patient's basic systems: structural, muscular, circulatory, nervous, and lymphatic is an absolute marvel of perfection. The same level of perfection exists in all of the organs of the body. This fine physical body is the product of millions of years of development by the Creator. (*See* photo section Fig. F1)

This point must be considered the foundation stone of the whole subject of healing.

2. Communications Capability

Most of the 60,000,000,000,000 cells of the physical body possess what science calls "information transfer capability." Lakhovsky[14] discovered in 1935 that the individual cell possesses two characteristics—capacitance and inductance—which are the elements of a tuned circuit. Like a radio, the cell must be tuned to the desired frequency. The desired frequencies are those involved in the life process. To put this into the vernacular, it is almost as though each cell carries its own walkie-talkie, permitting it to send and receive messages.

Since the days of Lakhovsky, the electron scanning microscope has come into being. James B. Beal points out that with this device we can now see that the cells are infinitely more complete than even Lakhovsky suspected. Beal observes:[15]

> What earlier seemed to be a "simple cell wall" was likely to be folded and convoluted—precisely the right kind of structure to *serve as a semiconductor*. And components of the cell are likely to include organic semiconductors such as liquid crystals, a material that is *hypersensitive to* temperature changes, *magnetic and electric fields*, stress, *radiation*, and trace contamination. To complicate matters even more, many cells have a double outer membrane; electrically, such a membrane functions as a capacitor with the characteristics of a leaky dielectric. [Italics mine]

Research in the U.S.S.R. has demonstrated that communication can, in fact, take place between cells. (When cells from a person's body were put into adjacent but separate quartz containers and one set was attacked and killed by a virus, the cells in the untreated container died simultaneously.)

The significance of this is that most, if not all, of the trillions of cells in the body are linked by a highly perfected communications system. Equally remarkable—and as we shall see, of great significance for healing—is that most of these trillions of cells possess a facility for generating energy to power the communications system. (Fig. F2 photo section)

3. *Rapid Cell Turnover*

The cells in the human body are dying at the rate of 5,700,000 per *second.* The fact that these are being replaced with the same number of new cells every second provides both the patient and the healer a golden opportunity to make certain that the replacements are healthy.

The human body is composed largely of protein and this protein is being renewed continuously. Liver and serum proteins are turned over *every ten days* and the proteins of the lungs, brain, skin, and principal muscles are turned over *every 158* days. Even bone, once thought to be permanent, is constantly replaced with new material. Only the *design* of our bodies, changing slightly with the passing years, remains constant. Thus at any one time it may be said that a large percentage of the cells alive at that instant in the body are new cells which were not in existence six months earlier.

If the healer and the patient can help these new cells to be born in a state of health and perfection rather than as a facsimile of the diseased and ailing cells which died, then the body is on the way back to health.

4. *Water, the Major Component*

The body is a soft, wet, plastic mass. Each of us was a fetus "assembled" in a world of water, totally submerged. Almost two thirds of the adult body is composed of water. A young woman would be astonished if she knew that it would take nine gallon jugs to contain the water in her body. Her brain (and that of the reader) is at least 80% water by weight. The significance of this for our understanding of healing is that water is *extremely sensitive* to many types of radiations. The American industrial research scientist Robert N. Miller and physicist Prof. Philip B. Reinhart have now devised four separate instrumental means (*See* Chapter 13) to show that some of the energy flowing from a healer's hands can trigger an alteration of the molecular bond between the hydrogen and the oxygen molecules in water. Sister Justa Smith, Ph.D., (as reported in that same chapter) has shown that the radiations from a healer's hands can affect the growth rate of one of the body's enzymes—trypsin—when the trypsin crystals are placed in distilled water in a test tube.

Since the body is composed largely of water; and since we have found that water is extremely sensitive to radiations from a wide spectrum of energies; and since we are increasing our ability to instrumentally detect and measure the flow of various energies from the healer's body, we can see the far-reaching implications of this.

5. *The Empty Body*   SPACE BWN ATOMIC PARTICLES

The soft, wet, plastic mass we were just talking about is found to be "empty"! By this we refer to the fact that our present-day insights into the nature of matter show us that most of the space taken up by the human body is 99 + % void (leaving aside the possibility of the so-called ether or equivalent). This situation is well described by Glazewski:[16]

> To illustrate this, imagine borrowing an atom from, for example, a hand. For the sake of convenience let us accept the Bolu model of the atom, magnified so that the nucleus is

the size of an apple—where would the next atom be? Between 1,000 to 2,000 miles away! Looking upon our bodies on this scale we would see a vast universe containing many millions of trillions of atoms forming billions of galaxies. If the nuclei of those atoms were shining, as they are centers of energy, we would confront a vast, celestial, starry sky of unimaginable spaces. So you see, our body, of which we have only a statistical perception when using our senses, is actually a great "void" with little centres of energy in forms of atoms dispersed at enormous distances. One biological cell contains many millions of galaxies of atoms.

So now we have arrived at the point where we see that the body *and* the brain are largely made up of water and that, in reality, both are largely "void" of any "solid matter". Obviously present medical thinking regarding the nature of the physical body may be due for some substantial revision.

6. *The Mind-Brain Relationship*

With the passing years it has become increasingly obvious that the terms brain and mind are *not* synonymous. Perhaps one of the most conclusive pieces of research was provided by the work of Penfield.[17] He was considerably surprised at how large a piece of the brain he could excise with little or no effect on the ability of the patient to carry on living as usual. To use a now out-of-date analogy of comparing the brain with a telephone switchboard, it was almost as though several of the "operators" went out for lunch but so long as there was still even one on duty, the calls could come in and go out much as usual.

In this same connection, it must be recalled that neither Penfield nor any other brain surgeon has been able to identify any specific brain cells as being what psychiatry refers to as the id, ego, and super-ego; or cells which correspond to what the psychologist calls conscious, subconscious, or super-conscious. Yet concepts attributing three levels or aspects to man's mind existed hundreds of years before the terms psychiatry and psychology ever came into existence.

For example, as noted in Chapter 17, both the native peoples of the Pacific and American Plains Indians recognized three levels of mind, and represented them in their tribal totem poles. Their medicine men or witch doctors—their healers—utilizing this knowledge of the three levels of mind knew how to accomplish healings so spectacular as to defy the comprehension of modern Western medicine. (Rolling Thunder still demonstrates these skills. Chapter 2.)

Any theory of healng must recognize that the levels of mind appear to be something quite distinct from the ten or twelve ounces of water which make up more than 80% of the reader's brain. Obviously, "the brain is not the mind(s)." As we shall soon see, the mind is something quite different.

7. *The Computer-Programmer Analogy*

In view of the foregoing considerations, let us replace the obsolete switchboard analogy with the computer analogy. This allows us to introduce the all-important concept of the programmer. No matter how sophisticated the computer, some *outside intelligence* is required to direct its activity.

As we shall postulate later, in the case of both healer and patient, *mind* serves the function of programmer for the cells that make up the brain.

(Incidentally, do not be dismayed at the growing tendency in our evolving theory to consider the physical body as "just an electro-biochemical mechanism." This does not do violence to the timeless concept of the soul or spirit. Quite the contrary, as we shall show later in this chapter.)

8. *The Crucial Role of Energy Fields*

In item 5, the quotation from Glazewski referred to atoms such as those in the healer's hands moving in vast galaxies. What makes these atoms work together organically as a unit in a biological cell? *Something* must organize them to make them cohere and work together toward one goal. The answer to this question is crucial to solving the mysteries of the healing process.

We are now beginning to find the answer in work initiated in 1935 by Harold Saxon Burr and F. S. C. Northrup[18] who published that year a little-noticed paper, "An Electrodynamic Theory of Life", In research during the forty years since, hundreds of scientists in many countries have been able to show that all living matter is enveloped in electro-magnetic fields, called L-fields. These are not readily detectable by our five senses, and until the development of modern vacuum tube volt-meters, it was not even possible to prove their existence.

In the case of the human body the electro-magnetic fields operate in a complicated manner as the molecules in the cells are constantly being torn apart and rebuilt or replaced with fresh material from food we eat and the oxygen we breathe. But, thanks to the controlling L-field, the new molecules and cells are rebuilt as before and arrange themselves in the same pattern as the old ones.

The situation is somewhat like a cook looking at a gelatine mold and knowing the contour she will turn out of it. If she uses a battered mold, she expects to find some dents or bulges in the gelatine. A "battered and bent" L-field will produce abnormal cells. The vistas and implications of this simple analogy for the health, happiness, and prolongation of life, are staggering.

Because understanding the concept of energy fields is so crucial to penetrating the mysteries of healing, and consciousness itself, we give still another analogy. Many readers will recall the experiment in high school physics in which a magnet was placed under a sheet of paper and wide-eyed students observed how the iron filings on top of the paper "organized" themselves according to the "fields" surrounding the magnet. In photo section Fig. F3, a strong electro-magnet is sending its "field" directly through the flesh, blood, and bone of my hand and "organizing" the iron filings. The magnetic force is so strong that it overcomes the force of gravity and holds the iron in precise formation along the "lines of force" in the magnetic field. There is reason to think that *similar "fields" surround all matter, animate and inanimate*, organizing it into its own distinctive form and then maintaining that form.

This is precisely the situation with all organs of the human body. If the electro-magnetic field around a given bodily organ—say the left kidney—is distorted then the cells in that kidney do not replace themselves with normal, healthy kidney cells. A field distortion will cause the atoms and molecules from ingested water, food, and air to be assembled into cells perpetuating the abnormalities of the "sick" cell. As we start to assemble the gigantic jigsaw puzzle of paranormal healing, we will see how this emerging knowledge of the electromagnetic fields of life fits in with the puzzle pieces which have been labeled "magnetic healing", "bioplasmic healing", and "mind and spirit healing".

9. *Placebo Effects and Spontaneous Remission*

Nothing more dramatically exposes the limitations of present medical science than these two terms. Actually they are daily used as terms of concealment. Literally translated, the medical practitioner or scientist is saying, "Well, to be honest about it, I have absolutely no notion of what is going on in this situation."

As Dr. Cioppa stated in Chapter 11, and I discussed in Chapter 16, the frequency of spontaneous remission and the well-documented existence of the placebo effect stand as two of the greatest challenges to the field of medical science. No theory of healing will be of much value unless it enlightens us on the underlying natural laws and the structure and functioning of the human body, and accommodates these two realities.

10. *The Attitude of the Patient*

Finally we will list one other factor that stands out from our years of observation of healers and their patients. Healing will seldom start, and it will not be permanent, unless there is a *desire* on the part of the patient to return to health. The patient cannot be made well unless he really wants to be well more than he wants to be ill, and once healed he will not stay well unless he *wants* to stay well. Often, of course, the patient is unaware of the duality of his wanting to be well/ill, unless he has had psychological counseling.

The importance of this discovery should be obvious. It brings a new dimension to what present allopathic medicine considers the sine qua non of illness—bacteria and virus. When bacteria are involved, the patient's attitude will help to determine if such unwelcome guests are allowed to interfere with health or are deactivated and expelled.

The unquestioned fact that the patient's attitude—that is, his thoughts and emotional patterns can often be more efficacious than medical prescriptions—is still one more item that must be accommodated in any workable theory of the healing process.

Less Solid Ground

Up to this point, our statements have had some basis in fact, and such untested or unproven statements as we may have made do not do too much violence to what we *think* we know of our physical world. But now we must move into areas which are in some cases unproven at this time, and in addition have been disdained by medical and material science. But let us take heart! It was observed by Prof. H. H. Price of Oxford University, "We should not be afraid of talking nonsense. Future generations will be puzzled not by the bizarreness or daring of our theories but by their timid and conservative nature."

Since organized science in its present form has had such a short time to unravel the mysteries of man, his minds, his sickness, and his health, let us turn to fields where these matters have been of concern for thousands of years, namely theology, mysticism, and the occult. Here we use the word occult meaning "deliberately kept hidden, secret."

One scientist who has had the courage to turn to this direction is Prof. William Tiller of Stanford University, author of the previous chapter. From teachings scattered through these fields over the last several thousand years by peoples living in all parts of this globe, Tiller has constructed Fig. 1. Prof. Tiller's rationale, explained in detail in my earlier book, *From Enigma to Science*[19] is as follows:

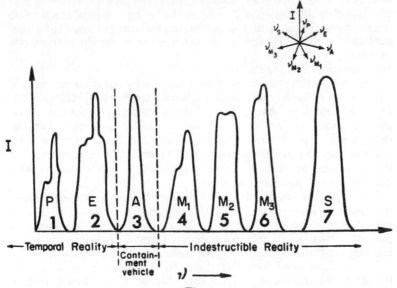

Fig. 1

Man exists on seven levels, with energy systems and substance involved in each. Going from the coarsest to the finest are (P) the physical level that we feel we know something about: (E) the etheric level—the Russians have called this the bioplasmic body; (A) the astral level; (M1), (M2), (M3), three levels of mind—instinctive, intellectual, and spiritual mind; (S) another distinct level which is spirit. These seven substances *interpenetrate* each other and may interact with each other. They may be brought into interaction with each other through the agency of mind. Mind—or what we refer to as thoughts and emotions, or consciousness—can actually bring about changes in the organization of structure in these various levels of substance. Prof. Tiller explains:

> Through mind forces, one can create a pattern, and that pattern then acts as a force field which applies to the next level of substance. In turn, that force field is a force for organizing the atoms and molecules into configurations at that level of substance. That pattern of substance at the etheric level, then, is in a particular state of organization and it has its own radiation field—its own force field if you like—and that force field then, is a field for the organization of matter at the next level of substance—the physical level of substance. These etheric forces, then bring about the coalescence and organization of matter at the physical level of substance.

The above paragraph provides one of the major keys to understanding paranormal healing. However, some non-technical readers may have difficulty interpreting Prof. Tiller's diagram (Fig. 1) and hence will not grasp the full significance of his crucial insight into what goes on between the healer and the one being healed. It is at the heart of the mysteries as to how the healing process works and what is at the basis of the great majority of mankind's aches, pains, illness, and premature death. So let us use an analogy. When standing between two mirrors to check the fit of a new garment at the store, one notices what seems to be a series of mirrors receding into the distance, each with a successively smaller image of one's self. In Fig. 2 we have given these mirror image bodies, the same names as used in the Tiller diagram.

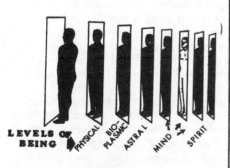

Fig. 2

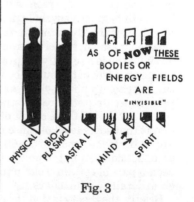

Fig. 3

As of now, our scientific instrumentation is such that we can detect and measure energy relating directly to *only the physical and the bioplasmic bodies.* The other so-called bodies or energy fields (Fig. 4) are "invisible", that is, we do not have instruments which will measure them. Actually this is not the serious barrier which it might appear to be. Modern physics grew up on many concepts which even today are not confirmed by anything more solid than informed speculation.

But this concept of multiple bodies gives us a method of visualizing

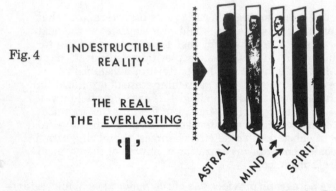

Fig. 4   INDESTRUCTIBLE
              REALITY

              THE **REAL**
              THE **EVERLASTING**

how parts of the individual person *might survive death.* (Fig. 4) If the minds and spirit or soul of the individual person are *non-physical,* it is not such a strain on the imagination to conceive of this portion surviving the death of the physical body. Recalling our brain-computer analogy, the computer may become damaged or even totally destroyed, but the intelligence which acted as the programmer for that and other computers is still very much alive.

In Fig. 5 we have separated the two sets of bodies to help us further visualize the above situation. This begins to suggest the mechanism by which a good clairvoyant sees what, since Biblical times, has been called "the silver cord" (c). Literature is full of accounts of how a good clairvoyant observes the gradual loosening and then the separating of the silver cord as a person is dying. This multiple body analogy also begins to help parapsychologists visualize how it is that while a person's physical body is totally relaxed and lying peacefully in bed, his consciousness can travel far from the body and describe scenes en route (provided he is a sensitive). In other words, this helps us to understand the mechanism of the out-of-body experience, or OOBE, to use present parapsychology phraseology, or what has been known for thousands of years in occult literature as astral travel.

Still another of these occult or hidden concepts now receiving attention is that some level of consciousness or intelligence extends all the way to the level of most of the 60 trillion cells in our blood, tissue, bones, organs, and even in the enamel of our teeth. This concept, which has been a part of certain Yoga philosophies for centuries is presented in great detail by Ramacharka.[20]

Briefly, the theory is that the physical body is built of some 60 trillion individual "cell lives", each of which has a given degree of development. Each cell is capable of independent action, and there is also a cell community action. Each cell appears to have sufficient instinctive knowledge of that which is vital to enable it to live, to maintain itself in a healthy condition and to reproduce itself. Each cell belongs to a cell group; each group forms part of a larger group; the whole forms a great group, a community, or even an organ of the body.

These cells act as though they have instinctive minds, and are able to communicate as discussed in earlier references to the work of Lakhovsky and current Russian scientists. Furthermore, recent work indicates that certain individual cells contain a holographic genetic replication of the body structure and, given the necessary conditions, can reproduce the entire structure. This has been proven in the case of plant cells, as in the Hawaiian Islands there are several acres of sugar cane, all of which were grown from just one single cell taken from a host sugar cane stalk.

In the case of the cells in the human body, the marvelous range of capabilities of the individual cell and the almost instantaneous information transfer up and down throughout the cell hierarchies is at the service of the three levels of mind and spirit of the individual whose physical body these cells constitute. To stay with our computer-programmer analogy, it is as though the subconscious or instinctive mind, the conscious mind, and the superconscious mind each *function as a programmer* whose thoughts and emotions are passed on down through the organization to the individual cell through the computer service performed by the etheric, or bioplasmic, and physical brains.

In all day-to-day matters, the three programmers have enough experience, and work sufficiently in harmony, to permit the individual to be a schoolchild, a wife, a doctor, a ditchdigger, a scientist, a soldier, an airplane pilot or a ballerina. However, history is full of examples where even the three programmers, wise as they are, have found it necessary to resort to a still higher authority, variously called God, Heavenly Father, the Great Spirit, Cosmic Mind, Universal Consciousness, etc., indicated by the connection (a) in Fig. 5. As a person passes through life and gains in wisdom and understanding, he finds that it is most rewarding to make a conscious contact daily with this higher authority (a) in Fig. 5.

Fig. 5

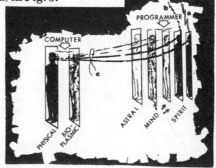

The communications network in the human body (awake or asleep) is ceaselessly busy carrying information in the way of thoughts and emotions. Certain thoughts and emotions are handled with no stress or strain. Other thoughts and emotions disrupt the organization even to the point of malfunction and "blown fuses". Conflicting commands, family discord, anger, fear, jealousy, confusion, hate, economic insecurity, avarice, etc., have the power to affect the life of a cell and a cell group just as surely as a bolt of lightning will blow out and make inoperative every appliance connected to the electric line which lightning strikes.

Relating all of this to the matter of health and healing, such stress or emotional disruption to the normal life of the cell perhaps triggers subtle changes in enzyme chemistry which impair the ability of the cell to fight off the bacteria or virus that are usually present. The disruption may be so extensive as to cause the cell to go berserk—to become cancerous to the point it attacks all normal cells within its reach. This portion of our evolving "theory" nicely accommodates the work reported in chapters 4 and 15 on the efforts in England and the U.S.A. to teach cancer patients to accelerate their healing.

Still another occult concept which has been around for a long time and which has been totally disdained by science is that of the chakras. The most useful information on these energy vortices of the body came in 1919 from Leadbeater and Besant,[21] two of the most gifted clairvoyants in recorded history. Present-day studies by Shafica Karagulla, M.D.[10] with clairvoyants in the U.S.A., have produced confirmation of the description of the energy vortices given by Leadbeater, and have clearly shown the relationship of these vortices and their respective glands, to health and to illness. Dr. Karagulla's studies have also described the changes taking place in these centers during the interaction between a healer and his patient. (Fig. 6)

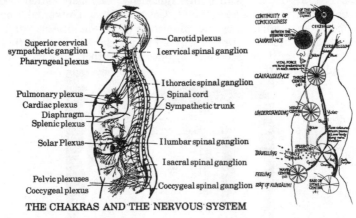

Superior cervical sympathetic ganglion
Pharyngeal plexus
Pulmonary plexus
Cardiac plexus
Diaphragm
Splenic plexus
Solar Plexus
Pelvic plexuses
Coccygeal plexus

Carotid plexus
I cervical spinal ganglion
I thoracic spinal ganglion
Spinal cord
Sympathetic trunk
I lumbar spinal ganglion
I sacral spinal ganglion
Coccygeal spinal ganglion

THE CHAKRAS AND THE NERVOUS SYSTEM

Fig. 6   (a)   (b)

Soon, for the first time, man may be able to measure the activity of these energy centers or transducers by using technology newly developed in Tokyo by Hiroshi Motoyama.

In connection with the chakras, it is necessary to mention acupuncture. Here, once again, is an idea whose scientific verification has come in time to help us unravel the mysteries of paranormal healing. In just the past decade, scientists in several countries have verified the 4,000-year-old teaching of the Chinese that the skin and body are interpenetrated with an invisible network of energy conductors known

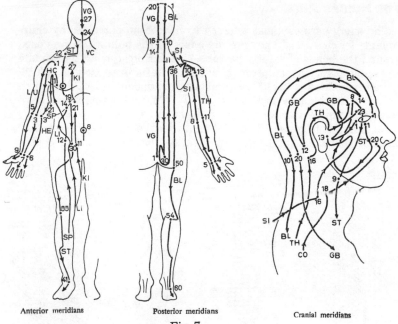

Anterior meridians Posterior meridians Cranial meridians

Fig. 7

as meridians. (Fig. 7) Dr. Motoyama is the first to create a computer ized electronic sensor which sends a small D.C. pulse through these meridians on a patient's body and then, with a high speed computer, prints out an analysis of the level of function of all the major organs in the body cavity. Motoyama's use of acupuncture meridians to diagnose illness just might clear up a mystery we encountered in our observation of one Filipino healer. We noted he would remove the shoes of a patient and then gently touch the toes. He would remain quietly in this position for a few moments—in what was obviously an altered state of consciousness or awareness—and then pronounce his diagnosis of the patient's ailment. Now we can see that perhaps he was using his own built-in and superb sensory systems to do *in part* what Motoyama has done with sophisticated electronic gear and computer technology.

Further indication of both the validity and the utility of the Motoyama chakra and acupuncture apparatus is said to be in its ability to detect whether or not a person has psychic abilities and to give quantitative and qualitative measure of such psychic abilities. Already it has been found that certain chakras relate to specific psychic abilities and that the equipment can indicate which of two psychics has the greater level of development of those specific abilities. These studies of course give further indication that the whole realm of the psychic is not involved with the physical body but with the energy systems making up the bioplasmic body, the minds, and the spirit.

The Human Aura

The energy systems just referred to have been perceived by clairvoyants for centuries. They are the basis for the halo which was used around the heads of saintly persons in paintings during the Middle Ages and in ancient sculpture. Leadbeater in India as early as 1902,[22] Kilner in London in 1911,[23] Bagnell (also in London) in 1937,[24] Regush in an aura anthology in the U.S.A. in 1974, and many others have established in-depth information on the aura.

As of now it is generally agreed that there seem to be three rather distinct components of the human aura, as diagrammed in Fig. 8. One

Fig. 8

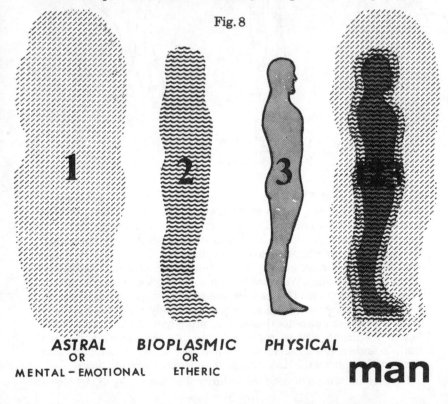

ASTRAL
OR
MENTAL – EMOTIONAL

BIOPLASMIC
OR
ETHERIC

PHYSICAL

man

component, #3, appears to be the overall energy field complex related to the physical body. It is said to extend some portion of an inch beyond the skin surface of the body. A second energy field, #2, interpenetrates the physical aura, and is reported to extend as much as several inches beyond the confines of the physical body. It is usually described as having striations, rays, or bands; and a highly skilled clairvoyant can often detect differences in the length and the slant of the striations which correlate with illness or disease in specific sections of the body. Finally there is what can best be described as a "zone of energy", #1, which interpenetrates #2 and #3, and may extent one or more feet beyond them.

These comments on the human aura are intentionally brief because the reality of the aura is too well-documented by too many people in too many parts of the world for science to continue to dismiss the aura as a figment of the imagination. We introduce the subject in this fashion however because those readers already familiar with these three components of the aura may be confused by the Tiller-Meek references in these pages to the *seven* levels of man's energy fields. To resolve this seeming conflict, let us now proceed to fit the pieces of the puzzle together.

Overall Concept Of Mind, Body, And Spirit

At this point, we have now verified with the aid of modern science and several thousand years of occult and mystical teachings a considerable number of the individual pieces of this gigantic jigsaw puzzle which must be fitted together if we are even to arrive at a "picture" or general statement of a theoretical framework for the healing process.

To simplify our task, let us use the Tiller-Meek multiple mirror technique (of course with due credit to Blavatsky, Bailey, and many others). Let us assemble enough pieces to result in the picture we present in Figures AA and BB.

The following points may aid in identifying some of the main concepts in Figures AA and BB.

1. Man's physical and bioplasmic bodies together constitute a superb electro-biochemical mechanism.

2. All operative functions within the envelope of skin, as well as the activities of the overall mechanism are computer-controlled by the brain in the physical body and its bioplasmic counterpart.

3. The computer-like brain is programmed by at least three levels of mind and spirit or soul.

4. The levels of mind and spirit (or soul), which appear to be non-physical in nature, are "contained" in an "astral body" (for want of a better term).

5. These levels of mind and spirit (or soul) can and do leave the physical body during deep sleep. Moreover, this activity is the basis of OOBE (out-of-body-experience) or

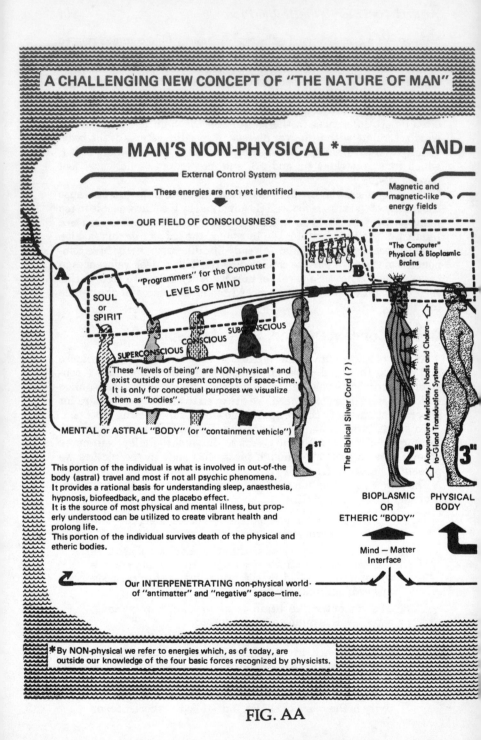

FIG. AA

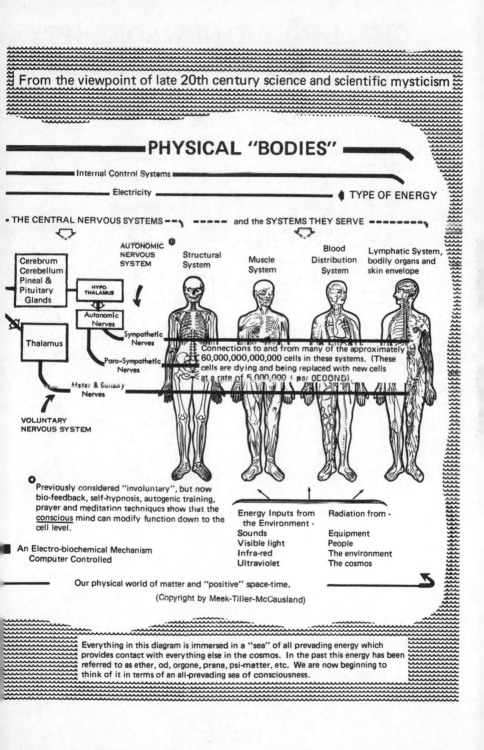

From the viewpoint of late 20th century science and scientific mysticism

PHYSICAL "BODIES"

Internal Control Systems

Electricity ◀ TYPE OF ENERGY

▪ THE CENTRAL NERVOUS SYSTEMS ⟶ ⟵ and the SYSTEMS THEY SERVE ⟶

| | AUTONOMIC NERVOUS SYSTEM | Structural System | Muscle System | Blood Distribution System | Lymphatic System, bodily organs and skin envelope |

Cerebrum
Cerebellum
Pineal &
Pituitary
Glands

HYPO-THALAMUS

Autonomic Nerves

Sympathetic Nerves

Thalamus

Para-Sympathetic Nerves

Connections to and from many of the approximately 60,000,000,000,000 cells in these systems. (These cells are dying and being replaced with new cells at a rate of 5,000,000 + per SECOND).

Motor & Sensory Nerves

VOLUNTARY NERVOUS SYSTEM

● Previously considered "involuntary", but now bio-feedback, self-hypnosis, autogenic training, prayer and meditation techniques show that the <u>conscious</u> mind can modify function down to the cell level.

Energy Inputs from the Environment -
Sounds
Visible light
Infra-red
Ultraviolet

Radiation from -

Equipment
People
The environment
The cosmos

▪ An Electro-biochemical Mechanism Computer Controlled

Our physical world of matter and "positive" space-time.

(Copyright by Meek-Tiller-McCausland)

Everything in this diagram is immersed in a "sea" of all prevading energy which provides contact with everything else in the cosmos. In the past this energy has been referred to as ether, od, orgone, prana, psi-matter, etc. We are now beginning to think of it in terms of an all-prevading sea of consciousness.

CHALLENGING NEW CONCEPT OF "THE NATURE OF MAN"

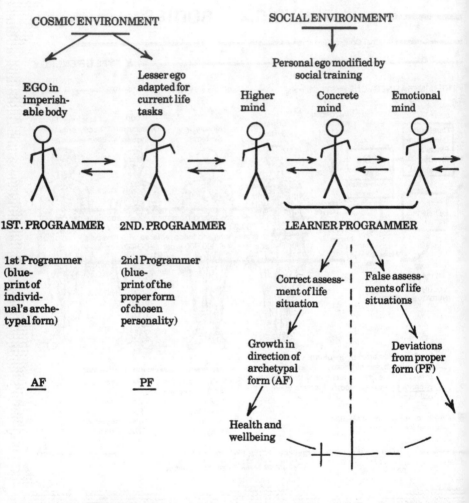

COSMIC ENVIRONMENT

SOCIAL ENVIRONMENT

Personal ego modified by social training

EGO in imperishable body

Lesser ego adapted for current life tasks

Higher mind

Concrete mind

Emotional mind

1ST. PROGRAMMER

2ND. PROGRAMMER

LEARNER PROGRAMMER

1st Programmer (blueprint of individual's archetypal form)

2nd Programmer (blueprint of the proper form of chosen personality)

Correct assessment of life situation

False assessments of life situations

Growth in direction of archetypal form (AF)

Deviations from proper form (PF)

AF

PF

Health and wellbeing

All programs constantly adjusted on basis of feedback learning.

FIG. BB

From the viewpoint of the psychiatrist and parapsychologist

PHYSICAL ENVIRONMENT

↓

Vital field and Body

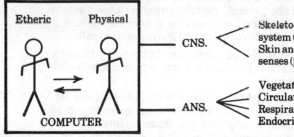

Etheric	Physical			
		— CNS.	Skeleto-muscular system (mobility) Skin and special senses (perception).	} Adjusts to outer environment.
COMPUTER		— ANS.	Vegetative system Circulatory system Respiratory system Endocrine system	} Regulates inner environment.

CNS-CENTRAL NERVOUS SYSTEM

Cerebrum
Telencephalon = cortex = new brain (self-awareness and control)
Diencephalon = older brain, major relay system, thalamus, pineal gland, hypothalamus and pituitary gland.

Cerebellum
Balance and coordination of cortico-spinal motor nerves; orientation via coordination of visual cues and cues from semi-circular canals in ears.

Illness and suffering.
Sin.
Annihilation

Brain Stem
Pons and medulla oblongata. Major lower relay station. Arousal centers.

Spinal Cord
Reflex nerve arcs and liaison with ANS.

ANS-AUTONOMIC NERVOUS SYSTEM
Spinal links, under the overall control of the diencephalon (see above)

FIG. BB

what has over the centuries been referred to as astral travel.

6. There is evidence that these non-physical levels of mind and spirit survive dissolution of the physical and etheric bodies at death and continue to function at another level of existence. This accounts, at least in part, for "spirits", "spirit guides", "discarnate entities", and "ghosts". This also would seem to account in part for the mental and behavioral abberration known as possession or obsession. (B in Fig. AA)

7. It is at these non-physical levels of mind and spirit where much of the interaction takes place between the healer and the patient, thereby bringing about actual physical and etheric changes as described in item 2 above—even down to the level of the individual cell.

8. The physical world, so inadequately revealed to us by our five senses, is just another segment of a single universal continuum.

9. All aspects of individual man are therefore totally immersed in an all-pervading substance or energy field which extends throughout the cosmos, totally interpenetrating what we call our three-dimensional universe.

In presenting the concepts embodied in Fig. AA we realize that medical and material scientists may be somewhat uncomfortable with pseudo-science aspects necessitated by inclusion of the centuries-old, but not yet fully scientifically documented, precepts of mysticism and the occult. But we are also aware that psychiatrists, psychologists, and parapsychologists will be even more uncomfortable. They seem to have a distaste for terms such as antimatter, negative-space-time, non-physical energies, chakras, energy fields, spirit, radiations, and electro-biochemical mechanisms. To make the basic concepts a bit more "comfortable" for these readers I present in Fig. BB a chart created by fellow researcher Mary Scott[25]. She provided this short commentary:

This diagram is an attempt to schematize personality theories common to various occult schools in terms of modern biology and the computer analogy. I have developed it in my ongoing research into man's energy fields and comparative occult theories.

From the standpoint of orthodox science only those functions which I call the "computer" and the "learner programmer" have verifiable existence, and only such parts are susceptible to experimentation and mathematical description. It is important to recognize that scientific "reality" is methodologically limited to physical reality. Paranormal states of consciousness, as well as the normal psychic activities of thinking, dreaming, remembering, etc. enjoy a sort of second order of reality as by-products of physiological processes which can be investigated experimentally.

What I call first and second programmer do not exist for science today but refer to entities postulated in all of the "theosophies" which I have so far researched. Theosophists of all schools set them in a context of reincarnation, distinguishing between an ego associated with a particular life-time and an EGO which is the core of individuality over many life-times. Both ego and EGO are seen as correlates of the human condition and are not ascribed to animals. They involve the presence of self-awareness and develop in complexity as growing intelligence increases one's capacity to adapt to and then manage oneself and one's environment.

The expression, "he has too much ego in his cosmos," indicates one way in which the ego can be distorted by inflation or hypersensitivity and so deviate from what I call PF or "proper form". In its proper form the ego is the incarnated self, suitably programmed for the tasks of daily living. It also gives each person a reference point by means of which he can discriminate between subject and object, himself and his environment. . . .

It is not necessary to accept any reincarnation theory to postulate an EGO. Any religious system which assumes immortality and an after-life would need to presuppose some such entity and give it similar priority as a programmer over the ego. It would then be necessary, however, to distinguish more clearly between soul and spirit than most religious people tend to do.

There is a sense in which each "body" shown here is both computer *and* programmer, computer in terms of the one above and programmer of the one below. Those which I have grouped together, particularly the boxed physical and etheric bodies, are so functionally interdependent that when distortions creep in at any level they tend to aberrate together.

From the standpoint of an individual's physical and mental health the "Learner Programmer" in Fig. BB is of crucial importance. Health, wholeness, and well-being stem from programming what Mary Scott calls "a correct assessment of life situations", or plus deviations from the vertical line which I have inserted below the heading "Learner Programmer".

"False assessments of life situations" result in negative deviations. In fact it has been suggested that the greater the negative deviation by the programmer, the *more serious* the physical and/or mental impairment. From just a minor deviation—say a head cold, backache or nervous headache—the false assessments of the life situation can program ever more serious dysfunction up to the point of heart stoppage, cancer, suicide, or insanity.

Actually these two very different diagrams complement each other nicely. It is somewhat analogous to using the wave and corpuscular theories to describe the behavior of light. As of now, however, Fig. AA gives insight into a wider spectrum of the phenomena observed in our research on healing.

From The General To The Specific—Healing Terminology

Having set forth these general concepts that certainly are not found in standard textbooks now on the library shelves of our medical schools, we shall start to formulate the "specifics" of a theory of paranormal healing. The first thing we encounter is a most confusing situation arising from the many names used to describe this healing relationship.

Over the centuries, words such as these have been in common use: Suggestion, Laying-on-of-hands, Psi, Metaphysical, Spiritual, Mesmeric, Magnetic, Spirit, Paranormal, Mental, Psychic, Type I and Type II, Pranic, Etheric, Divine, Bioplasmic, and Psychic Surgery. Little wonder that confusion abounds as to just what is actually taking place.

A terminology consistent with our level of understanding at the time this chapter is written is shown in Fig. 9. There are three classifications, which we tentatively propose to call Magnetic, Bioplasmic, and Mind-Spirit. (We certainly have no objection if it is decided to refer to these as types A, B, and C.). The reasons for this terminology will soon become apparent, as will be the classification of all of the previously mentioned names for healing.

Fig. 9

A TENTATIVE CLASSIFICATION OF HEALING TERMINOLOGY		
TYPE "A"	TYPE "B"	TYPE "C"
MAGNETIC	BIOPLASMIC	MIND & SPIRIT
———————————— LAYING-ON-OF-HANDS ————————————		
	PRANIC	SPIRIT
	ETHERIC	SPIRITUAL
	——— TYPE II ———	TYPE I
		SUGGESTION
————————— PSYCHIC "SURGERY" —————————		
————————— PSYCHIC —————————		
		METAPHYSICAL

Now let us begin to think of the relationship between the *healer* and *patient* in terms of Prof. Tiller's diagram (Fig. 6) and then with Figures 2, 3, 4, 5 and AA, which in effect give you a "peek into the mirror" as a means of understanding the concept of the seven levels of man's being. Of course we know that there are not, in fact, six bodies separate and distinct from the physical body. Rather all of these "bodies" or "energy fields" INTERPENETRATE EACH OTHER: and therefore occupy substantially (but not quite) the same space as the physical body.

Therefore for the purpose of our present discussions we will visualize the various levels of man's being *all in one body,* with the seven rainbow colors (representing the seven bodies) merely shown as vertical bars confined within the outline of the body. (From red for the physical body—the lowest vibrational frequency, up to violet—representing the spiritual aspect. Fig. 10)

To facilitate discussion of the energy channels involved, consider Fig. 10. Here we show the healer and patient—each with his seven levels of being—meeting in what we have previously called a "healing environment." Usually the healer and his patient are in immediate proximity of each other. But due to the fact that at least some of the energies involved seem to be relatively unaffected by distance (*See* Chapter 13)—in total contrast to most of the energies now known to science—the so-called healing environment, or attunement concept applies to *absent* healing as well as to the face-to-face situation pictured in Fig. 10.

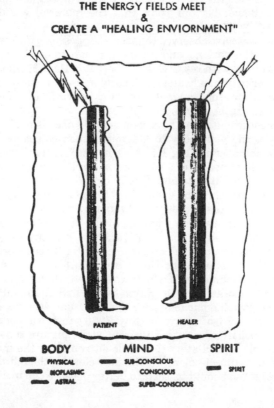

THE ENERGY FIELDS MEET
&
CREATE A "HEALING ENVIORNMENT"

PATIENT   HEALER

Fig. 10

BODY	MIND	SPIRIT
PHYSICAL	SUB-CONSCIOUS	
BIOPLASMIC	CONSCIOUS	SPIRIT
ASTRAL	SUPER-CONSCIOUS	

Type "A", Magnetic Healing

The first and simplest type of healing involves a flow of vital energy to the patient through the minds and body of the healer. You, the reader, first experienced such an energy flow when as a child you had a bad fall and your mother lovingly picked you up, put her hands on the injured area, and consoled you. This flow involves energy that seems to be surprisingly similar to the lines of force which come from a permanent magnet. In the Western world this type of healing is usually called "Magnetic" healing. This term originated in 1767 with the activities of Anton Mesmer, who first used magnetized bars of iron in his healing activities in Vienna and Paris. Later he learned that he seemed to get similar results when he made passes with his own hands. While he was judged by his peers to be a fraud, the term "magnetic healing" remained and is still widely used in Brazil, England, and the Philippines—perhaps with good reason.

It was shown in Fig. F3 how the magnetic lines of force pass through the flesh, blood, and bone and continue to organize the iron filings, overcoming the force of gravity. Energy, in the form of an invisible magnetic "field" passes through the blood, bone, and tissue just as easily as light energy passes through a thick plate glass made of soda and sand. (Remember our point that the material world is almost completely a "void"?)

Many healers have observed that the energy seems to flow from their *left* hand to the patient, and return through their *right* hand. This correlates nicely with research by Albert Roy Davis[26] who has shown that the energy from a healer's left hand appears to be similar to that from the north pole of a magnet—and that both tend to reduce swelling and have a strengthening effect. (Fig. 11)

Further confirmation of the responsiveness of cells in plants, domestic animals, and your body to magnetic energies comes from many sources. In photo section Fig. F4 we see in this "Kirlian Type" photo the magnetized steel needle of a compass in a research laboratory of Dr. Dennis Milner of Birmingham, England.[27] The lower tip of the needle seems to be attracting and displacing the energy field of a freshly cut plant leaf. The opposite pole would have a repelling effect.

Look closely at the area adjacent to the pointed ends of the magnetized compass needle in this photo, and note that there is a difference in the patterns around each end of the needle. This difference in the magnetic fields between the North and South Poles was even more perceptible in a photograph which was taken when I was working in the research laboratory of Dr. Ralph Sierra in San Juan, Puerto Rico. In this photograph a bar magnet of 3/4 inch diameter, six inches long and with a strength of approximately 1,200 gauss, was suspended on a piece of transparent tape just in front of the picture tube on a color television set. Immediately the fields surrounding the magnet were displayed in brilliant colors which show clearly (though the original color photograph should be seen to better observe the intricacy, sym-

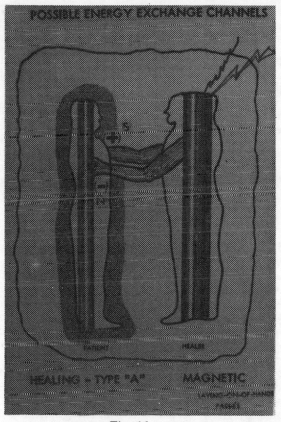

Fig. 11

metry, and complexity of the different lines of force.)

In Chapter 13 we reported that Miller and Reinhart have shown that the energy from a magnet will change the surface tension of water, affect the hydrogen bond of water, and change the color and shape of copper salt crystals suspended in water in precisely the same way as the energy from a healer's hand. (While some further refinement of these techniques may be required, they suggest simple and inexpensive tests for evaluating the healing ability of a person training to become a healer.)

Do you recall our earlier references to the brain being 80% water and the nine gallon jugs it would take to contain the water in a girl's body? With our new knowledge of how the surface tension and molecular structure of water is modified by the energies emanating from a magnet and/or the hands of a healer, we get our first real insight into how magnetic energy emanating from a healer can have a *physical* effect on the cells making up the wet, plastic mass of a patient's body.

Research by George Starr White, M.D.[28] showed that cows gave more milk and hens produced larger eggs when their bodies were given a certain alignment with respect to the earth's magnetic lines of force.

Yet another confirmation of the part magnetism plays in the most subtle workings of the body and its minds comes from an experience of the English medium Bertha Harris.[29] She learned that her clairvoyance is greatly enhanced if she sits with her back to the North Pole of the earth when in the northern hemisphere and to the South Pole when she is in the southern hemisphere.

The role magnetic fields play in human physiology is reported in the work of A. I. Likhachev of the Ukraine Institute of Cybernetics. He reported[30] on studies that indicate the magnetic field is a controlling factor for the central nervous system and that magnetic fields, steady or slowly varying, can affect the flow of blood and tissue.

In Fig. AA we noted that electricity is the principal form of energy used in driving the biochemical mechanism we call the physical body. With the evidence presented here, and much more which is rapidly being assembled in the laboratories the editor has visited in his worldwide travels, there can no longer be any doubt that another form of energy—which for now we call magnetism—is probably *one* of the energies which powers the etheric body. There is still much to be learned about magnetism as indeed there also is about other energies. Even the electricity which powers our homes and industrial civilization is still a mystery. When Albert Einstein was asked to explain electricity, he fell back on what he considered the best definition then available, "Electricity is the way nature behaves." At least we have progressed to a point where we can now say, "Man has an etheric or bioplasmic body and it seems to use an energy which behaves like magnetism."

This chapter is not the place to evaluate the strengths or shortcomings of Type A Magnetic Healing. It is used with apparently great success by thousands of healers in Brazil. Some healers in England, very successful ones, say magnetic healing is a figment of the imagination. But now that science has isolated this form of energy exchange in the healing process, it will be possible to plan new and meaningful research.

Today it appears that the much ridiculed Anton Mesmer was perhaps not as much of a charlatan as he was thought to be in 1767 with his magnetized steel bars in tubs of water and then the magnetic passes of his hands. It took just two hundred years for science to build a basis for examining the subject in a realistic way.

Before leaving Type A Healing, it should be observed that very seldom is it carried on in the absence of at least some aspects of Type B and/or Type C. Only in the case of a beginner or a completely inexperienced healer is the healer-patient exchange limited to Type A.

Type "B", Bioplasmic Healing

Next we briefly consider Type B. Fig. 12. For the present we will call this Bioplasmic healing. The term bioplasmic was first suggested by Russian scientists and we prefer it to etheric, psychic, and psi as it is a bit more *energetically* oriented. It acknowledges the fourth state of matter which physicists have now labeled "plasma" (the others being solid, liquid, and gas). The bioplasmic body apparently does not involve energy in the form of electricity as does the physical body. It begins to seem as though such bioplasmic energy it may be getting through the chakras and acupuncture meridians is *in part* magnetic in nature, possibly what Worrall called "paraelectricity". It will be some years before the work of Motoyama, Chapter 14, and other researchers in acupuncture can yield a clearer understanding of the energies involved.

POSSIBLE ENERGY EXCHANGE CHANNELS

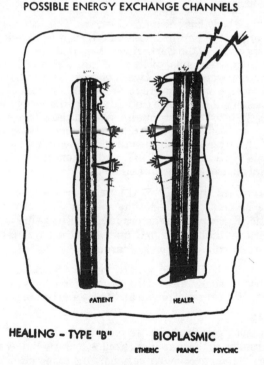

Fig. 12

PATIENT   HEALER

HEALING - TYPE "B"   BIOPLASMIC
ETHERIC   PRANIC   PSYCHIC

Knowing as little as we do about the chakras and their functions, we can merely describe them as invisible "energy vortices", which channel a possibly non-physical energy to and from the major glandular systems in the physical body. (Figures 6A, 6B, AA, 12) In ways we do not presently comprehend, there appear to be energy exchanges between chakra systems of the healer and patient. Until scientific research begins to yield useful data on the acupuncture meridians, the chakras, and mutual interaction of chakras and meridians, and their relationship to the major glands of the body, we can continue to ponder the wealth of information in the writings of Alice Bailey.[31] For example, on this matter of the part played by the acupuncture meridians on chakras, the Tibetan "source", speaking through Mrs. Bailey, said:

> The etheric body is a body composed entirely of lines of forces which cross each other and thus form (in crossing) centers of energy. Where many such lines of force cross each other, you have a larger center of energy, and where great streams of energy meet and cross, as they do in the head and up the spine, you have seven major centers. In addition to these major centers, there are twenty-one lesser centers and forty-nine smaller ones known to the esoterics.

This same "source" discusses the crucial role played by the etheric, or bioplasmic, body:

> The etheric body has one main objective. This is to vitalize and energize the physical body and thus integrate it into the energy body of the Earth and of the solar system. It is a web of energy streams, of lines of forces and of light. It constitutes part of a vast network of energies which underlies all forms whether great or small (microcosmic or macrocosmic). Along these lines of energy the cosmic forces flow, as the blood flows through the veins and arteries. This constant individual human, planetary, and solar circulation of life forces through the etheric bodies of all forms, is the basis of all manifested life, and the expression of the essential non-separateness of all life.

We have reported that only in the past few years many medical doctors have become convinced that roughly 70% of all illness is psychosomatic. The causative factors in most illness are thought and emotional patterns that trigger malfunction of the physical body. Alice Bailey's "source" spoke of this forty years ago when he said:

> In these two bodies, the etheric and astral bodies, (the astral body is sometimes called the emotional body), ninety percent of the causes of physical disease and trouble is to be found.

Thus, with such corroboration as modern medical practice is now supplying for many of the statements made by Mrs. Bailey's "source", we have every reason to consider seriously his pronouncements about the reality of the etheric (or bioplasmic) and astral bodies; the energy systems through which they operate; and the key role of thought and emotion in illness, health, and healing.

With the above quotations from Mrs. Bailey's books still in mind, the reader may find it useful to pause for a moment and turn back to Fig. AA and look again at these relationships in diagrammatic form.

Finally, just to make the researcher's task a bit more complicated, it must be observed that Type B healing (Bioplasmic) probably does not occur completely independent of Type A and Type C! It is only for the purpose of simplifying the theoretical aspects of these studies that it is set forth now as a separate classification.

Type "C", Mind And Spirit Healing

Finally, we consider what I have classified as Type C healing—Mind and Spirit. While of necessity this type of healing also includes Types A and B, the comments which follow will relate only to the *added* dimensions introduced by "mind" and "spirit". (Fig. 13)

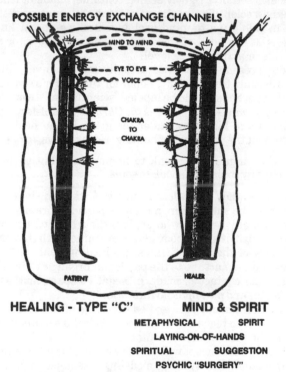

POSSIBLE ENERGY EXCHANGE CHANNELS

MIND TO MIND

EYE TO EYE

VOICE

CHAKRA TO CHAKRA

PATIENT   HEALER

Fig. 13

HEALING - TYPE "C"   MIND & SPIRIT

METAPHYSICAL   SPIRIT

LAYING-ON-OF-HANDS

SPIRITUAL   SUGGESTION

PSYCHIC "SURGERY"

In this type of healing our energy-flow paths are so numerous that even a good communications specialist could be excused for becoming a bit bewildered. He would have to call for the assistance of psychologists, psychiatrists, clairvoyants, clairaudients, healers, parapsychologists, hypno-therapists, neurologists, biochemists, microbiologists, plasma physicists, and communication engineers. In addition to all of these he would have to ask for help from persons with a deep grounding in the religious, occult, metaphysical, and mystic teachings accumulated over the past several thousand years of mankind's mental and spiritual advancement. All we can hope to do in this initial effort to build a hypothesis of paranormal healing is to point out

some of the additional energy-flow channels involved in Type C healing
and leave it to researchers in the many fields mentioned above to fill in
the details over the decades ahead.

1. *Mind-to-Mind and Spirit-to-Spirit Channels*

First let us consider "mind-to-mind" transfer. Research in the past
decade by Russian scientists[32, 33] has clearly documented existence of
the phenomena of mental telepathy—the ability of one person to influence the thoughts and physiological reactions of another person,
even if the persons are hundreds of miles apart and even if the "receiver" is encased in a tightly sealed container made of lead. At this
point we know scientifically almost nothing of the nature of the energy
involved in this mind-to-mind exchange and we do not know if the
exchange is at the level of the subconscious, conscious, or superconscious minds, or at the chakra level.

Since our present-day science actually knows so very little about
"mind" as distinct from "brain", I offer for the reader's consideration a
thought that perhaps should be labeled "scientific mysticism". Chapter
23 of *The Aquarian Gospel of Jesus the Christ*[34] tells of Jesus' purported
visit to India and his study under the great Hindu healer, Udraka.
Speaking about the pathways of healing, Udraka says, in part:

> ... The tongue may speak to human ears, but souls are
> reached by souls that speak to souls. ...

Our years of study of healers in many parts of the world indicates
that this may be more than merely a poetic expression. We have
encountered many healers who explain their healing by saying that
their soul or spirit or astral body gets into contact with the soul or spirit
or astral body of the person who seeks healing. Once this contact is
made they can then attune to the particular organ or tissue that needs
assistance. The contact is made in negative space-time so distance
between healer and patient is no limitation.

Since science has not yet verified existence of the soul or spirit we
cannot expect it to place any credence in Udraka's statement that the
healer and the patient are in contact at the level of soul or spirit. Be
that as it may, this concept will be more believable *when* and *if* science
begins to find some reality in the modeling assembled in the left portion
of Fig. AA. Using the concepts presented there we have developed Fig.
14, which shows MENTAL or ASTRAL BODY (or "containment vehicle") of the healer tuning in to the electro-biochemical computer of
the patient's etheric and physical brain. It then beneficially supplies
healing energies to that portion of the patient's body needing re-
inforcement.

2. *The Visual Channel*

Let us call attention to the energy exchange involved in the visual or
eye-to-eye pathway. Medical thermographic images of the face during
meditation show greatly increased heat (10-um infra-red) being ra-

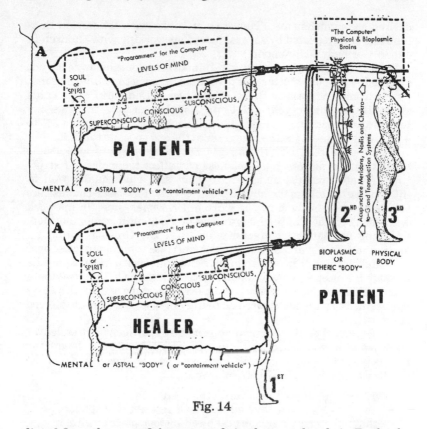

Fig. 14

diated from the eyes. Other research in the past decade in England, U.S.S.R. and the U.S.A. has given some indication that energy flow by this channel is capable of moving physical objects with a mass of several grams and modifying the crystalline structure to a point of distorting objects made of metal.

In the latter connection consider Prof. John Taylor's[35] experiments with a ten-year-old boy who had developed "metal bending abilities" after watching the Israeli psychic Uri Geller on British TV. Taylor, working in his laboratory in King's College, inserted a piece of aluminum bar eight inches long into a clear plastic tube, sealed both ends, handed it to the boy and instructed him to use his mind to bend the encased aluminum rod. (*See* photo section figures G1, G2, and G3.) Three minutes later, *without having been touched,* the bar was in the condition shown in photo section Fig. G1. The same ten-year-old boy produced the multiple bends in an aluminum rod shown in photo section Fig. G2, again *without any physical contact.* A fifteen-year-old boy bent stainless steel spoons without contact, photo section Fig. G3. At least twenty other English children developed the ability to modify the molecular structure of metals solely by focusing their minds on the desired accomplishments. (The work of Taylor with children in England has been repeated by several scientists working with children in Japan, Germany, and Austria.)

Further evidence of the ability of human consciousness to reach out and modify physical matter was presented to the Second International Psychotronic Congress by Dr. R. D. Mattuck of Denmark.[36] One of his students, seventeen-year-old Lena Ilsted, was able to raise the temperature reading of a long glass clinical thermometer from 35° to 40° C. while she held the thermometer at the end opposite the bulb.

Perhaps the reader is thinking, "Yes, there appears to be some indication that *focused consciousness* can affect the molecular structure of water, metals, and mercury, but can it do equally well in influencing the cells of the physical body?" One of the clear-cut answers to this question is given by the work of Dr. Elmer Green in his work with Jack Schwartz in the laboratories of the Menninger Foundation. Speaking at Stanford University in 1972, Dr. Green reported investigation of Schwartz's ability to demonstrate voluntary control over pain and bleeding.[37] In the first test Schwartz stuck a knitting needle through his bicep as shown in photo section Fig. H. On this trial there was considerable bleeding when the needle was removed, but Schwartz maintained that he experienced no pain even though the needle pierced the muscle.

Dr. Green asked Schwartz to repeat the experiment but endeavor this time to prevent bleeding. Schwartz complied and even though the needle passed through a small vein there was no bleeding when the needle was removed. Dr. Green reports:

> The wounds closed up around the needle, as Jack pulled it out, leaving two small red spots. Of interest was the fact that no detectable subdermal bleeding took place on either trial. No discoloration was present the next day, and in 24 hours one of the holes had disappeared. In 72 hours none of the spots were visible. His skin was as smooth and unblemished as at the beginning. Jack said he had performed this demonstration hundreds of times, but his skin was smooth and unmarked.

Not only did Schwartz demonstrate conscious control of bleeding and pain, but he demonstrated *control of infection*. Although the needle had fallen to the floor, Schwartz was unconcerned. He said, "Infection is not possible because my mind will not allow it."

Space does not permit additional examples, but there is no longer doubt that consciousness can control the physical body at the level of the cell groups. (Refer once again to Fig. AA to see the pathways by which a "thought" accomplishes this purpose.)

Earlier we said that no single scientific discipline could possibly "explain" what is going on in paranormal healing. The implications of "mind over matter" research, such as that of Dr. Green, Dr. Mattuck, and Prof. Taylor recall the severe limitations of a single discipline such as behavioral or Skinnerian psychology. For almost sixty years observers have been peering intently at pecking pigeons and bar-pushing rats, trying to fit *man* into the same "cage". But how can we accommodate into behavioral psychology of man the ability of a ten-year-old child to accomplish metal bending merely by an act of focused consciousness? How can we explain the ability of a seventy-year-old healer, Olga Worrall, in Baltimore, Maryland, to focus consciousness strongly enough to cause a photographically recordable disturbance in an atomic cloud chamber and to cause 845% increase in the growth rate of plants—both cloud chamber and plants being located in a physics laboratory 600 miles away? How can we "explain" the ability of Frances Farrelly of St. Petersburg, Florida, (through an act of focused consciousness) to determine the red and white blood cell count of a patient 1,000 miles away—and with precisely the same accuracy as the best clinical laboratory using an actual blood sample? (Reported in various public talks and in private correspondence) How can we explain the psychometric ability of medium Bertha Harris, sitting in London, England with only a photograph and sample of the handwriting of Frances Farrelly—at that moment across the Atlantic in the Bahamas—to "read" these tokens and give the most intimate details of Ms. Farrelly's life with an accuracy of 84% ?

Of course we have not singled out behavioral psychology for criticism. Precisely the same questions can be asked of the parapsychologists, medical scientists, biochemists, and every other scientific discipline, or combination of disciplines.

The significance of the foregoing, as it applies to our theorizing on the healing process should be obvious. We learned first that the healer can manipulate energies to the end that he modifies the molecular structure of the water which makes up so much of the physical body. Then in another area of research we saw that energy brought to focus on a piece of metal by the mind or consciousness of a ten-year-old child can function at the level of the molecules in a solid piece of stainless steel, aluminum or copper to physically tear the metal apart. Why should the reader doubt the possibility that the mind of the healer, working at the level of atoms and molecules in the cells of a patient's diseased organ, can bring about a desired change in the structure of that organ?

3. *The Audio Channel*

Having considered mind-to-mind transfer, and the visual (or eye-to-eye) pathway, let us now consider the audio or voice channel. Here we enter into the domain of the psychologists, hypnotherapists, psychiatrists, metaphysicists, and theologians who are involved with the spoken word. I will mention only two examples of the type of energy exchange that can take place at this level using only sound. (Let it be understood that in the two examples the action does *not* result from the direct impingement of the sound vibrations or energy but rather from the psychological impact of the spoken words at the level of mind in the patient. However, if the words were not spoken by the healer, thereby using energy to set up the sound waves in the air that impinge on the diaphragm of the listener's ear, there would not have been the psychological impact at some level of the patient's mind which in turn carried the message electrochemically to the cells of the listener's body.)

Picture in your mind this incident which I observed: Two patients from Switzerland were standing in the lobby of the healing center maintained by Tony Agpaoa in an exquisite setting high in the mountains of northern Luzon in the Philippines. One patient says to another, "Did you see Mr. Jones on the dance floor last night? He was twisting and turning with the music just like a teenager, and yet prior to his arrival here last week the old codger had not been out of his wheelchair for ten years!"

Or picture in your mind an incident in the Bay View Hotel in Manila in which a forty-five-year-old American housewife says in the presence of other patients, "Mr. Cunanan, I want to make you a present of this white blindman's cane. I have had to use it for the past four years since an auto accident caused me to be totally blind, and my American eye specialists could not restore my sight. After the second treatment by Marcello, I could read a newspaper." Then with tears rolling down her face she added, "But best of all, I will be able to look into the faces of my loved ones when I return home." Yes, spoken words such as these (energy exchange at the audio or sound level which may or may not also act as carrier waves for still other types of energy) can of themselves be picked up by the ears of other patients and have a profound and beneficial effect on the very cells of the bodies of all who take these words into the sensory systems of their own body, minds, and spirit. (In this connection, recall that repeatedly in the Biblical accounts of the Nazarene it is reported, " . . . and He spoke the WORD and they were healed." (*See* Bibliography C)

The Role Of Emotions In Healing

At this point in our study of the nature of illness and the healing process it should be obvious that if the patient's mind is fed a daily diet of anger, remorse, revenge, hate, jealousy, suspicion, and envy the very cells of the patient's body are sure to reflect this environment. When the psychiatrist, psychologist, or healer helps the patient replace these emotions with their positive mirror images, the patient is able to cope with life and can enjoy both physical and mental health.

As has been observed in Chapter 12, the healers almost invariably possess the emotional constellation of qualities including empathy, harmony, unselfishness, devotion, tenderness, consecration, kindness, fellow-feeling, love and compassion as previously discussed in connection with self-healing in Chapter 17.

We do not profess to understand at this time all of the precise mechanisms by which these emotions of the healer help the patient to re-energize the weakened or diseased cells of his body but there can no longer be any doubt that love and compassion are the very cornerstones of the edifice of health, healing and wholeness.

One of the most striking demonstrations of how "love" can beneficially assist the reprogramming capability of the human mind and spirit is to be found in the work of C. Norman Shealy, M.D.,[38] a neurosurgeon who established and operates the Pain Rehabilitation Center of La Crosse, Wisconsin. (He is author of the Postscript). The "statistically average" patient at the clinic during the past four years is as follows: An average of four operations, an invalid for more than six years, with a medical expense record of from $50,000 to $75,000, and in some cases taking from ten to fourteen different drugs.

Dr. Shealy has discontinued all neurosurgery and describes his approach to the handling of such patients as follows:

> By the use of autogenic visualization or guided imagery and biofeedback techniques and many exercises, both mental and physical, we undertake in just twelve days to help the patient stop off all drugs and then through his own effort restore the necessary balance and harmony to the body, the autonomic nervous system, and to the emotions.
>
> All healing involves what I call "love energy". So we start with follow-up with the mate, the children, or any others in the home environment, in an effort to replace the life script which triggered the illness in the first place. The fact that in many cases we are not able to extend our reprogramming to the family environment is one of the reasons that our records show that at the end of six months roughly one third of our patients have slipped back to their pre-treatment condition.

Considering the average patient profile and that 80% of the patients leave the clinic at the end of only twelve days significantly improved, we feel that Dr. Shealy has provided dramatic proof of the validity of the portion of our overall theory that relates to the ability of the mind and spirit to produce profound physiological effects in the patient's body.

Dr. Shealy's work is also useful in showing that biofeedback, autogenic training, and self-hypnosis techniques make it possible to reprogram the patient's thoughts and emotions. (Recall Fig. AA and BB) These painless, drug-free, and relatively low-cost techniques produce results not generally achievable with neurosurgery. Moreover this work is proving our point that the underlying mechanism of what is today considered paranormal in the work of the healers can be effectively incorporated into the framework of modern medicine.

The Placebo Effect, Spontaneous Remission And Self-Healing

In Figs. AA and Fig. BB we have for the first time a rational basis for understanding the modus operandi of the placebo effect. We can comprehend why the patient benefits from a sugar pill; from a powerful medicine or pharmaceutical which physiologically does nothing but poison the patient's system and add to the complications; from a pilgrimage half way around the world to the Philippines or to the shrine of

Lourdes; from a few painful pricks by an acupuncture needle in an area which may, in fact, have no connection with the patient's ailment; from the reading of inspirational passages from the Bible or other revered books; or from the release which comes from sharing a stressful thought while kneeling in the confessional box or reclining on the psychiatrist's couch.

Should we cast scorn on one of the healers taught by LeShan when she proudly announced that 50% of her patients benefit—when we know that the love, compassion, and understanding she gave merely triggered the same sequence of mind over matter actions inherent in any of the above-mentioned placebos? Not at all! The benefited patient cares nothing about the process—he is just happy to be well again. But with the new insights we have into the nature of illness, healing, and health it behooves us to do everything in our power to enhance the placebo effect.

The concepts in Figures AA and BB now enable us to understand why and how it is possible for the patient's own God-given capabilities to carry on the self-healing process and produce what the medical profession labels "spontaneous remission". If it is possible in the decades ahead to bring self-healing concepts to the populace, billions of dollars can be saved *annually* in the area of public and private health care.

The research reported in this book shows that, important as self-healing is, there seems to be a practical limit at this point as to how far the average patient can go in throwing off his centuries-old burden of misinformation about the causes of illness and disease. This misinformation severely limits the patient in consciously accepting and fully utilizing the self-healing process. Hence it is important to recognize that the primary role of the healer and the medical practitioner is to supplement the patient's own self-healing capabilities. The mind-to-mind and spirit-to-spirit interchanges between the healer (or medical practitioner) and patient, presented in detail in the preceding pages, greatly stimulate and enhance the self-healing process in those organs of the patient's body which may be debilitated or may be under attack from bacteria or virus.

The work of the thousands of healers who are annually helping millions of patients in all parts of the world provides irrefutable proof of the reality and the utility of psychic, faith, spiritual, and mental healing—call it by any term you prefer.

The "Sticky" Matter Of Discarnate Entities Or Spirits

Finally we come to what may be one of the most important energy pathways involved in the healer-patient relationship. It is certainly the most controversial and one which present-day materialistic Western science has refused to dignify by any serious research and, for that matter, even refuses to acknowledge the theoretical possibility of its existence. I refer to the world of "spirit" as that level of man's being as it is diagrammed in Figures AA and BB.

No study into the nature of man will ever get very far if it rigidly insists that it will not utilize the analytical and reasoning modalities of the scientific method to at least "have a look" at the subject of spirit. After all, medical science, to give just one example, has found that many herbs or plant extracts used over the centuries by witch doctors or medicine men to cure an illness have been found to contain chemical compounds that are a great addition to present-day medical therapy. (Examples: quinine, digitalis, and rauwolfia) By the same token, when *all* peoples in *all* parts of the globe, at *all* times in recorded history have instinctively postulated somewhat similar beliefs in "spirits" and in an individual after-life, might it not be worthwhile for science to at least examine such a possibility?

Can any scientist worthy of the name fail to recognize that in all geographical areas of the world where paranormal healing is today practiced extensively, all of the healers have basically the same belief system as it relates to what they loosely describe as "the spirit world"? How can any medical scientist even begin to explain the fully documented performance of Arigó? How could this relatively uneducated part-time church janitor make instantaneous on-the-spot diagnosis of the ailments of 500 patients and score 95% agreement with the carefully made diagnosis of a team of American medical men? By what means did Arigó acquire the knowledge that enabled him to give prescriptions for a vast array of medicines—some of which were newly developed drugs just placed on the market by the manufacturers in Switzerland and not yet on the shelves in Brazil? How did the American Edgar Cayce over a period of decades diagnose the illness of many thousands of patients, often at great distances, and prescribe medication that proved effective even though he—like Arigó—had no training in medicine or pharmacology? What parapsychologist has made even a small beginning toward a respectable answer to any of these questions?

Did Arigó, in fact, get his knowledge and his skills from the spirit world, via the alleged discarnate spirit known as Dr. Fritz and associates? Do the thousands of other healers working today in Brazil, the Philippines, Britain, and the U.S.A. have similar connections as they claim? All of these situations over the centuries and around the world—looked at objectively—should give sufficient incentive for the more courageous scientists to begin to take a tentative look at the energy exchange channels that are symbolically shown by the zig-zag lines (a) and (b) in Fig. 15.

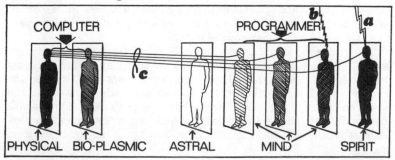

Fig. 15

Actually the steps I am asking scientists to take in exploring these questions would be so much easier to take if it could be found there are some elements of truth in these two diagrams, insofar as (a) and (b) are concerned. *If* the entities who are purportedly speaking in Chapter 2, and *if* the thousands of healers in Brazil, England, and the Philippines are correct, then it does not seem so preposterous that *former* medical doctors, surgeons, and scientists, having passed through a door labeled "death", might be interested in using the delicate sensory systems of mediumistic persons (who tend to make the best healers) to energize and heal the weak or diseased cells in a patient's body. Comments on these matters, purportedly from discarnate medical doctors, will be found in Appendix B.

While references to paranormal healing in the foregoing pages have been confined largely to ailments of the physical body, it is also possible to throw valuable light on many mystifying aspects of mental and emotional illness. Therapy which utilizes the conceptualizations presented in this chapter and practiced for a period of twenty years by medical doctors and psychiatrists in England and Brazil reduces treatment time by 80% or more in the wide spectrum of mental and emotional problems.

The concept embodied in Fig. 15 is helpful in conceptualizing the centuries-old mysteries of "possession" and discarnate entities. Let us assume for the moment that on death, the "silver cord" (c) is cut, thereby disconnecting the "programmer" from the "computer". All parts of the physical and etheric bodies disintegrate, including the brain which served very well as the computer to control these two "bodies". Except for the loss of the connection to the physical and bioplasmic bodies, the individual is perfectly alive and well. His minds and spirit continue to exist in the very same negative-space-time world that has always been their home. (See *left* portion of Fig. AA) Thus the living, vibrant, and pulsing bundle of energy fields continues living and retains all of the thoughts, emotions, and experiences garnered before being disconnected from the more materially oriented bodies.

It has not suddenly become God-like. It still has all of its good and bad traits. It has not departed to some far-off spot waiting for the great day of judgment. It is still "right here" in that vast void which is also the material world. It is still "right here", in another dimension which interpenetrates what we call our physical world—a world which is just as insubstantial and full of empty space as the thick plate glass window which holds the water in the aquarium and yet allows you to peer through it and see the fish and the water.

The Nazarene said, "In my Father's house there are many mansions." This lovely poetic language was the only way the subject could be covered at that time. Today we can even more readily grasp the concept that there are likely to be many levels to which the "mind and spirit entity" may advance after shedding the physical and bioplasmic bodies. If, for example, the individual had frequently been in an alcoholic stupor, he will find himself in the lowest and least desirable level or "mansion", totally confused and still feeling an attraction to former companions who are still frequenting bars. In such a situation, it is a simple matter for this discarnate "bunch of energy fields" to get locked into the magnetic aura of one of the flesh and blood patrons of the local bar or pub. Dr. Carl Wickland[39] gives some of the best documentation on this.

If the bundle of energy fields pictured in Fig. 15 had been a medical doctor with a moderately high level of intelligence, emotionally mature, and dedicated to serving his fellowmen, he will soon find himself at a level or in a "mansion" considerably higher than does the unfortunate alcoholic just referred to. He finds that he can continue to pursue his interests, and continue to progress in his professional development. If his emotional constellation includes a goodly measure of love and compassion, there is nothing to prevent his "looking in" on some person who is still in the physical body and giving aid to that person in his efforts to serve as a healer of the ills of his fellows. Such discarnate entities as Dr. Lang, Dr. Fritz, and the so-called "healing intelligences" in Chapters 2 and 3, and Appendix B, are quite possibly examples of medical persons who have chosen to follow precisely this course. Diagramatically, their connection—as well as the connections of the alcoholic suffering "possession" mentioned above—is shown as B, the small astral body in the upper left portion of Fig. AA.

Of course it would be a great inducement for scientists to start to research in this area if they were able to pick up the phone or the ship to shore equivalent of an "interplane communications device" and communicate directly with such purported doctors and scientists. What are the prospects for such a breakthrough?

A Breakthrough?

Writing in 1972 *(From Enigma to Science)*, I told how Thomas A. Edison and Guglielmo Marconi had unsuccessfully turned their remarkable inventive abilities to the development of devices to permit communication with individuals who have walked through the door labeled Death. During the last ten years reports have been received through reliable deep-trance mediums in several countries that Edison, Marconi, and Tesla continue to work on the problem in whatever place of being they currently enjoy. They are reported to have provided guidance—intuition?—for serious researchers in Austria, Sweden, Germany, England and the U.S.A. Because of the crucial importance of the "discarnate entity problem" to paranormal healing research, as well as to the whole question of the nature of man, we will briefly summarize recent research of great significance.

Following in the footsteps of Edison, Marconi, and Tesla is a new generation of pioneers: Attila von Szaley, Raymond Bayless, William A. Welch,[40] Joseph and Michael Lamoreaux and others in the U.S.A.; Friederich Jurgenson[41] in Sweden; Dr. Konstantin Raudive[42] and

Theodor Rudolf[43] in Germany; Ing. Franz Seidl[44] in Austria; and Richard Sheargold[45] and others in England. These men and others have used various techniques for recording on magnetic tape, words, phrases and complete sentences from what are purported to be the spirits of persons who have died.

By any standard, the content of such transmissions as reported up to now must be judged as having no practical value. The significance of the work lies entirely in the fact that a first step has actually been taken in the direction of interplane communication. Radio communication as we know and use it today did not exist and was almost impossible to imagine when the author, as a boy in 1920 used a small crystal of galena and a wire cat's whisker to pick up his first radio signals. Any of the readers listening today to some of the current efforts of the above-mentioned researchers would have great difficulty imagining that static-free communication might someday be possible.

Only the passage of time will show whether these efforts will eventually confirm the discarnate entity concept just as the Miller-Reinhart research in magnetism (Chapter 13) has validated the 200-year-old work of Anton Mesmer and the work of Motoyama is starting to validate the ancient Chinese teachings on acupuncture meridians and the ancient Indian teachings on the chakras.

Consider what happens when and if interplane communication is established to the satisfaction of science. Mankind would perhaps be forced to recognize:

1. That individual man is a spirit which is temporarily occupying a physical body.

2. That individual mind and spirit (and personality) pass through the door marked Death, and promptly continue existence on another plane of being.

3. That it may well be productive to examine the extent to which mind and spirit (consciousness) are the principal determinants of illness, healing, and health.

Thus when and if interplane communication is scientifically confirmed, the whole field of medicine and health care would be due for nothing less than a revolution.

Implications of interplane communications would show man that he is far more than the reward-seeking rat or pigeon the behavioral psychologist says he is. Social, economic, and political philosophies now based on the concept that man is a mere automaton would, in perhaps only one or two centuries see a greater revolution than anything seen in the history of man to date. (Further implications of the totally unexpected insights generated by a decade of research into the paranormal healing will be the subject of the last three chapters of this book.)

Summing Up

At this point in our theorizing it is certainly obvious that no *one* scientific discipline can solve the many remaining mysteries of paranormal healing. There are challenges to and opportunities for each of the following specialists:

clairvoyant &
  clairaudient psychics
communication engineers
deep trance mediums
healers
medical doctors

microbiologists
nuclear chemists
parapsychologists
physicists (plasma)
physicists (wave
  mechanics)

physiologists
psychiatrists
surgeons
theologians

It would be hard to name any other single area of man's research which has a need for so diverse a group of investigators.

In recent years the efforts to fathom the mysteries of the paranormal have relied increasingly on the word "consciousness". Since this word and its many connotations, conceal more than they enlighten, let us avoid it and fall back on the two words "minds" and "spirit", unacceptable as these words are to both the physicist and the parapsychologist. Thus, using these terms in the framework developed in the foregoing pages, we suggest that the answers to the remaining mysteries of psychic, faith, spirit, spiritist, mental, and self-healing lie at least in part in these two deceptively simple statements:

> All of these seeming miracles of paranormal healing, materialization and apport phenomena, and psychoenergetic activities are normal and completely natural manifestations of the energy exchanges initiated by the mind and spirit of the healer and the patient, and

> Any further increase in understanding and mastery of disease, illness and health, as well as understanding man's place in the cosmos, depends largely on gaining ever deeper insights into the energy exchanges which can be initiated and controlled by the various levels of man's mind and spirit.

On this note we end our first effort to draft a general theory of healing. Until science devises more useful terminology and develops data that indicate otherwise, we suggest that further research in the field of paranormal healing place increasing attention on mind and spirit.

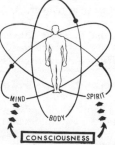

REFERENCES

1. Itzhak Bentov, Private Correspondence, 1974-1975.

2. Andrija Puharich, *Beyond Telepathy* (London: Dartman, Longman and Todd, 1962).

3. Jule Eisenbud, "The Mind-Matter Interface". In *Journal of American Society for Psychical Research,* Vol. 69, #2, April, 1975.

4. C. D. Broad, *The Mind and Its Place in Nature* (London: Kegan Paul, 1925).

5. Robert N. Ashby, "In Search of a Theory to Explain the Psychic Realm". In *Fate,* April, 1975.

6. Lawrence L. LeShan, *Toward A General Theory Of The Paranormal* (New York: Parapsychology Foundation, 1969).

_____, *The Medium, The Mystic and The Physicist* (London: Turnstone, 1974; New York: Viking, 1974).

7. R. H. Thouless, and B. P. Weisner, "The Psi Processes in Normal and 'Paranormal' Psychology". In *Proceedings of Society for Psychical Research,* Vol. 43, Part 174, December, 1947.

8. Lyall Watson, *Supernature* (London: Hodder and Stoughton, 1973).

9. Joan Fitzherbert, "The Nature of Hypnosis and Paranormal Healing". In *Journal of Society for Psychical Research,* Vol. 46, #747, March, 1971.

10. Shafica Karagulla, *Breakthrough to Creativity* (Los Angeles: De Vorss, 1969).

11. John White, ed., *Frontiers of Consciousness* (New York: Avon Books, 1975).

12. Jeffry Mishlove, *Roots of Consciousness* (New York: Random House, 1975).

13. Charles Musés, and A. M. Young, *Consciousness and Reality* (New York: Outerbridge and Lazard, 1972).

14. Georges Lakhovsky, *The Secret of Life* (London: Heinemann, 1939).

15. James B. Beal, "The New Biotechnology". In *Frontiers of Consciousness,* edited by John White. (New York: Avon Books, 1975), Chapter 13.

16. Andrew Glazewski, "The Pattern of Telepathic Communication". Talk at Annual Conference of Radionic Association, March, 1973.

17. Wilder Penfield, "Engrams in the Human Brain: Mechanisms of Memory" Lecture at the Royal Society of Medicine, London, April, 1968.

18. Harold S. Burr, and F. S. C. Northrup, *An Electrodynamic Theory of Life* (New Haven: Yale University Press, 1935).

19. George W. Meek, *From Enigma to Science* (New York: Samuel Weiser, 1973).

20. Yogi Ramacharka, *The Science of Psychic Healing* (Chicago: Yogi Publication Society, 1934).

21. Annie Besant, and C. W. Leadbeater, *Occult Chemistry* (London: Theosophical Publishing House, 1927).

22. C. W. Leadbeater, *The Chakras* (Adyar, India: Theosophical Publishing House, 1927).

_____, *Man, Visible and Invisible* (Adyar, India: Theosophical Publishing House, 1910; Wheaton: TPH, 1976).

23. Walter J. Kilner, *The Human Aura* (New Hyde Park, N.Y.: University Books, 1965).

24. Oscar Begnall, *The Origin and Properties of the Human Aura* (New York: University Books, 1970).

25. Mary Scott, "Science and Subtle Bodies: Towards a Clarification of Issues", Paper No. 8, 1975, at College of Psychic Studies, London.

26. Albert Roy Davis, and W. C. Rawls, Jr., *The Magnetic Effect* (Hicksville, N.Y.: Exposition Press, 1975).

————, *Magnetism and Its Effects on the Living System* (Jericho, N.Y.: Exposition Press, 1976).

————, *The Rainbow in Your Hands* (Hicksville, N.Y.: Exposition Press, 1976).

27. Dennis Milner, *The Loom of Creation* (London: Neville Spearman, 1976).

28. George Starr White, *The Story of the Human Aura* (Mokelume Hill, CA: Health Research, 1969).

29. George W. Meek, and Bertha Harris, *From Seance to Science* (London: Regency Press, 1973).

30. A. I. Likachev, A paper on magnetic fields and the central nervous system presented at Monte Carlo, June, 1975. In *Paraspychology Review*, Vol. 6, No. 5.

31. Alice A. Bailey, *Esoteric Healing* (New York: Lucius Publishing Co., 1972).

32. Helena Pralnikova, and Victor Popovkin, Report on Moscow Congress on Telepathy, 1968. In *The ESP Papers*, edited by Ostrander and Schrocder. (New York: Bantam Books, 1976).

33. L. L. Vasiliev, *Experiments in Mental Suggestion* (Hampshire, England: Institute for Study of Mental Images, 1963).

34. "Levi", *The Aquarian Gospel of Jesus the Christ* (London: L. N. Fowler and Co., 1907).

35. John Taylor, *Superminds, An Inquiry into the Paranormal* (London: Macmillan, 1975).

36. R. D. Mattuck, Paper and film presented at Monte Carlo, July, 1975. In *Parapsychology Review*, Vol. 6, No. 5.

37. Elmer E. Green, "How to Make Use of the Field of Mind Theory". Paper presented at the meeting of Academy of Parapsychology and Medicine, Stanford University, 1975.

38. C. Norman Shealy, *The Pain Game* (New York: Celestial Arts Press, 1975).

————, *Occult Medicine Can Save Your Life* (New York: Dial Press, 1975).

39. Carl A. Wickland, *Thirty Years Among the Dead* (Hollywood: Newcastle Publishing Co., 1974).

40. William Addams Welch, *Talks With The Dead* (New York: Pinnacle Books, 1975).

41. Friedrich Jurgenson, "Voice of Phenomena". In *Esoteric* (Freiberg, West Germany) October-November-December, 1975.

42. Konstantin Raudive, *Breakthrough* (Gerrards Cross, England: Colin Smythe, 1971).

43. Theodor Rudolph, "Electronics in Parapsychology". Paper presented in Calderola, Italy, 1974.

44 Franz Seidl, *The Psychofon* (Vienna, Austria: 1971).

45. Richard K. Sheargold, *Hints on Receiving the Voice Phenomenon* (Gerrards Cross, England: Van Duren Press, 1973).

VI

CHALLENGES AND OPPORTUNITIES

- **Medicine**
- **The Church**
- **Science**

It became obvious when our healing research finally led us into a study of the nature of man, that we had opened a veritable Pandora's Box. As has been noted in Chapter 14, we came face to face with realities of man and the cosmos which just did not harmonize with the current world views held by the medical profession, leaders of The Church, and Scientists.

The concepts embodied in Figures AA & BB in the preceding chapter, if substantiated, even in part, present challenges and opportunities of great magnitude.

In this closing section of the book, three of our co-authors provide specific insights on both the challenges to and the opportunities for these three major segments of our society.

Some of the techniques of unorthodox or paranormal healing are examined for the light they throw on the nature of reality.

It is suggested that they provide the best available means for challenging the established orthodoxy of biology and medicine and for provoking a revolution of the kind that quantum mechanics produced in theoretical physics.

20

CHALLENGES AND OPPORTUNITIES

● Medical Science

Lyall Watson

I have no difficulty in swallowing the saliva in my mouth. It is there and it is part of me and the whole process of secretion and ingestion goes on automatically. But there are very few things that could make me drink my saliva if I had first of all to put it into a wine glass and look at it carefully as a good scientist should.

And yet it is the same saliva. Nothing has changed and there is not necessarily anything wrong with it, but a wedge has been driven between us. Science does that. It is a valuable instrument, essential to the process of analysis and description that has made it possible for us to forge our way of life and our patterns of belief. But it does alienate us. Making observers of us when we ought now to be more concerned with our role as participants.

As a biologist, I have a fundamental bias in favor of the system as a whole. I see connections between all its parts and I feel party to at least some of its intrigues. We didn't come into this world, we came out of it like butterflies out of a cocoon. We were produced by the world and are still very much attached to it, but our traditional sciences insist on descriptions which emphasize individuality and an order based on a point-to-point correspondence between individual particles.

Tradition of course is giving way in the face of the revolution produced by quantum mechanics. Heisenberg's principle of uncertainty is phrased in terms of particles whose location and velocity it is impossible to determine exactly, but its essential conclusion is that there are no particles at all. The order implicit in the particle model no longer applies. Likewise, there are no fields in the sense that the continuous field model makes no sense either. Theoretical physics has had to put up a sign reading "Temporarily Closed for Reconstruction" as the specialists set about their search for some fundamentally new notion of order.

The most hopeful new paradigms all embody some notion of

connectedness and the identification of separate levels of reality. In practice it is almost impossible to distinguish the axioms of the newest physics from those of the oldest philosophies. A reconciliation has been effected, but it is taking an unconscionably long time for news of it to get about. Most laymen aren't aware that some of their leading scientists are raving mystics, and very few scientists even in the areas most directly affected by the revolution, have begun to embody the new concepts in their work or in their way of life.

The two worst culprits are biology and medicine. They are still descriptive sciences like old-fashioned geography, stuck with a reductionist thesis that keeps their workers fussing about at an atomistic DNA level, worrying about cells (the biological equivalent of the physicist's nonexistent particles) and apparently totally unconcerned about the whole organism and the possibility of its holistic operation.

This particle orientation in biological thinking is absurd, but fortunately it is almost entirely confined to the West. As research begins into areas like acupuncture and the control of autonomic processes, the field-oriented ideas of the East are beginning to influence us. The emergence of a new field approach to the life sciences is under way, but it still needs a lot of help. It needs special pressures and an incentive to change. I think that the phenomena involved in the area of unorthodox healing provide just such a stimulus. They present a challenge that is hard to ignore.

My first direct experience in this area took place in the Philippines at a daily clinic held by a local healer at his home in the Pangasinan lowlands near Manila. José Mercado begins his ministrations each morning by lining up all potential patients against the wall of the concrete brick building in which he works. He then passes along the line and, with his forefinger held out like a kid playing cowboys, gives each proferred arm one of his "spirit injections". At no time does he come within three feet of a patient, and yet each one in turn feels a pin-prick sensation on his skin, and about eighty per cent produce a tiny spot of blood at the appropriate point.

I joined the line. When he pointed his finger at my bicep and made the squeezing motion of giving an injection, I felt a sharp localized pain. When I rolled up my sleeve, there was a tiny puncture wound of the kind one would expect to have been produced by a needle, and a drop of blood. The shirt seemed to be totally undamaged.

As a Western scientist, one thinks first of mechanical solutions. I toyed briefly with the notion of a concealed laser beam, but soon discounted this on the grounds that this man could not have concealed, would not have been able to afford, and could never have manipulated a laser in this way. I thought of equipment capable of firing minute projectiles of water, ice or even blood—and then discounted this line of enquiry for similar reasons.

But I couldn't leave it alone. I came back the following morning with very simple equipment designed to test some of the possibilities inherent in the situation. I placed a folded sheet of polyethylene, four layers thick, over my bicep held it in place with a rubber band beneath my cotton shirt. I then joined the line again.

Mercado made his customary gesture in my direction from a distance of about five feet. I felt nothing and told him so, asking if he would try again. He repeated the process from a distance of approximately three feet. This time I felt the prick and when I removed the pad, I found the usual puncture and a drop of blood which I collected on a microscope slide for analysis. Five minutes later, I squeezed out a second drop for the sake of comparison.

I found also that the sheet of plastic had been pierced in the area directly over the wound as though a cold needle had been run right through all four layers. An inch away from this point, probably in the area corresponding to Mercado's first "injection", there was another puncture in the plastic, but this time passing through only two of the four layers as though his strength from a distance of five feet was not sufficient to penetrate my experimental barrier. But it was the innermost two layers, those closest to my skin, that had been punctured.

When the blood samples were typed in a laboratory in Manila later that same day under my personal supervision, the second one proved to belong to a group appropriate to my own, but the first was totally foreign to me. It was not even human—the red corpuscles had nuclei.

This gave me food for thought. The presence of holes in the plastic ruled out the possibility of my being responsible for producing blood by some sort of hysterical response akin to those that cause religious stigmata. And yet the presence of one set of holes in only the innermost layers of plastic, seemed to cancel out the possibility of Mercado being responsible by the exercise of any known energetic projection. The existence of non-human blood made it seem unlikely that I alone was involved in the phenomenon and yet the presence of a puncture wound through which my own blood did ultimately ooze, made the whole thing very personal. The dilemma was complete.

Since my experience, others have tried to identify the phenomenon by using capacitor plates and a variety of sophisticated electronic apparatus, but without success. On occasion the apparatus fails to work, but more often the response fails to appear in the presence of instrumentation that could establish its reality beyond all reasonable doubt. After more than six months of research into these types of phenomena in the Philippines, I am satisfied that their elusiveness has nothing to do with deliberate fraud or an unwillingness to perform in the presence of scientific instruments for fear of being found out. The fault seems to lie in the instruments themselves and in the experimental attitude which they engender. Our tools are designed to cope with objective everyday reality, because that is the only one our system recognizes. They are not designed to deal with mental and psychic factors or the kinds of interaction which can occur between two or more minds—and I believe that in many types of unorthodox healing we are dealing with events in this area, with an order that is based on another level of reality.

Theoretical physics, with the help of Heisenberg, has come to terms with this problem, and it is high time that our life sciences followed suit. We need to rid ourselves of preconceptions about how things work, because the likelihood is that our descriptions are all more or less misleading. Non-preconception is a necessary pre-condition to true discovery. Being open is a unique and powerful state of mind. When you do not preconceive, then you go about finding out. There is nothing else you can do so you really explore.

But being open is very difficult. I think that there is already sufficient evidence to show that the child who sits day-dreaming in class is using his mind more creatively than the one who pays attention, but you will find few teachers who can accept that. They are the experts, and by definition and by custom they are required to tell our children how it is, not to encourage them to explore. We have all become specialists, and specialists don't welcome discovery, we welcome only new proofs of what we already know. We have all acquired a dogmatic certainty in the validity of our own particular perceptions, in the specific interpretations of reality that we have learned to make in common and to accept as exclusive fact. And of all the life sciences, probably the most dogmatic, the one most set in its ways, is the theory and practice of modern medicine. This is another reason why I find the phenomena inherent in the practice of unorthodox healing so challenging.

The quality of the healing provided by unorthodox means is dealt with very fully in other sections of this book. I think there is no longer room for doubt that many of the systems are appropriate in that they use cultural, and sometimes very dramatic, techniques for putting patients in direct touch with the unconscious areas in their own minds that are, in the end, entirely responsible for health. They give patients back the responsibility for their own health. This is tremendous, but what excites me more are the related phenomena which are in direct conflict with the established explanations of how things work. I think that in unorthodox healing we have the potential not only for making ourselves well, but also for making ourselves very much wiser.

Central to all these unorthodox healing methods as found now in the Philippines, in India, in Africa and in South America, is a series of visual effects, a kind of window dressing which dramatizes the healing taking place at another more fundamental level. Invariably, these techniques involve the production of macroscopic matter in a most unusual way. In a word, they involve materialization.

Conventional physics cannot countenance the production or destruction of matter without the utilization of enormous quantities of energy. Quantities far too large to be produced or controlled by any biological system. Physics is right, things do not happen that way, but they do nevertheless happen and they cannot be shrugged off as delusion, hypnosis, fraud, conjuring, or sheer wishful thinking.

On at least one occasion in the Philippines, I was able to control the circumstances in which materialization took place so rigidly that there was no possibility of fraud. A healer came to have a meal with me in my hotel in Manila. While we sat together, he was approached by an American lady whom I knew by sight. She had never met him, but wanted to know if he could possibly find the time to treat her before she returned to the U.S. the next morning. He was reluctant to do anything at that late hour, but when I offered them the use of my room, he agreed to try. He agreed also to give me this chance to eliminate any suspicions I might have about the source of tissue that customarily appears on the surface of the patient's body in his treatments.

I took him immediately to my room. He stripped and allowed me to search him thoroughly and to lock his clothes in my cupboard. He wore only a pair of my thin cotton shorts. The patient was similarly searched and agreed to be treated lying on my hotel bed, with not even the usual towel as covering. A friend and I drew up chairs and watched the entire procedure from a distance of less than two feet. We took several polaroid pictures to make certain that the action was as it appeared to our naked eyes.

The healer used no water, no cotton wool, no oils—nothing which could be prepared in any way to produce chemical reactions that would simulate blood and tissue. And yet, despite all these precautions, after he had been manipulating her skin for about three minutes, a red liquid appeared on it that proved on subsequent analysis to be blood of a group appropriate to her own. A little later in the treatment, the healer also succeeded in producing a small quantity of tissue, about ten grams, which I collected and sealed in a specimen jar with the object of typing it when I could get to a laboratory the next day. But I never did get that analysis. Although the jar was still sealed the next morning, it was empty. The sample had vanished without trace, as though it had never been completely materialized in the first place.

After several years of exposure to healing situations, I am certain that part of the procedure takes place in areas which make nonsense of our normal concept of space and time. Not only do materializations take place, but very often the objects involved are so totally appropriate that their production would require a knowledge of circumstance and psychology on the part of the healer that is even more difficult to believe in than the creation and destruction of matter.

On one occasion in the Amazon I was traveling in a narrow river boat with three Brazilian *caboclos* when one suddenly developed a fever as a result of an inflamed abscess beneath a wisdom tooth. I had no anti-biotics with me and struggled in vain to remove the tooth with a pair of the engineer's long-nosed pliers. I was about to turn back when one of the boatmen mentioned that a famous healer lived just a few hours up a tributary not far away. We left the muddy mainstream and moved into a quiet pattern of lagoons of clear green water. Eventually we reached a place where the forest had been cleared to plant a crop of cassava, and we drew in to the bank opposite a group of huts thatched with palm fronds.

The healer agreed to treat our patient and did so immediately by seating him on a log in the clearing in front of his house. The preliminary consultation was concerned not at all with the patient's symptoms but with the particular circumstances, the exact time and place, they were first noted. An agreement was reached which took the blame off poor dental care and placed it squarely on some malevolent outside influence, an evil spirit force, which as it happened, the healer knew well.

He stirred around in the patient's mouth with his crooked forefinger and lifted out the offending molar as though it had been lying loose there under the tongue. We all got to examine the tooth and to peer into the empty socket which was only bleeding very slightly. There was great satisfaction all round, but the healer wasn't finished yet. He said that he still had to get rid of the pain.

He massaged the swollen glands on the patient's throat, made him sit back with his mouth wide open and then sat down opposite him and began to sing softly in an Indian dialect. After a few minutes a trickle of blood began to flow out of the corner of the patient's mouth and following it came a column of live black army ants.

Not a frantic confusion of ants such as would have resulted if the healer had merely dropped some container into the patient's mouth; but an ordered column of ants, marching two and three abreast, coming from somewhere and going somewhere. They kept on coming until there were a hundred or more moving in a stream down the patient's neck, along his bare arm and down to the log on which he sat. Then he and I and everyone present watched the column move across the clearing, into the grass and away.

The patient got well very quickly after that. I was flabbergasted, but for him, in his culture, with his expectations and belief, the treatment was totally appropriate. Right from the very beginning, the healer had concentrated on exploring with the patient, his entire life situation and all the circumstances leading up to the illness. He never once concerned himself with symptoms or with giving fine-sounding diagnoses. He tried to tackle root causes and to set up the condition so that it would be available for treatment. He gave it a meaningful handle—an identity.

He may not have been right in attributing the toothache and the fever to evil spirits, but by recognizing anything of the sort he was providing, in addition to his highly effective dental treatment, appropriate psychiatric and social care at no extra cost. And he made the judgment stick and ensured that it would work by the performance of an extraordinary piece of sleight-of-mind. I am certain the ants were real. I think they must have been materialized, but what impresses me most of all is the shrewd choice of that particular manifestation.

When the ants came pouring out of our patient's mouth, everyone present burst into roars of laughter. They thought it was very funny, but I didn't see the joke until it was explained to me later. The local word for pain is the same as that used to describe the ants. The healer had said the pain would leave and so it did. It walked out in the form of an elaborate and extraordinary visual pun. The materialization, however it was produced, was wonderfully appropriate. It was tailored in an imaginative and delightful way to the needs of the patient. It was couched in the kind of symbolism that the unconscious mind can most easily deal with. It gave the patient the incentive and the means for making himself well.

That to me is very good medicine.

It is also a kind of magic with overtones of intelligence. An awareness of need and an accuracy in diagnosis which is impossible to explain in any normal way. It is the kind of phenomenon that occurs quite often in unorthodox healing techniques and which must make medical and physical scientists think very hard indeed.

It worried me a great deal. I was reluctant even to talk about it until I became more familiar with the work of some of the new theoretical physicists. I find one of their models particularly appropriate.

David Bohm, at Birbeck College of the University of London, has suggested a new concept which he calls the enfolded or implicate order. He uses the hologram to show that a photographic plate can record interference patterns of laser light in such a way that an object cannot only be recreated three-dimensionally, but can be recreated in its entirety from any small fraction of the plate. Each part of a hologram contains it all. What it in fact records is an order inherent in the movement of light taking place at the position of the plate. And what is characteristic of this order is that all the information about the whole object is enfolded in every region of the space occupied by the plate.

Bohm calls this order, implicate, and describes it as the folded state of matter. This state is invisible, inaudible and intangible, but it becomes possible to see, hear, and touch an object once the light waves, sound waves and moving electrons of which it is constructed have been unfolded from the hidden folded flow of things.

In the old Newtonian physics it was possible to use the laws of motion to describe the successive positions occupied by an object at a series of successive times. The new quantum mechanics shows that the objective world in space and time no longer exists, and forces us to deal, not in hard facts, but in possibilities. Bohm suggests that the most logical possibility is that an object does not move physically from one place to another, but is created anew in each new position. He proposes that an unfolded visible object folds itself, disappears, and then reappears when it unfolds again in the new position. Its form in the new position will be generally similar to what it was, but there will be differences in detail. It is not the same object.

If he is right, we may begin to make sense of apparently contradictory phenomena like materialization. If matter is merely an appearance, abstracted from the basic folded order, then there will be no need to assume the expenditure of vast quantities of energy for its appearance and disappearance. Such things are happening all the time. They are part of the normal behavior of all unfolded order. We, and the plants on which we feed and the rocks on which all of us stand, are nothing more than relatively stable forms derived from the underlying universal flux. Our matter has sufficient independence for it to be investigated in its own right, but only up to a point. We may know a particle's velocity or its position, but never both. When any exploration of substance gets to this fundamental level, it breaks down. It founders on the principle of indeterminacy which demonstrates that some things can never be known because they are not there to be known. The folded order cannot be investigated with the methods and the instruments designed to explore unfoldings.

Theoretical physics arrived at this point some years ago, but now with the growing attempt to explore and explain fringe phenomena like those attendant on unorthodox healing, the life sciences are being brought face to face with the same situations of scientific stalemate that forced physics to stand back and rethink. We are at last catching up with ourselves.

The important thing to realize is that the tools for this reconstruction have always been available. They are today in the hands of those still young enough, or those still remote enough from us, to permit belief in other kinds of reality.

This other kind of knowing is not something new. Quantum mechanics has produced a sort of statistical mysticism that has made conjecture along these lines respectable, but it has always been there, allowed to persist alongside our scientific system because it was never seen to be a threat to organized science or religion. It is there in the mouths of babes, in the mind of everyman, in old wives tales, in folklore, in superstition and in mythology and all the cosmologies constructed by so-called primitive people. It is made possible by the fact that we are all unfolding and retain some sort of basic contact with the system. We are the eyes and ears of the earth and all of its mysteries are embodied in every one of our cells like the tiny fragments of some cosmic hologram. The keys are there for the taking, but we generally find them very hard to recognize except in retrospect.

The conceptual essence of the special theory of relativity was formulated more than two thousand years ago by the Jaina thinkers of India in their philosophical doctrine of ayadvada. Something very like the general theory was outlined in detail by the Greeks Heraclitus and Zeno of Elea as far back as the sixth and fifth centuries B.C. In the natural sciences, Darwin's work was clearly anticipated by Anaximander in the 7th century B.C., and though Freud is credited with the invention of psychoanalysis in our time, it is a system that has been in use by the Plains Indians of North America for centuries.

How much time we could have saved by having the courage to go directly to those sources. And how much time we seem now to be wasting by continuing to be too clever and too proud to take these sources seriously.

There are practical possibilities inherent in a recognition of techniques of unorthodox healing. We may be able to reduce the work load on physicians by setting up some kind of filtering system that would take patients first through the hands of trained healers, most of whom are more effective than traditional Western doctors in handling problems of psychosomatic origin—and that eliminates 95% of a general practitioner's problems at one fell swoop.

The extraordinary skill of some healers in diagnosis would also undoubtedly be useful at a second level in this system, where they could work side by side with physicians in more advanced consultation over difficult cases.

I don't think there are great problems in getting the Western public to accept healers; they already put a great deal of faith in the few available. But it is not going to be easy to get the physician to accept what he sees as a threat to his livelihood and to the emotional vested interest he has in one particular description of reality.

So I see the doctor and not the patient as the stumbling block in this situation. I continue to look for and at unorthodox systems, not with hope of co-opting them into an establishment—I believe that is a hopeless cause—but in the hope that exposure of these systems will excite public interest and force legislation that will permit these systems to be set up in our society as viable and legal alternatives to Western medicine.

The public interest in acupuncture forced a situation of this kind and now not only do we have traditional practitioners of the art setting up in business in the West, but we have trained medical scientists deserting their disciplines to study these techniques and practice them instead of their own.

In time the two competing systems will inevitably find common ground. Western medicine is clearly superior in the technology involved in treating radical injury, for instance, but it has a lot to learn about the control of autonomic processes such as those that govern rejection of foreign implants. There are obviously areas in which "particle" and "field" medicine can be complementary and all should be carefully explored.

I do not really expect to find that the Asmat headhunters hold a cure for cancer, nor that the secret of long life has come to a Hopi Indian in a dream or is embodied in a game played by children in the streets of Cyprus. But I think we cannot afford to ignore even these outlandish possibilities.

I suspect that the big breakthrough in the coming medical and biological revolution will be made on the frontiers of genetics, molecular biology and cell dynamics, but I feel certain that the new creative insights necessary to make these discoveries will come not from inside the relevant disciplines, but from some totally undisciplined outside source.

And that is why I am spending most of my time these days in pursuit of the unorthodox and the unaccountable, trying to find some way of reconciling scientific investigation and mystic revelation. Trying to find some system of natural knowing that is so much in tune with the total environment that it will bring us, our methods and our minds, back into synchrony with things as they really are, and not as we would like them to be. And of all the practices I have taken part in, of all the mystiques into which I have been initiated none is more basic nor deals with matters more directly relevant to all of us, than alternative systems of healing.

We need new answers of the sort that can only be found by asking radically new questions. And, on balance, I find more inspiration, more excitement and a greater sense of challenge and achievement in a study of questions raised by unorthodox healing than I do in any other single area, because this one is concerned at heart with balance—with the notion of equilibrium.

In these troubled times, there is nothing that we need more than a new and certain sense of equilibrium.

21

CHALLENGES AND OPPORTUNITIES
• The Church

In the British Isles more than 3,000 healers who make up the membership of the National Federation of Spiritual Healers have practiced the
admonition of Jesus Christ with respect to healing their fellow men,
but they do this completely outside the framework of the Church of
England. In the U.S., except for the Order of St. Luke in The Episcopal
Church, few of the organized religions have taken any serious interest
in carrying on a healing ministry, hence only a few of the American
healers have church sponsorship. In Brazil we have a similar situation
where some thousands of healers work completely outside the Catholic
Church—the one to which the majority of healers belong.

While serving as a priest, Michael Wynne Parker developed great
interest in healing and actually became a good channel. He found it
necessary to leave the Church in order to carry on his healing ministry
in the most effective manner. Therefore he is in a qualified position to
discuss this involved matter and the challanges and opportunities
which healing poses for organized religion.

Michael Wynne Parker

The worldwide research into paranormal healing, some of which has
been reported in the foregoing chapters, presents challenges to and
opportunities for religion no less than those posed for medicine and
science. It is the purpose of this chapter to identify and then discuss at
least some of those challenges and opportunities.

Generally speaking, "the Church" is the composite of all religious
organizations, each one set up to promulgate a particular set of beliefs
relating to a Supreme Being and to provide dogma, creed and worship
practices and procedures.

However, in this chapter, "the Church" will include only the Christian Church since we will be referring only to the religious doctrines and practices which stem from the life and teachings of Jesus Christ.

Even here we will find significant differences of interpretation and meaning.

For example, I have heard many people involved in paranormal research and practice refer to church-goers as being "orthodox". This poses a problem of terminology. Within religious circles the term "orthodox" can only properly refer to the Orthodox Church, which in a Western sense appears to be extremely *un*orthodox.

Whereas the Western Church (both Catholic and Protestant) has, since the Reformation, been largely identified with material development leading to present-day Christian Humanism, which has in turn led to the reactionary charismatic and psychic movements, the Eastern Church has followed more closely the mystical path. Therefore, what may appear to Western Christian eyes as being paranormal may very well be to the Eastern Christian perfectly normal.

So to define our terms even more carefully, we must in this chapter think of the Church as being the established norm of Western Christianity.

Three things must now be said:

• First, the Western Church, because of its humanistic tendency, has on the whole been *unable* to reconcile itself to the manifestation of the paranormal as set out in the examples contained in this book.

• Second, let it not escape our attention that, despite the fact just mentioned, there has been a steadily growing awareness of paranormal phenomena within the Established Church.

• Third, there is a tendency for fringe members of the Established Churches to underestimate the practice of paranormal healing within the Church. The Anglican Church has its Burrswood, founded by the saintly Dorothy Kersin who manifested the strange phenomenon of the stigmata at the end of her life.[1] The Roman Catholic Church had its Padre Pio from whom "psychic" phenomena flowed daily. These two examples could be repeated many times throughout Europe.

Having made the above points, let us now single out four points that emerge from the implications of the phenomena contained in this book. They are:

1. that Healing is not the prerogative of the Established Church;
2. that illness cannot be "the will of God";
3. that man is far more than a physical body;
4. that life continues beyond the grave.

Healing Is Not The Prerogative Of The Established Churches

This is a fact. According to Gilbert Anderson's account in Chapter 4 of this book and George Meek's observations in Chapter 5, the number of actual healers outside the Church far outweighs the number practicing within it. This may be because of theological objection to healing, but it is in fact more likely to be because of lack of encouragement (and even opposition to healing) on the part of the Church hierarchy. The theological aspect of this is interesting. Kenneth Clark in his classic work, *Civilization,* makes the point that whereas the early church was involved in healing and the constant manifestation of *spiritual gifts* which provided an attraction to the Faith, the Church ultimately became preoccupied with *the Cross* and its sufferings which naturally did not have such a popular appeal.[2] The point here is that the manifestation of healing is an evangelizing factor which is why those sections of the Church that practice it are now thriving (at least numerically) and why the fringe healing sects continue to flourish.

Old Russia had a saying. It was that if there is a doctor in the village the priest must be neglecting his work. This reflects the attitude of Eastern Christianity. Sadly, it could not be said of the average Western situation.

The fact that healings do happen despite the Church's general attitude obviously presents a challenge. If the Church will not heal, the healers will!

The opportunities for the Church are enormous. The priest and minister are in a splendid position to act as healing channels. They have the training, experience and self-discipline, in addition to a faith in God, which would combine to ensure that healing practices were balanced and safe. Furthermore, there is no reason why the lay members of the Church should not be encouraged, recognized and authorized to act as healers within the Church organization. This would certainly meet with the approval of St. Paul who stressed the importance of the exercising of individual gifts within the framework of the whole.

Something should be said here about the laying-on-of-hands which is the most commonly used method of healing within the Church today. The main difference between the Church usage of the laying-on-of-hands and the method used by the majority of healers in this book is that the former normally confine the hands to the head of the recipient while the latter tend to place the hands on the diseased part of the body. I have personally witnessed the helpful effects of *both* methods.

The laying-on-of-hands, as I point out in Chapter 4 of my book, *The Wholeness of Man,*[3] is regarded by some Christians as purely symbolic, by others as an act of faith and by others still as the actual means of conveying the "gift" of healing. There is great room for flexibility here—and flexibility is vital. Some will respond best to healing in an atmosphere heavy with incense surrounded by candles and blue Madonnas, while others require an almost clinical approach. We must recognize that for every individual ill somewhere there is a cure.

Illness Cannot Be "The Will Of God"

This is a vital matter for consideration. For centuries, the attitude of the Church has been negative. There has been little clear conviction that God's will must always be to make whole. Indeed, in many instances, the theologians have taught that sickness is sent as a punishment for wrong doing. This belief has caused an enormous amount of suffering and has contributed considerably to the obsessions with guilt that lie behind some of the many psychological disorders today. The Biblical message rang out—"Repent and be saved." The trouble today is that we have not learned to repent and forget.

What is the significance of medical science here? Doctors have gradually come round to the view that perhaps 80% of all patients have ailments triggered largely by emotional stress and inappropriate thoughts. Watson, in the preceding chapter, goes even further. If this is so, does it not emphasize the importance of human responsibility? Is it not therefore blasphemy to attribute the blame to God? Let us try to look at this objectively.

First, God created us with enormous resources with which to meet the problems of life. Second, God has placed within us an automatic system of healing—the cut finger immediately begins to heal. Third, Christ healed people and taught his followers that he always followed God's will. Fourth, all Christ's teachings were designed to create an emotional balance needed for perfect health—*see* the Sermon on the Mount.

From the above four points, how can anyone possibly believe that God desires people to be ill? One of the most important tasks, therefore, is to help people change their attitude toward sickness, for if healing depends on a man's WILL TO BE WELL, his conscience must be persuaded that this is RIGHT.

Man Is Far More Than A Physical Body

Philosophers, saints and poets have always known this, now scientists are joining their ranks. As I have already pointed out, Western Christianity has been overly preoccupied with materialism during the past four hundred years. This is understandable because Christianity was the means of bringing civilization to many parts of Europe; it encouraged art, music, morals, education, health and social justice. But while Christianity employed itself in building Western democracy, it tended to overlook the fact that material man has also a spiritual life. Hence, our present surprise at the manifestation of the paranormal.

The Western emphasis on the physical and the material prepared the way for the development of humanism in the Church. By humanism I mean man's belief in his own complete self-sufficiency. What he has experienced, witnessed and is capable of he believes in—of everything else he must be skeptical. The present example of this is the Church's deep involvement in politics and sociology instead of spirituality and philosophy. "Seek *first* the Kingdom of God," said Christ!

One of the Church's problems over the resurgence of healing is the very fact that this phenomenon does not depend on man at all, man being merely the "channel" or "instrument". The assertion that "the healer does not do the healing" is a total contradiction of the humanist belief in the total self-sufficiency of man.

The Church must rediscover its faith in God, the Supreme Power and

Source of all. A revival of true Christian mysticism within the Church would surely bridge the gap between "established Christians" and "fringe healers".

Everything written in this book presents a challenge to those who believe that man is confined to his physical body. Its challenge to the Church is obvious. Let the Church point out and again emphasize the reality of the *spiritual* and that the inspiration flowing from the spiritual must inevitably lead to positive action for the good of mankind as well as better physical and mental health for each individual.

Life Continues Beyond The Grave

For centuries, religions all over the world have proclaimed this. St. Paul described belief in the resurrection as being the central theme of Christianity. "Oh death where is thy sting, Oh grave where is thy victory . . . ?" However, modern man, immersed in his material jungle, has begun to doubt, while the Communist world denies that the life of the individual is eternal.

At this time science cannot be dogmatic over any claims that life continues beyond the grave, despite the fact that this is a firm belief among several scientists (and is the reason why two top Russian scientists have been assigned to concentration camps in the past two years). However, if the phenomenon described in earlier chapters of this book is true, is any further proof required?

Having just used the word "proof", I should immediately say that of course proof is not something that any of the great Christian saints have regarded as necessary at all. Indeed, on the contrary, they were as skeptical as to the validity of the desire for proof as many people today are of the validity of religious faith. This is the main difference between Religion and Science, the latter requires proof whereas the former, at least traditionally, does not. Personally I have never found that any so-called proof of life beyond helped my belief in it, though I have known of those who have been helped thereby.

The questions posed by the implications of belief in life after death are legion. Are the departed aware of what we are doing? How much, if at all, can they influence us? Can we help them? And so on. I have often thought that Spiritualism and Catholicism have much more in common here than would appear at first. The Catholic belief in praying for the departed and the Spiritualist belief in the departed helping us both imply the possibility for cooperation, such as would leave the Protestant amazed!

Let us try to gather our thoughts together.

First, "There are more things in heaven and earth than are dreamt of in your philosophy, Horatio." This pertinent remark of Shakespeare applies to the establishment in general and the church in particular and *should be taken more seriously*. The Western Church has far too long ignored the impact that psychic discoveries are having upon it.

Second, the Church must provide a positive alternative to the mood setting trends of negative materialistic philosophy. If Healing is true; if God wills *health;* if man is not limited to his physical body; if life is not confined to its physical expression, *then there is hope.* We should indeed recognize that phenomena described in this book provide what could, in New Testament terms, be described as SIGNS—pointers to the limitless potential of mankind. Possibly they provide the greatest antidote to the FEAR which, since the explosion of the atomic bomb, has cursed mankind, the fear of complete extermination. The bomb cannot exterminate the soul! Hence the material "signs" of healings and other strange physical phenomena could help the Christian Church back to the *spiritual reality* which provides the only hope for man's future.

Finally, if we accept that there is indeed a challenge to the Church to be again an agency of healing in the world, then I would suggest a few practical points for consideration.

● First, the "gifts of healing" should be brought into greater prominence in the Church than they are at present. In most existing churches the emphasis is largely on the sacramental approach being combined with medicine. People with actual gifts should be employed to work along with the doctor and the priest to the greater benefit of the patient. Many who use the healing gifts are professionally qualified in other directions which greatly adds to the patient's faith in their ability to help. There are, however, many remarkably gifted people without professional qualifications who should be integrated into the healing team.

● Second, natural healing methods should be encouraged to play a far larger part than at present. In the area of natural healing I include acupuncture, osteopathy, naturopathy, dieting and fasting.

● Third, state health services should give serious consideration to integrating the methods of healing outlined in this book into its system.

● Fourth, there is a great need for serious research into the whole area of non-medical healing. The Church should include a "research department" where many of the problems surrounding the newly revived healing ministry can be solved and all its many variations be investigated.

● Fifth, any good center of healing must necessarily be a center of education also. By this I mean that prevention is better than cure and people should be taught some of the principles behind the conditions that make for a healthy life. Furthermore, there is terrific need for both the clergy and the doctors to become aware of the implications of their ministry of healing and wholeness. Many of them still have far too limited a view of the work with which they are involved.

All people of all time are involved in and therefore concerned with sickness. And all people of all time are directly or indirectly influenced by religion. These two aspects of life are inseparable because they are both dealing with LIFE itself. I hope therefore that a serious contemplation of the "paranormal" will be a means of turning mankind from the path of self-destruction and set his feet on the way of LIFE.

Over the past two centuries there has been a widening gap between the religions and science. It has not been recognized that the world of matter has its roots in the world of spirit. Hence, few people today are aware of the actual role of *spiritual* influence on *material* life.

However, change is in the air! The scientific research reported in this book seems to have reversed the trend. Now we have scientists telling us that man is *more* than a physical being, that there are definitely *non*-physical aspects to his being, and that for want of a better term, this non-physical part may be called spirit.

The purpose of this chapter is to identify the challenges to and the opportunities for today's Church. Will the Church now utilize this new-found support for its ages-old belief in the spiritual component of man? Will the Church help people to recognize that illness can be avoided? That prevention of illness is surely better than cure? That our Lord taught the importance of the preservation of life?

Will the Church teach that disease is not inevitable? That healing and good health are the will of God? That methods of spiritual healing by the laying-on-of-hands are now compatible with scientific findings presented in this book?

Will the Church help people to realize that we are given our lives to live to the full for the benefit of all and that healing can indeed help people to extend their *useful* life span?

Above all, will the Church accept the challenge of all that is outlined herein to acquaint men with his inner spiritual world, remembering the words of Appollonius of Tyana who said,"No creature can be sound so long as the *higher part* of it is sickly."?

Spirit, Mind and Body are one and derive their being from the one source whence they came—and in which they "live and move and have their being."

REFERENCES

1. D. M. Arnold, *Dorothy Kerin: Called By Christ To Heal* (London: Hodder and Stoughton, 1968).
2. Sir Kenneth Clark, *Civilisation: A Personal View* (London: British Broadcasting Corporation and John Murray, 1969).
3. M. W. Parker, *Healing And The Wholeness And Man* (London: Regency Press, 1974).

22

CHALLENGES AND OPPORTUNITIES
● Material Science

The contemporary world-picture of scientific materialism is described. Limitations of this concept of reality are emphasized by quotations from many scientists of repute.

The inability to accommodate the observed facts of paranormal healing in this world-picture makes it imperative for science to carefully consider the growing gap between scientific materialism and the reality of paranormal healing.

Admittedly, changing one's worldview is difficult and painful, particularly for the eminent members of the world of learning. On the other hand, those who refuse to even consider the need for such change as is suggested by our rapidly expanding knowledge of man's consciousness and the psychic aspects of it are placing themselves in an increasingly untenable position.

Fortunately this situation is now changing as the new generation begins to glimpse the opportunities for up-dating our world-picture.

Sir Kelvin Spencer

This book presents a challenge. It is a challenge not only, indeed not primarily, to material science. It challenges the way most educated people think and act in the contemporary world.

The way people think is their "world-picture", which means the way they interpret the experience of life. The way each of us does this results in a philosophy of living, though most people would say that they know little of philosophy and have no interest in it. In the last century or so philosophy has fallen on bad times. There is an uncomfortable truth in such gibes as: "philosophy is a learned discourse that confuses thought, conducted in a language specially devised for that purpose;" and "a philosopher stirs up the dust and then complains that he can't see."

What is this world-picture that modern man holds? How long ago did it take shape? Throughout history we can trace a succession of world-pictures which have dominated the thinking of communities of different kinds, and of the same community in different epochs. We get glimpses of the earliest of these from deductions made by archaeologists. The first coherent world-picture that has come down to us in writing is that of the Greeks during their Golden Age of Socrates, Plato and Aristotle. Since then many quite different world-pictures have displaced their predecessors. Most were of a religious kind, many of specialized dogmatic variety. This is not the place to give a summary of them. The subject has now become academically respectable under the general title, "The History of Ideas", and many books about it are available.

My task is to state the challenge to the contemporary world-picture posed by the findings recounted in preceding chapters. In what ways is this world-picture now challenged?

Most of us, as parental guidance wanes, look elsewhere for help in finding our way through life's perplexities. Modern educated man now looks to Science in much the same way as his forebears looked to the Priesthood. And the kind of Science which makes up his view of the cosmos is, in historical perspective, of quite recent growth. It can be roughly dated from the sixteenth and seventeenth centuries, to such innovators of thought as Descartes (1596-1650), Leibnitz (1646-1716), Locke (1711-1776), Kant (1724-1804), Hegel (1770-1851), and to poets, among whom Goethe (1749-1832) takes, perhaps, first place.

The nineteenth century saw the rapid development of what is now called scientific materialism. According to this world-picture, Matter is primary; consciousness, if indeed accepted at all as a realistic concept, is but a by-product of Matter. During the nineteenth century knowledge made great strides, but it was knowledge of a special kind. It took as self-evident that the starting point of all orderly, coherent thought was Matter, originally in a very disorganized and diffused form. Over the aeons, according to nineteenth century cosmology, these unorganized diffused "particles" of Matter cohered into atoms, and then into molecules of ever greater complexity. At some stage in the history of planet earth, certain complicated molecules began to manifest characteristics which later developed into living matter. From that point onwards, Darwinian evolutionary theories (of which more and more varieties are thought up every year) seemed to hold promise of ultimately "explaining" everything that is: of giving an adequate account of the totality of Man's potential awareness.

This line of thought, reinforced by highly sophisticated techniques of observation, deduction, and experiment, proved highly successful in its own field. It is to this kind of Science that modern man owes most of the advances in the comforts and easements of life today. No one who benefits from these advances—and which of us doesn't?—should decry the great achievements of scientific materialism. It is in striking contrast to the dogmatic religious outlook that held sway in previous centuries; and the struggle to break out of that former way of thinking was at times grim, and always hard. But freedom of thought and experiment was finally won during the nineteenth century. A landmark for Englishmen is, perhaps, the famous meeting at Oxford in the

1860's of the British Association for the Advancement of Science, when Thomas Henry Huxley soundly trounced the religious dogmatism of Bishop Wilberforce and won acceptance for the fact that the *physical* body of Man evolved from primitive forms of life and was not a special creation.

But this victory for freedom of thought and the uninhibited search for "truth" brought with it the seeds of its own decay. These seeds have now, in the last quarter of the twentieth century, grown into formidable crops. We are now reaping the harvest. One aspect of this harvest is the resistance to acceptance of most of the facts, happenings and experiences described in this book.

Sir Allister Hardy, F.R.S., now in his eighties and still working in a research unit under the aegis of Oxford University, England, has posed the issue in eloquent terms, in *The Divine Flame*[1]

> For three hundred years the doctrine of monism [i.e. scientific materialism] has been gathering force. Could it be possible that modern humanistic Man, excited by the success and neatness of the scientific method, and exalted by the sense of liberation from the intellectual absurdities of mediaeval thought, has been carried away into a new realm of intellectual folly quite different from but only a little less absurd than that which preceded it? Could he be making a gigantic mistake?

Sir Allister's rhetorical question has a respectable ancestry. One of the great adventurers in the realm of thought in the decades spanning the nineteenth and twentieth centuries is Alfred North Whitehead (1861-1947). He was a contemporary of Bertrand Russell at Cambridge University, England. At an early stage of their careers they collaborated in a magnum opus which has become a classic and is generally accepted as the culmination of one line of mathematical-philosophical thought: *Principia Mathematica* (1910). In 1924 Whitehead was appointed to the Chair of Philosophy at Harvard University; and in the remaining years of his life he won for himself a unique place in the intellectual world of the U.S.A. and of Europe as a philosopher, mathematician, and scientist. In 1925 he delivered at Harvard a set of eight Lowell Lectures, subsequently expanded into the classic *Science and the Modern World.*[2]

In this book he sums up in masterly fashion the limitations of scientific materialism as it had then developed; and his pungent criticisms of these limitations are as relevant today as they were half a century ago. It is these limitations which make modern educated man so resistant to taking seriously the ever increasing well-attested manifestations of the paranormal.

The following is an extract from Chapter 3 of his book where he is defining scientific materialism:

> In the first place we must note its astounding efficiency as a system of concepts for the organization of scientific re-

search. In this respect it is fully worthy of the genius of the century which produced it. It has held its own as the guiding principle of scientific studies ever since. It is still reigning. Every university in the world organizes itself in accordance with it. No alternative system of organizing the pursuit of scientific truth has been suggested. It is not only reigning, but it is without rival.

And yet—*it is quite unbelievable.* This conception of the universe is surely framed in terms of high abstractions, and the paradox only arises because we have mistaken our abstractions for concrete realities. (My italics)

In the present century more and more eminent scientists have echoed this misgiving so eloquently stated by Whitehead. For instance:

1. G. N. M. Tyrell, a science graduate of London University and a pioneer in development of radio communications, in *Grades of Significance*:[3]

Understanding is knowing on one definite grade of significance, and it is on this account that intellectual concepts are all abstractions. This is also the reason why knowledge intellectually gained is so clear and precise—so satisfactory to the tidy mind; so unsatisfactory to the mind that hungers for meaning.

2. Henry Margenau, Professor of Physics at Yale University:[4]

Physics did not adhere slavishly to the Greek rationalistic formulations that preceded it; it was forced to create its own specific constructs. . . . The parapsychologist, I think . . . must strike out on his own and probably reason in bolder terms than present-day physics suggests—tolerate the strident critical voices of hard-boiled, pragmatic, and satisfied scientists without too much concern and continue his own painstaking research for an understanding of new kinds of experiences, possibly in terms of concepts which now appear strange.

3. Sir James Jeans, F. R. S.:[5]

Today there is a measure of agreement, which on the physical side of science approaches almost to unanimity, that the stream of knowledge is heading toward a non-mechanical reality; the universe begins to look more like a great thought than like a machine. Mind no longer appears as an accidental intruder into realms of matter.

4. A. S. Eddington, F. R. S. (Quoted by Koestler in *Roots of Coincidence,* p. 59):

The stuff of the world is mind-stuff.

5. Werner Karl Heisenberg:[6]

... the human ability to understand may be in a certain sense unlimited. But the existing scientific concepts cover always only a very limited part of reality, and the other part that has not yet been understood is infinite. Whenever we proceed from the known to the unknown we may hope to understand, but we may have to learn at the same time a new meaning of the word "understanding".

These are but a few of many comparable dicta of eminent scientists of the last seventy years or so. They all emphasize the arbitrary and limited confines in which contemporary Science has imprisoned itself. This self-constricted science is what is now expounded by run-of-the-mill professors and researchers within the pale of orthodoxy, and it is this which forms the climate of opinion current today.

An increasing number of well-informed people are beginning to recognize that contemporary science gives but one way of interpreting experience. Professor William A. Tiller (Chapter 18) gives expression to the wider view now becoming acceptable to the pioneers of new thought. I particularly draw attention to three passages in his chapter:

- We may liken conventional scientific understanding of the universe to the visible tip of an iceberg.
- We are so chained to our view of reality as perceived with the five physical senses that we are unable to give credence to our true nature.
- Our perception mechanisms at the space-time vehicle level lock us into a very narrowly restricted view of reality and the Self.

The founders of the scientific way of thinking that has held sway for the last three centuries recognized the limitations of that way of thinking as does Professor Tiller today. For instance, let us remind ourselves of Isaac Newton's (1642-1737) famous confession: (Brewster's *Memoirs of Newton,* Vol II, chap. 27)

I do not know what I may appear to the world, but to myself I seem to have been only a boy playing on the seashore, and diverting myself in now and then finding a smoother pebble or a prettier shell than ordinary, while the great ocean of truth lay all undiscovered before me.

If, in Newton's parable we take the small boy as representing Science, we can extend it thus: That small boy has now grown into a sturdy adolescent. For the greater part of his life he has confined himself to exploring the seashore. Many pebbles, some far smoother and prettier than any Newton could have conceived, have been found. And many horrible ones, too! Those of us who have lived through the second World War and through the Vietnam War do not need to remind ourselves of these: napalm, nerve gases, defoliants and above all, the atomic bomb.

During the present century, that boy has begun to venture on the great ocean of undiscovered Truth. The physicists have been in the vanguard. One can picture them as having fashioned very primitive boats, and in these they have embarked on an ocean vast indeed, and not always calm. Some of the more adventurous have voyaged out of sight of land, and are indeed "at sea". Lyall Watson, that all-too-rare savant who has studied both biology and physics, outlines in Chapter 20 the revolution in thought brought about by quantum physics and the Heisenberg principle of uncertainty. He writes, "Theoretical physics has had to put up a sign reading, 'Temporarily Closed for Reconstruction' as the specialists set about their search for some fundamentally new notion of order." Translating this into Newton's parable: those who have embarked on the great ocean of Truth have lost their bearings, and have not yet invented the compass or discovered how to navigate by observation of the heavens. In that same chapter Lyall Watson acknowledges that a few scientists have embodied new concepts in their work or in their way of life, but he singles out two branches of science as being especially nervous of going beyond the search on the seashore for newer and better pebbles. He writes, "The two worst culprits are biology and medicine." Those working in these fields, he writes are still "stuck with a reductional thesis that keeps their workers fussing about at an atomistic DNA level worrying about cells . . . and apparently totally unconcerned about the whole organism and the possibility of its holistic operation."

Lyall Watson, in singling out biology and medicine as the two worst culprits, is being a little unfair to doctors, most of whom are easing the pains from which we mortals suffer. Do not let our plea for a wider awareness degenerate into an attack upon such doctors. Many of them give unstintingly of their time, knowledge and mental energy to succor the ailing; and vital statistics show that the expectation of life of middle-aged doctors is, as a consequence, significantly less than that of those in many other professions. Those of us who strive to win recognition for paranormal healing and allied "impossibilities" should aim *not* at attacking orthodox medicine but at encouraging its practitioners to open their minds to therapies which often *do work,* but to which they at present turn a blind eye. Remember that if they show such a widened awareness in their practice of medicine they may well lose cast with their peers in what, for all its limitations, is a profession from which few of us have not benefited at some time, and to which some of us, in fact, owe our lives.

The physicists, in their search for the fundamental constituents of matter, have had to postulate more and more "elementary particles", some of whose characteristics are very odd. In early 1930's three elementary particles were recognized, and these could be pictured in comfortably mechanistic ways. There were the negatively charged electron, the positively charged proton, and the chargeless neutron. Protons and neutrons made up the nucleus of the atom, and the electrons revolved around the nucleus as planets do around the sun. But by 1972 over one hundred elementary particles had been discovered, and more have been discovered since then. Some of them exist for only a tiny fraction of a second; some, like the photon, have a virtually unlimited life; some are very odd indeed; one has attributes which are referred to by the technical term "strangeness". Arthur Koestler writes:[7]

> M. Gell-Mann has proposed a theory of elementary particles which, with acknowledgments to Buddha, he called the 'eightfold way'; and which enabled him to predict the discovery of yet another previously unknown particle called the omega minus . . . for which he got the Nobel Prize in 1969. Gell-Mann and his co-workers have even suggested that the 'elementary particles' may in fact not be elementary at all, but may consist of even more elementary entities which they decided to call 'quarks'—with acknowledgments to James Joyce in *Finnegan's Wake*.

These researches of the physicists have shown that the universe is indeed a mysterious one. They have a very significant implication for the problem set by the present book. For it seems that *matter*—the hard unyielding stuff of common sense *and the stuff of our own bodies*—does not exist in any acceptable scientific sense. It has dissolved into "fields", and man's experience of matter—and the physician's experience of the human body—is in fact an experience of the relationships between disturbances in "fields". When the concept of what the human body is made of sinks in, maybe orthodox medicine will have less difficulty than now in widening traditional ideas to embrace unorthodox and "impossible" types of healing and surgery.

The physicist's reduction of matter to "fields" prompts the question: fields in what? Four "fields" are at present recognized by science; gravity, electromagnetic, and the Strong and Weak fields within the nucleus of the atom. But—fields in *what*?

When one presses this question in discussion with theoretical physicists they become evasive. One such professor whom I know justified his not even trying to answer by saying that the acceptance of "fields" as a valid concept had enabled a great body of theoretical mathematical knowledge to be built up which was self-consistent, intellectually satisfying, and enabled predictions to be made from time to time which could be translated into factual terms admitting of experimental verification in the laboratory: "Whose job was it, then," I asked, "to puzzle about what 'fields' were?" My professor friend was not very interested in this; it wasn't *his* job; perhaps the theologians or the philosophers should take it on.

Alas, neither theologians nor philosophers have taken it on. Maybe none of them is capable of doing so. For by the time a man has reached a high position in the world of learning he has become so acclimatized to the particular worldview within which he won his high position that he has a strong vested interest in resisting all attempts to change it. Furthermore, eminence in a field of learning seldom comes before a man is well on in years and has lost the mental agility needed to change his pattern of thought. In the academic world, for instance, professors are usually appointed to their chairs in their late thirties or early forties, and they don't retire till their middle sixties.

Thus for some thirty years these aging priests of learning are conditioning each rising generation into ideas that become more and more out of step with the latest findings of those few who have ventured on Newton's great ocean of undiscovered truth. This is one cause (there are many others) for worldwide student unrest.

It is difficult to devise a humane cure. To retire a professor at, say, fifty, would be to throw him onto the labor market with little chance of anyone wanting to employ him. Climbing the academic ladder involves narrowing one's interests and competence till, in the too famous gibe, he knows everything about very little. It has (facetiously, I hope!) been suggested that aging professors should be culled by shooting a few to make room for promising younger men whose minds are still agile. A more realistic, but probably impracticable, idea mooted in some circles is that a professor should be required, as a condition of being appointed to a Chair, to take a first degree in some subject remote from his special subject within, say, ten years; failing which, he would be demoted but not retired (or shot!)

Professors have been singled out rather unfairly in this criticism. There are many others whom the cap fits. Presidents of Learned Institutions, editors of Learned Journals, and science journalists, for instance.

The concept, so acceptable to physicists, that matter as manifested to common sense is the outcome of one, but only one, interpretation of sense data, and that on delving deeper, matter is found to dissolve into immaterial fields, is of high significance to Life Scientists. Without some such concept it is impossible to accept any of the paranormal happenings described in this book. These happenings *cannot* be fitted into the concepts now governing biology and orthodox medicine. Hence those whose whole way of thinking is conditioned by these present concepts *know* that, however many happenings of this kind may be reported, and however eminent those who bear witness to them, they *cannot* be true. Some method must be found to "explain" the happenings within orthodoxy, or to discredit those who allege that they have observed or experienced them. There must be a catch somewhere. So those imprisoned in orthodoxy spend their mental energy in devising possible flaws in the evidence or in the reliability of those testifying to it. And these compulsive skeptics draw disproportionate attention to the failures of unorthodox healing conveniently forgetting that orthodox medicine has its failures, too. Alternately the compulsive skeptics may ignore the whole subject. Most of them do. And they are helped by the trivialization of the mass media. But ignoring the subject is becoming more and more difficult; in fact, those who adopt this attitude are already getting into disrepute.

It is because of this that the present chapter is devoted to what, using an old-fashioned term, is the metaphysics of the paranormal. The physicists have not flinched from re-assessing the metaphysics of their specialty; how long will it take the Life Scientists to show comparable courage?

The purpose of the present book, as stated in the author's preface and elsewhere, is to evoke a wider awareness of the *facts* of paranormal healing, and to encourage scientists to refine this knowledge by well-conceived research, to the end that the knowledge now becoming available may be used for the health and welfare of us all. The significant word in that sentence is "well-conceived". Research always starts with some theory, explicit or implicit. What facts are regarded as relevant, and hence what facts are sought for and collated, depend on that starting theory. So long as it is of a materialistic mechanistic kind it *cannot* lead to the kind of research that will much advance our understanding of paranormal healing. It cannot even countenance the great er part of Figures AA and BB in Chapter 19

In that chapter, Meek has attempted the task of creating a new system of concepts preferable to the currently established one because it is capable of embracing facts which, to current concepts, are manifestly impossible. It would be only too easy for the critic to attack Meek's attempt. But, if he has courage comparable to Meek's, (and Lyall Watson's sentence quoted above shows it will be needed!) he will not take the easy path of destructive criticism. Of course, this tentative theory is wide open to criticism. All theories throughout the whole history of science have been attacked when first advanced, modified, and attacked again. This is the very life-blood of scientific advance. But let the attack be constructive. If Meek's theory is demolished, let the demolisher have the intelligence, knowledge, and courage to advance an alternative. Let us have no more of the cowardly criticism that explains away every uncomfortable fact by putting it down to faulty observation, badly contrived experiment, emotion-tinged interpretation, or a conspiracy of fraud. Will any critic be bold enough to accuse of fraud the goodly company of Nobel Prize Winners, Fellows of the Royal Society, England, and university professors of academic eminence, whose views and observations abound in this book? To evoke fraud would be the nadir of the bankrupt critic.

And let those specialists immensely learned in their own specialities but illiterate over a wider span of knowledge, spare their critical efforts for subjects within their ken. The substance of this book transcends the currently accepted boundaries of knowledge. The time is ripe for an epistemological revolution. This revolution will come. The question is: will it come from within the conventional world of learning, or must it be forced on orthodoxy by freelancers?

Some, especially maybe those now in positions of eminence and influence in the scientific world, will be unable or unwilling to accept the challenge. Let them, if such there be, take to heart the quotation by Max Planck which headed the editor's preface to this book:

> A new scientific Truth does not triumph by convincing its opponents and making them see the light, but rather because its opponents die and a new generation grows up that is familiar with it. . . .

REFERENCES

1. Sir Allister Hardy, *The Divine Flame* (London: Collins, 1966).
2. Alfred North Whitehead, *Science and The Modern World* (Cambridge, England: Cambridge University Press, 1933).
3. G. N. M. Tyrell, *Grades Of Significance* (London: Ryder, 1930).
4. Henry Margenau, Address to American Society for Psychical Research, 1969.
5. Sir James Jeans, "The Mysterious Universe". In *A Religious Outlook For Modern Man,* Raynor Johnson (Cambridge, England, Cambridge University Press, 1930).
6. Werner Karl Heisenberg, *Physics And Philosophy* (London: Geo. Allen & Unwin, Ltd., 1959), p. 172.
7. Arthur Koestler, *The Roots Of Coincidence* (London: Hurchinson, 1972), p. 60.

POSTSCRIPT

C. Norman Shealy

Probably this is the most comprehensive collection of information by authorities in the field of alternate medicine, the healing arts and, indeed, *physics*. Implications are all too obvious so no repetition is required at this point. Hopefully, there will be enough enlightened scientists who have learned from the narrow, restricted viewpoints of the past that we shall not continue ignoring this important information. As Linus Pauling stated a couple of years ago, "All progress is heresy." In this case, heresy seems good, for the material in this book suggests very safe alternative ways of handling many problems.

Strictly from a medical point of view, I believe it is imperative that the American public demand safe health care. If, as has been frequently reported and suspected, 85% of the symptoms that plague mankind are due to stress, then effective techniques for teaching everyone how to cope with stress must be taught. Preferably such teaching should be begun in kindergarten and remain part of the curriculum throughout the school years. At the present time a combination of biofeedback, autogenic training and physical exercise seems to be the most effective way to control systemic problems of stress. We must insist that the so-called health insurances, which really are "disease-treatment" insurances, cover preventive medicine and health maintenance. Courses in combating stress need to be widely available as an integral part of our society. Patients should demand psychophysiologic treatments rather than tranquilizers, for stress-related diseases. At least 90% of the use of tranquilizers and many other drugs could thus be curtailed to the great benefit of the health throughout our country.

When surgery is indicated—and certainly there are times when it is—the biorhythms of the patient and the surgeon should be taken into account. Elective surgery should not be undertaken at a time of the full moon because of the increased bleeding associated with that particular cosmic event. Also, it seems extremely wise that three independent opinions be obtained before patients agree to undergo elective surgery. When there is any doubt on the part of one of these physicians, then faith healing or spiritual healing, coupled with biogenic training would seem to be a much more reasonable alternative.

In addition, spiritual healing should be available as an integral part of the healing process, even in conjunction with the traditional medical and surgical approaches. The only harm in spiritual healing and some of these alternative methods will come if they remain split from the establishment. If they can be integrated and used as useful humanistic adjuncts, there is little question that tremendous benefit from a psychological, physiological and ulimately physical point of view will ensue. Ultimately we are talking about a blending integration and synchrony of *will* and *imagination*. When the average individual is capable of inherent knowledge that these two major mental forces are working in conjunction with the highest spiritual goals of the individual, then true health can obviously flow through.

So much for the medical implications of this book. But it has implications over a much wider field.

No one with intellectual integrity can any longer ignore or deride *all* of the strange phenomena described. Maybe some of them, in the light of further knowledge, will be found to have been misinterpreted; some may be found to have been based on observations which turn out to have been insufficiently rigorous. But no matter how ruthless and passionate the effort to discredit the work, there will remain a substantial residue of unchallengeable fact which does not fit into the current world-picture accepted by orthodoxy. *This is the challenge of the book.* Will scientists and others respond worthily? Can scientists look *objectively* and *scientifically* at the evidence?

APPENDICES

APPENDIX A
American Healers Association

During the past ten years as the doctors and scientists carried out the research on which this book is based, it was necessary to travel to many foreign countries at considerable expense in time and personal funds, since donations were meager for such "far-out" research. Often the studies were frustrating because of the language differences and because the healers had little if any educational background which would permit them to describe what they thought was going on in their interaction with patients.

However such foreign travel and research was necessary because ten years ago there were very few Americans who had any established records as healers. Moreover, the "academic climate", to put it politely, was not highly conducive to carrying on such research in the U.S.A. Only the most intrepid researcher would dare to accept the ridicule and danger to his professional status by having it become known that he was looking into faith, spirit, magnetic, etheric, or spiritual healing.

Fortunately the pioneering work of those who did do the research in foreign countries is now paying off. Research into the work of the healers has suddenly become "respectable", partially as a result of the rapidly growing dissatisfaction with many aspects of Western medicine, including skyrocketing costs of medical care and the lack of even minimal medical care for much of the world's population; and additionally because of the rapidly expanding insights into the nature of human consciousness and the realization that a very large portion of all illness is triggered initially by inappropriate thoughts and emotions.

Since the first edition of this book, there has been a most gratifying explosion in the concept known now as holistic health and holistic healing. For example, Dr. Norman Shealy helped organize the American Holistic Medical Association. In only three years time the new organization has a membership of hundreds of medical professionals. Many of these doctors are quite open to the role that healers can play in providing better health care for the general public. Also, individual healers, such as Olga Worrall and William Brown, have appeared before audiences which cumulatively have numbered tens of thousands of people. Hence in a few short years, the acceptance or "climate" surrounding the work and the results of the healers here in America has improved more than in all of the preceding decades.

At the time the first edition of this book appeared, it was hoped that plans then in formation could be executed and result in establishing a much-needed organization—The American Healers Association. For various reasons those specific plans did not come to fruition. The need for and the potential benefits of such a group are now even much greater than they were then.

In the hope that individual healers and those interested in the cause of healing will now come forth and do what is necessary to make the American Healers Association a reality, the following statement of objectives (originally conceived by Prof. Douglas Dean and his friends) can serve as a starting point for a statement of objectives for such an organization.

1. **To assemble a referral list of CERTIFIED healers who will be available to work with doctors, psychiatrists and the clergy.**

2. **To upgrade the status and ability of "natural" and "spiritual" healers.**

3. **To establish standards and to screen and certify healers.**

4. **To provide training courses for unorthodox healers.**

5. **To educate the public to know that healers are available, worthy and helpful.**

6. **To work on reducing the risk of legal harassment of healers through the gradual revision of laws.**

7. **To sponsor, coordinate and publicize scientific research into healing.**

8. **To seek the right of patients in hospitals to call in a healer when the patient wishes to supplement what he is receiving from traditional medical practice.**

It is obvious that with such objectives, a healers organization could rapidly qualify as a government-approved tax-free foundation. With the rapidly exploding interest that now exists in the cause of holistic health and healing, and the growing realization of the effectiveness of the healing services rendered by devoted healers, substantial grants should be obtainable for furthering the activities and research of such a healers organization.

APPENDIX B

The Role Of "Discarnate Entities" In Healing

George W. Meek

If you have had no interest in the psychic, occult, or metaphysical fields, it is likely that your encounter with "Dr. Fritz" in Chapter 3, as well as "Dr. Lang", the "guides", "protectors", or "controls" of the other healers in Chapter 2, served as your first contact with discarnate entities. If so, you cannot be blamed for muttering, "Preposterous! This is just a figment of the imagination. This is obviously a crutch the healer uses for impressing his patient or for fitting his actions into his own belief system."

Let it be said that more than twenty psychiatrists, clinical psychologists, medical doctors, parapsychologists, psychical researchers and scientists who have been associated in the research reported in part in this volume are a long way from understanding whether the view of the healer or that of the skeptic is correct.

A careful reading of the Old and New Testaments shows that the idea of "spirits" was already established 2,000 to 4,000 years ago. (*See* Bibliography C) There is some evidence that in the early versions of the New Testament there were perhaps even more such references. It is also a possibility that much of man's inspired writings down over the centuries in both East and West may have come from so-called "spirit" sources.

Only in the past few years have parapsychologists and psychiatrists begun to take a really serious look at the whole question of some part of man surviving death of the physical body—and the question of whether or not the surviving part fits the role which spiritualists have for one hundred years ascribed to "discarnate entities". One such study was that of psychiatrist Robert Laidlaw, M.D. (reported in Chapter 2) in which an "interview" was had with "Dr. Lang", the discarnate medical doctor purportedly working through the consciousness of George Chapman, British healer.

At the present time no branch of science has even the slightest basis for coming to grips with this question—a question which puts the whole concept of discarnate entities in its true perspective.

In what role, if any, did a deceased German Dr. Fritz assist an *uneducated* Brazilian named Arigó in making medical diagnosis *instantaneously* with at least the same accuracy as did a team of American M.D.'s using sophisticated diagnostic equipment; in performing "operations", including physical removal of a cataract in 30 seconds with a rusty knife and resulting in no pain to the patient; in prescribing a great variety of known and unknown remedies with good results; and in treating up to 300 patients a day during the few hours of each day taken from his part-time jobs as a church janitor and civil servant?

In the absence of any really sound scientific data—and almost no agreement among scientists as to how such a research program should be devised—we might in the meantime consider what some of the discarnate entities themselves are supposed to have said in answer to this baffling question.

In our studies of altered states of consciousness we have searched around the world for sensitives or mediums who can go into such a deep state of "trance" that for all practical purposes their conscious mind seems to be either "turned off completely" or to have temporarily left the body. In this state, a totally different consciousness or personality appears to take over and it will oblige the researcher by indulging in questions and answers.

Because of their willingness to help enlighten mankind, we have asked some of these "mediums" or "sensitives" and their discarnate helpers to enlighten us and the readers of this volume by giving *their* thoughts on the reality of discarnate entities and their role in helping the Philippine, Brazilian and English healers. For whatever value such replies may have, we share them with the reader.

The first question-and-answer session was conducted in Florida in February, 1975, when Henry A. Mandel, an experienced healer (*See* Chapter 2) had available the services of Sarah Gran. Mrs. Gran, herself a healer, is a deep-trance medium who occasionally works with Mr. Mandel, while the latter seems to act as a "battery" or supplementary source of power to increase Mrs. Gran's receptivity. The editor supplied Mr. Mandel with a set of six questions. Mrs. Gran went into trance and the transcription of the resulting tape recording is presented here. (This material is verbatim except for a few changes in sentence structure or terminology which will help to clarify the intent. Italicized portions result from particular emphasis in the voices recorded on the tape from which this transcription was prepared.)

MANDEL—George Meek writes that he is working with a team of medical doctors, psychiatrists, scientists, and psychologists who are preparing a book on the work of healers in the U.S.A., England, Brazil, and the Philippines. They intend to have a chapter, most of which will be written by discarnate entities who serve as guides, helpers, or controls to the healers. It is their intention to use in this book answers such as Dr. Bernard, Elihu, or others care to make to these questions. They will appreciate any information you can give on these questions and they ask for permission to quote your answers.

Question 1—To what extent do healers in U.S.A., the Philippines, Brazil, England, and elsewhere obtain their diagnostic and treatment capabilities as a result of help from entities on your plane?

Answer—I am Barnard. There are innumerable teams of intelligent and energy-expressing beings on the highest levels of spirit who are interested in the betterment of conditions on the plane of earth. They work together much as I do with teams of from five to twenty of such entities trying to perfect every possible means of alleviating pain and suffering of entities who are still in the physical existence. These teams go into your hospitals to observe operating techniques. They are interested in such work so as to help perfect your techniques and implement tools, instruments, and training for those who are the operation teams. These are perfected here in the spirit level of existence and given to those on your plane who are devoting their lives to this work, a little at a time in a way you call "intuition" or "inspiration". There are many things which we bring through in this line which make it much easier and on a much more efficient scale than existed in any time in the past, except perhaps in the far past when there was a tremendous knowledge of brain surgery among ancient Egyptians.

There are those who have been family physicians, general practitioners or specialists in the realm of child medical care, or gerontology, or obstetrics, or urology, etc. Many times in hospitals there are those surgeons who are willing to be guided and many times those of us who are present as observers and who are very knowledgeable will assist in various difficult cases by aiding the operating instruments and giving inspiration.

I myself am interested in general practice, especially as related to energy fields of man. We have found that in the lower abdomen there is a center [Ed: Chakra, *See* Chapter 14] which, when adversely affected by many factors, will cause energy imbalances which then outpicture in the aura or the general health energy field in and around the person. This is a great indication of trouble within and may be traced by the general wave lengths and the shortness and deficiency in either portion of this organ which is, as called by physicians, the spleen or pancreas, not only affecting the liver but also affecting the general energy output to all the lower sections of the body. This is something for the future.

Now there are many other entities who like to work in different ways and work according to the intelligence of the patient, suiting their treatment to what the patient can understand and accept, and this is the reason for the many, many different manifestations through various channels of expression. I myself work through the hands of my instrument, Dr. Mandel, and also by telling him ways he understands [Ed: clairaudiently] how to deal with various cases. He has been most successful and I in cooperation with him very often bring in my associates. I have various ones, including, Dr. White, Dr. Williamson, Dr. Lorraine Mandel, Dr. Evans, and Dr. Aaron Silver. At times, one or two or three or four of us participate in working on any one case. Your research and cooperation, your contacting us across the boundaries or dimensions is more productive of results at this time because of the difference in thinking and the growing knowledge of energy fields which is now manifest on earth as compared to the slower more negative reactions of the past. Does that answer the question?

Question 2—Sometimes exceptionally effective healers, for example, the American healer Edgar Cayce and some of today's good healers in England, claim they are getting NO help from discarnate entities. Are they in error in their opinion?

Answer—No, I would say they are not totally in error because in this area, through long training, the spirit within a healer is able to disassociate itself from the healer's body and go forward into the spiritual dimension and look at the physical body from within or without, seeing with the "eyes" which are the "seeing eyes"—in the old times such people were called "seers". This is a manifestation of what is known among psychics as X-ray vision. It comes to those who are usually able to lift themselves in a consciousness and concentrate upon that which they desire to see and if, as in Cayce's instance, the "spirit" which was Cayce (who was many other expressions of spirit and physical being in past centuries) was able to "see" (project himself) and become aware of what was inside the human body. We also know that there are those enlightened individuals who are aware that the universe is teeming with expressions of energy and, by opening themselves completely as a channel, they may pull in the cosmic energy from the greater sources and allow it to flow through their hands to help and to heal distress in human bodies.

This has been taught in various places throughout history. It can be worked in cooperation with those on higher spiritual planes or it may be done strictly as an activity of the spirit within the healer, that which is his real, his true self. Usually these individuals have had a long history of being able to work with higher, finer energies. We feel that each person should go his own way. Working with a human healer as I do (and many others I know) gives the healer a *deeper experience* and a *wider range of knowledge* than if he depends entirely upon his own ability to travel out from his body to gain the knowledge needed at a distance or to open himself to the cosmic influence. Also, we are delighted to have the privilege of being of service to persons serving as healers. This is our life. We *must* be of service. In becoming the "light" ourselves, we must serve the light. Remember also that we continue to do pioneering research and thus we are able to give many new ideas and inspiration to the healer we work through.

Question 3— What determines which particular entity will work with a particular healer—or, put in another way—How did the former German Dr. Fritz and his associates happen to work with

a poorly educated Brazilian healer, Arigó, or Dr. Lang with Geoge Chapman, or you with your healer?

Answer—First of all, may I remark that appearances on the plane of physical phenomena are often deceitful. Who knows and who can judge what is in the background of a person who is able to be a channel for healing? Who knows how wide his outreach is? In our humble opinion, most lasting associations for healing between those who work from dimensions of spirit and entities incarnate with those upon the physical plane are determined by *compatibility of the radiations* or the vibrations on the spiritual plane and on the physical. Not only must the body be in tune with the common vibration but the emanations must be able to be attuned to combined power.

In other words, it is the same thing as transfusions of blood. One does not put just *any* kind of blood into a patient's veins during transfusions, because of the incompatibility of many types which cannot meld together to become a working influence in the body. Therefore, the vibrations of the physician-in-spirit and the healer-in-the-physical must be compatible and they must be able to put together their vibrations in order to maintain a very high frequency of radiation. These are matters of individual selection. Usually those who desire to become healers must be willing to give up many old ideas and be able to enter into an *intellectual concentration* and a *devotion* and *dedication*.

As the time goes by and they continue to work, their efforts will attract one whose vibrations are similar and in harmony. The outward appearance of many, as I said, is judged by standards on the material plane. If you say a man is poor or not educated, this is the appearance on the physical plane. Those of us in spirit see what is the state of health of the being within his or her body, *notwithstanding* all physical conditions, *notwithstanding* any outward appearance or lack. The healing vibrations which enable us to work with an entity are *not* affected by lack of education or lack of anything in the line as judged on the material plane! Many times the entity had some experience in previous lifetimes which has specially fitted him and raised his spiritual vibration to the point of power which can be used by the team of doctors or the one doctor-in-spirit who desires to use him as the channel.

Question 4—**When a person wants to serve his fellowmen as a healer, what steps can he take to make himself a more suitable channel of guidance from a discarnate entity?**

Answer—There are various teachings which have been given through selected channels over the centuries which express it thus: A dedication of ideals, a feeling of compassion, and a desire to reach out to touch those who are in need of healing. There must be a great ability to shut out from oneself all influences which would interfere with the objective. These are characteristics or qualities for which we look in an individual. The next thing is to guide if possible, or throw into his path, some learning or to let him learn by experience if he accepts the fact that he is a healer.

There are various ways and levels of understanding in healing just as there are in all areas of intellectual pursuit or spiritual pursuits or scientific pursuits. There must be some understanding and we will lead him gently to the understanding.

Perhaps the healer does not know why his hands placed on a certain position on a patient will cause a disease to disappear or help an organ to return to utmost efficiency or the desired result of any kind to be effected, but as time goes on, the dedication and the deep desire to be of service will lead to understanding. As he attunes himself, he is more able to find out, to learn, and to accomplish those things which make him a better healer as his understanding progresses. In case of dire need and where there is great compassion in the heart of the healer, many healing "presences" will work through his hands regardless of whether he knows of their identity or not! We refer to the great channel of healing called Harry Edwards. He has a deep compassion for human suffering. He has a need for help from those who are able to assist him and he often exclaims, "Oh, healing presences, manifest through my hands" and he uses those who are able to help, *regardless of whether he has any particular healing presence known to him by name*. This happens with many healers when they do not take the time to pursue the knowledge or to inquire deep within their own consciousness as to where the healing ability comes from. Many just "know", in their subtle way of knowing, that something happens when the hands are laid on someone and so they do it because they cannot bear to feel that another person, another human being, is in pain and they can help. They can alleviate the pain, they can remove the cause. Is this the answer you seek?

Question 5—**Whatever you answer is perfectly all right with me! It was George who asked the question. Now, do you work with more than this healing channel here on the earth plane?**

Answer—On this plane of existence I do not work with more than this channel, except in a very special case which is going on at this time and on which I will not elaborate. I have worked with Dr. Mandel from the very beginning and before that when we were preparing him for his career in healing.

My personal work through a channel is done through Dr. Henry Mandel. I also was his personal physician when he was a child and as he grew into manhood, as he went through the rigors of life and felt the battle of life, I helped to keep his physical body in condition to meet the work that he needed to do and then when he was able to turn his entire attention to being an expression of the compassion that he is, I felt that I needed no other channel. However, as I have said, I, too, work as a team member or collaborator in other cases.

Question 6—**It has been observed that occasionally Philippine healers seem to produce blood and tissue when working on foreign patients and also produce so-called witchcraft items, such as tobacco leaves, broken glass, etc. when working on** native patients. Can you tell if this is an apport or materialization phenomenon and, if so, is this carried out by entities on your sphere of evolution or on the level of nature spirits or elementals?

Answer—This poses a question which extends into the spiritual nature of the patient. If a patient's mind is not in condition to receive the changing of his vibration and the restoration of his balance of energies, sometimes physicians who work with healers will manifest such materializations in order to help the patient in very serious cases to accept the idea that *something* had been done so there will be positive results. Emanating from the "faith", as you might call it, or acceptance, the body of the patient will accept that much has been done; that the operation has been accomplished. Therefore their minds accept that the healing *is* done as an offset to the brain-washing teaching of so many in civilized countries to the effect that nothing can be done without the knowledge that healing is a *physical* thing!

Now, in the evidence produced by these healers on the native patient, the native mind is conditioned to accept that certain things will cause certain ailments. Therefore the doctors will oblige and give their faith a basis in fact by materializing certain things which they accept the fact of and know that once these are removed the body is healed. It is as simple as that. Just as the ones who work in this area are intent upon the healing and they will work in accordance with the understanding of the patient.

In *my* level of understanding and of the ones with whom I work, we do not work in such a manner. We use applications of energy to melt, to tear down, old calcium deposits, to change the vibrations of the organ to manifest it into perfection, to remove the poisons that the body is continually creating under abnormal conditions, and replace it with good, positive cell-building vibrations, going back to the premise that each cell is an electrical unit which has its own energy pattern and works with other cells so that together they produce that certain amount of energy the body needs to be maintained in perfect harmony. Once this energy pattern is disturbed and has become unbalanced, then there is trouble, there is illness, there is disease. This may come by continual negative suggestions from the rational mind which the sub-conscious mind seizes on and uses in ways which cause distorted energy fields. It may result from suggestions from others, such as *doctors,* who have unthinkingly suggested negative results to patients who have undergone healing, and immediately outpictures, because the subconscious of the patient is not conditioned to continually accept the positive and reject the negative suggestions. All of these factors come into play. We would like to discuss with you at some other time the greater implications of the energy fields of man and their relationship and inter-relationship with all other energies. It would perhaps prove interesting to you.

Mandel—This is all of the questions George had but he says if

you want to talk in general terms of your own, or if Elihu wants to say something, or Lorraine, or anyone else, this is the time to let us hear from you.

Dr. Barnard—We will state the hypothesis that all states of being are *expressions of energy*. We have said in many sessions here through this channel that many speakers have referred to "the one power". We have postulated that each body is an intricate expression of energies of various levels, so we are going forward into the future working along this line of research so that when the equipment, you might say the sensors, or the flow of energy is interrupted or malfunctions occur in the circuits of the human system for any reason whatsoever, the energy fields become imbalanced and therefore generate certain conditions of abnormality. This is what we work with. We do not go in and look at the patient and say, "Oh, yes, he has got chickenpox—he has got cirrhosis of the liver," and give him a long list of stuff to do. But we do believe that patient participation in his own care is *very necessary* to give the patient something to help his own condition. This means programming him in a positive manner, as this aids his own ability of regeneration and restructuring. This is the system we are using. We could go into reams of pages of discussion on this as it has been our theme of research for the last five years. We have pioneered in many instances in this type of thing, especially with the giving of information leading to development of certain instruments which measure wave length of the brain, which measure different types of energies and there are still greater things in progress at this time.

Healing is perhaps the greatest of all the fields to which man on earth can dedicate himself inasmuch as it is an expression of the higher energies of compassion and unselfishness. Here on our plane of being, we have those whose hearts and minds are dedicated to the healing of others and altogether it sets up a most positive pattern through which we can work. We condemn no manifestation or type of healing. There are many ways of working from our realm with healers upon earth. Dr. Lang [Ed: *See* Chapter 2] preferred that his instrument be in deep trance and he would take him over completely and work through him, as he was accustomed to do in the lifetime he lived as a very excellent physician. Also, we would say that there are many surgeons who prefer to work through an instrument in trance and their work is done by operating on the etheric body which serves as the connection between the astral and the physical. One of the most gratifying things that this type of healer does is cut down the time needed for recovery from such an operation. For example, in open-heart surgery, as done through one eminent healer channel and his team of surgeons, the recovery time or the outpicturing from the etheric into the physical of the benefits of the operation takes only three days. In this period the body must be very still in order that the energy patterns may emanate from the etheric through the physical and create the physical conditions desired. This is certainly a great deal less time than your conventional open-heart operation would take to manifest completely in recovery and healing of the body. Any physical surgery is a great shock to the system and therefore the energy fields of the patient take a long time to be regenerated in complete balance and some never do.

Healers are more effective when working in trance. There is a great need for more trance channels for healing. A being such as I needs to find a healer who is dedicated and whose vibration is in perfect accord. It is very difficult to work through a channel who is completely conscious and whose rational mind may at any time reject the instructions or the collaboration offered by the physician-in-spirit.

There is a lack of deep trance channels today due to the fact that with the higher, finer atmosphere in which the age of the air and the age of energy is now manifesting on earth, it is much easier for channels to work in complete consciousness—*but not in this field.* As I said, it is a thing of matching energies, matching emanations, of the human channel being able to quiet his conscious mind, and let the physician-in-spirit feed him the needed information. The physician-in-spirit is a specialist in his field, is highly educated in his field, and is deeply engaged in research in his field, whereas the human instrument has only a great desire and the ability to open himself to guidance and a great and deep compassion for those who are suffering whom he is able to help.

Now, the limitations of this: Only so many can be helped in this manner through any one channel. There must be a taking care of the healer's own body. There must not be the complete depletion of energy of the human channel or healer who many times throws all of his own energy into the healing. This he should not do, because it is better to use the cosmic energy flowing through the spirit physician. This way the channel does not become depleted.

If the healing channel does become depleted, the physician-in-spirit must take time and effort to again build up the healer's body before the healer can again be of maximum service.

Moreover, it is necessary that the healer wash his hands frequently and that he take a shower with soap at the end of the day. Otherwise there is a build-up of the effluvium which has come from the body of each patient.

Thus there are certain rules to be followed in healing as in any other pursuit, certain laws which are in effect and which work impartially and impersonally; and obedience to these laws by both physician-in-spirit and healers-in-the-physical will make for a much better team. Would you like to make any comments on that, Dr. Henry?

Mandel—No, it is your day. George wants YOUR dialogue in this book. Whoever wants to speak is most welcome.

Elihu—I am Elihu. [Ed: An elevated intelligence who was Dr. Barnard's spiritual guide or teacher when Dr. Barnard was a physician in New England about 100 years ago. Elihu now serves as Mandel's spiritual teacher.] I merely want to say that from the plane of wisdom on which I work, we see the reasonably complete picture and know that all energies emanate from *one* source, that all energies are an expression of intelligence plus free will. This is true whether energy works as a being without a body or works through those who have physical form. Many times as I watch the healing work in this center, I frequently see Bernard give way to another who has more knowledge of a particular condition. This way the energies become increased and the physician-in-spirit and the healer become more efficient and open a better expression for the compassion they are.

Dr. Barnard: It is a waste of time for a patient to go to a healer and continuously question the healer's ability. This is a tearing-down of the energy fields built for his benefit. The patient will promptly return to his old suffering.

Patients who cannot receive should stay away and allow the healer and the physician-in-spirit to collaborate on those who *will* receive. An educated man has much false ego. The meek and lowly, and all those willing to receive healing will be benefitted—and this is as it should be. *Love,* the great healer, *cannot flow where there is controversy.*

The energy that I am—and all other healers, poets, musicians, scientists, engineers, philosophers, teachers, etc, just name them—flows as intelligence. Each of us seeks to find his own level. That is the purpose of existence—to accomplish on one plane or another, one vibration or another—the working out of the intelligence or the energy that we are.

Lorraine - [Ed: Henry Mandel's daughter who "died" many years ago and who in her plane of being has become a medical specialist.] I also work in the area of experiment and research, specifically I am involved in changing certain conditions through the correction of the energy fields as related to the brain and nervous system of the newborn child. This is a field of great interest because much can be done for the body when it is still in the formative state, very soon after birth. Frankly, I would like to get those children even before they come into physical manifestation outside the womb, but we can do very much with them by replacement and rebalancing of their energy fields as they are affected by the body chemistry of the mother, for one thing, and also certain other imbalances due to conditions before birth. I will not say too much about it because we are still working on this, but we feel that with the methods we are pioneering at this time, fifty percent of babies who are diagnosed as having brain damage could be completely normal in the future.

Dr. Barnard—Henry, this is the extent of our discourse. We feel that it has been a wonderful opportunity to express ourselves and to answer these questions for friend George. We are delighted to have been of service.   *   *   *

Communications between planes of existence will probably not receive much credence until the trance medium is replaced by some non-human electronic marvel of communication equipment. (Thomas

A. Edison is one of many who endeavored to develop such equipment, as was reported in my previous book, *From Enigma to Science*. Research on the development of such equipment is underway in at least two countries.) The next communication to be reported resulted from work in one such research laboratory where the transmission is accomplished by the use of a superb deep trance medium *in combination* with sophisticated electronic gear, which, although hardly making a start at eliminating the trance medium, has been found of use in boosting the energy level of the medium.

Paul—[An electronic engineer and inventor of certain portions of the equipment being tested.] Do you have one or more medical doctors there on your plane today who would be interested in contributing to a new and comprehensive handbook which George and his fellow researchers are writing on the subject of paranormal healing? Your comments would be a valuable addition to their work.

Dr. Holmes—[Ed: At one time a professor at Swarthmore.] Yes, we will arrange for one of our medical doctors to speak to you, although this type of communication is new to him.

Dr. Defoe—I am Defoe.

Paul—Dr. Defoe, formerly of Canada and the Dionne quintuplet fame?

Dr. D.—Yes. This is a new experience for me. I have not participated in such a communication channel as this. What would you like to know from me? You said a book?

George—Yes, in the last several years I have been cooperating with a group of scientists from the fields of medicine, surgery, psychology, physics, chemistry, parapsychology, and biology. We have now teamed up to prepare a book on the subject of paranormal healing. One of the problems that we had to face is the question of how much help are the healers in various countries getting from your plane of existence. To be specific, one of our questions in this area is: Could you tell us whether or not you or any of your associates work with healers on this plane of existence in matters of diagnosing illness and/or treating the illness of a patient who comes to a healer?

Dr. D.—Yes, Holmes is correct. This is my province. Many of us work together in research in the fields of surgery techniques, particularly as relates to obstetrics, which is my field. One of our functions is to select individuals on your plane who possess harmonious vibrations with which we can work. Some of us work only through entranced individuals. [Ed : As in the case of Rev. William Brown (Chapter 2) George Chapman, also in that chapter, and Arigó in Chapter 3.] One of my associates is McKenzie, a doctor in the time of Queen Victoria. He and several other surgeons have a healer through whom they perform many intricate operations on the etheric body. They also gave your surgeons the information, the intuition, if you want to call it that, which led to the open-heart techniques.

When McKenzie and his associates work through their entranced healer, they work on what we call the "light body", the "etheric mold", and *not* on the physical shape. This etheric body may be molded by the mind, by the consciousness of the spirit which dwells within both the healer and the patient. Then the physical is shaped by the etheric back into a condition of health.

It is desirable for the patient to rest for a few days after such work to allow the physical body to change. Just think what a big help this is to the patient who does not have to undergo the shock of anaesthesia, the scalpol and the drugs. The putting of drugs indiscriminately into the physical body without tailoring the dosage to the chemistry of the individual, is one of the horrible conditions of what you call modern medicine. Every internist knows that taking medicines internally results in chemical change in the body. Now, if you do not know precisely the chemistry of the body itself, and who does, then how can you be sure that the results are going to be favorable in the long range?

We are familiar with what you have been studying in the Philippines. There are many among us who are experimenting with such healers, in a certain manner. Now we have to point out that the whole method of thinking and acceptance in that area is very different from Occidental thinking. It does not tend to be Oriental, yet it is not truly Western. If it is believed that spirits, per se, are very active, then the healer and patient can more readily accept the healing. . . . So there is a necessity to enlist help on the lower planes to deal with these lower consciousnesses.

In this connection, you are knowledgeable enough to know there are many forces in nature, especially under the primitive conditions which exist in parts of the Philippines. There are many types of energies at work in such healing. Each healer is limited to such energies as he or she can use.

Often there are several of us in attendance at one of the Philippine healing centers and we laugh to see what the "elementals" manifest in some of these "operations". [Ed: Reference here is to the action of a very elementary life form being able to cause some material object—tobacco leaves, fish, broken glass, nails, coconut husk, lace panties, etc.—to suddenly appear, seemingly from nowhere. *See* Chapters 6 and 7.] "Elemental" forces sometimes go a little bit farther in their idea of what should be done to instill faith in a patient than healers in the Western world would do!

Paul—Are you saying the "elementals" are responsible for some of these phenomena?

Dr. D.—Yes, indeed.

Paul—So-called nature-spirits?

Dr. D—Yes, yes, in many cases they do the actual manifestation under the supervision of higher level intelligences carrying out the treatment or healing. In the Western world, of course, it does not work that way. In different areas of the world, we tailor our assistance to the level of understanding of the healers and the patients. Where there is a religious orientation, then the healers are encouraged to call upon the spirit helpers in the name of Jesus Christ or the Blessed Mother, whatever is acceptable to the consciousness of the patient and the healer. It makes no difference if they call on Isis or the Virgin Mary. The important thing is to see that the desired healing is accomplished.

In my life, I was one who went to the Blessed Mother for help. How do you think I kept those five frail premature babies alive, with no instruments, no help, no nothing—till we could get word out of what happened?

They lived because I was a channel of healing to them. . . .

Today I still work to save little lives, to help mothers who are in trouble. Much of our trouble is with mothers continually poisoning their bodies and those of their unborn babies by cigarette smoking. . . .

Many of us do not work with just one channel. There is a great healer in England who said, "All healing presences come manifest through me to help get this poor one well." Oh, how happy we are when someone says this to us!

We do not seek fame for ourselves. We do not care if men know what we individually do. All a person needs is the courage to seek spiritual healing and say, "Come, healing presences, manifest the healing flow through me. I'll be the channel." This is very, very good.

Paul—George, perhaps Dr. Defoe can check out the validity of that picture you recently took which apparently shows an energy beam passing a Filipino healer's hand enroute to the patient's eyes. Neither you nor the many photographic experts you have consulted have been able to explain it away as a light leak, a manufacturing error, processing error or an electrostatic discharge.

Dr. D.—I can only report that all healing is done by some manifestation of energy. You have been told that there are many of us who supervise the work of the healers and whatever is necessary to be done by the lower forms of intelligence.

You have been fortunate to capture such an energy manifestation because many times the cameras as we know them, do not pick this up. This energy comes from up and over. It comes directly from what we call healing presences.

Now you cannot prove this with paper and pencil and you cannot test it in a machine but for just a brief instant your film caught the picture of energies that were going on in this operation. The healing intelligences manifest these as pure energy in the hands of the healers or beam these directly into the area needing help.

So if you will accept your photograph for what it seems to be, it *is that*. [Ed: The final two words were emphasized.]

George—Thank you, Dr. Defoe. We thank you and your associates for making this information available to us this afternoon.

Dr. D.—We have many others who will be glad to talk and give you information. Of course, *we know there will not be acceptance of these communications among the great masses.* Even the Master had to speak in stories to illustrate what he wanted to teach. But to those who *knew,* he spoke a different language.

So it is today. We must have doctors, hospitals, improved medical-operation-laboratory techniques. All these are necessary for how else will people find health when they have no faith in anything else? Their minds are solely on the conscious level of the material world. So the many thousands of intelligences like me do what we can to help increase knowledge and to work through those healers who can accept our services.

Geo.—Thank you, Dr. Defoe. We will explore these matters further in another session.

Observations

What do these communications *prove* about the existence of discarnate entities? Nothing! Proof of the reality of the "many mansions" which the Nazarene said were in his "Father's house" is not yet available in a way that materialistic Western Science considers valid.

In the meantime we do point out that:

■ There is excellent correlation between the content of the interviews just presented. (Lack of space prevents the use of four additional transmissions from different sources, of equal quality and almost identical content.)

■ The material presented here correlates well with hundreds of books written on the subject of discarnate entities in England, France, Brazil, and the U.S.A. over the past century.

■ This material correlates well with the experiences and statements of many of the most accomplished healers now working in many nations.

■ There is no motivation for fraud on the part of the communication channels whose transmissions have been quoted here in some detail.

■ Chapter 19 shows that we can begin to accommodate the discarnate entity concept into the theoretical framework now being constructed to cover all facets of paranormal healing and psychic phenomena. (The editor takes the position that no "theory of paranormal healing" will be of lasting value if it cannot include some basis for accommodating the thousands of years of experiences which mankind has had with the "spirits". In this connection let us hasten to say that the favorite "explanation" of the psychologists that this is just an example of the human mind's ability to fantasize, is no explanation at all!)

Perhaps the only sensible and truly scientific attitude to adopt with respect to this subject until there is a further breakthrough—such as strictly instrumental electronic communication capability—is that suggested by Sir Francis Bacon:

> Read, not to contradict and refute . . .
> nor to believe and take for granted . . .
> nor to find talk and discourse,
> but to weigh and consider.

APPENDIX C

(Presenting the concluding portion of Chapter 7
by Alfred Stelter)

The Basis for the Psychoenergetic Phenomena

Any serious researcher of the Filipino healing scene very early becomes aware that water seems to play a key role in the work of many healers. Sometimes they will merely have an open container adjacent to the patient. Sometimes they will sprinkle the water on the patient. Sometimes they will first dip cotton into the water before pressing it onto the patient's body. A magician leaning to the idea that *all* actions must be considered in their deceptive role, is prone to say, "Ah, ha! That is part of his trickery in producing the phony blood."

Those of us who have researched this matter in depth are convinced that there is far more to the explanation than that. At one level it may have a psychiatric or psychological function. Since the earliest times, water has played a part in religious ceremonies in many parts of the world. Baptism has been a part of the Christian rite for two thousand years. The Bible contains numerous references to water and its relation to "spirit". [Ed.: As we saw in Chapter 19, the concept of "spirit" as an active part of consciousness, begins to play an important role in our efforts to theorize on the underlying processes in paranormal healing.]

The role of water in the work of the Filipino healer also deserves to be examined from the energetic standpoint. The human body is more than 60% water by weight. The brain of the healer and the brain of the patient are mostly water—at least 80% by weight! Hydrogen and oxygen certainly play crucial roles in all bodily processes. Dr. Lyall Watson, author of Chapter 20, discussing in his book, *Supernature*[1] key role of water in all living organisms, says, in part:

> Water is sensitive to extremely delicate influences and is capable of adapting itself to the most varying circumstances to a degree attained by no other liquid. Perhaps it is even by means of water and the aqueous system that the external forces are able to react on living organisms. . . .
>
> Every high school student knows that water is H_2O, a chemical compound of two simple elements. And yet scien-

tific journals are full of articles arguing the merits of various theories on the structure of water — and we still do not understand exactly how it works. . . .

The clue to some of water's strange behavior lies with the hydrogen atom, which has only one electron to share with any other atom with which it combines. When it joins with oxygen to form molecules of water, each hydrogen atom is balanced between two oxygen atoms in what is called the "hydrogen bond" but having only one electron to offer, the hydrogen atom can be attached firmly on only one side, so the bond is a weak one. Its strength is ten per cent of that of most ordinary chemical bonds, so for water to exist at all, there have to be lots of bonds to hold it together. Liquid water is so intricately laced that it is almost a continuous structure, and one worker has gone so far as to describe a glass of water as a single molecule. . . .

So water is tremendously flexible. The tenuous links between its atoms make it very fragile, and little external pressure is necessary to break the bonds and destroy or change its pattern. Biological reactions must occur quickly and take place with very little expenditure of energy, so a trigger substance such as water is the ideal go-between. In fact, all living processes take place in an aqueous medium, and most of the body weight of every living organism (in man the figure is 65%) is made up of water.

No scientist now doubts that water behaves like this inside a plant or an animal.

I think it is reasonable to speculate that water plays a significant role in many materialization and dematerialization phenomena. It may also play a key role in the energetic reaction in the cells of the patient's body with the energies channeled by the healer from his body and from the cosmos.

I have seen, alone and with companions, many hundreds of treatments by many different healers. When I was in the company of some people, we observed extraordinary things, while in the company of others, nothing unusual happened. I am convinced that some people block the action of paranormal events by their mere presence. The healer senses at once their thoughts, emotions and belief systems. He asks some people to come closer and even to participate. In the presence of others who obstruct him, he may exclude them from the treatment room or limit himself to a simple magnetic treatment.

Soviet scientists have confirmed this effect in experiments with the medium Nina Kulagina. Eduard Naumov has stated that emotions have a great bearing on the medium's performance. The energy fields of the observers have a substantial effect on the medium. In tests before sympathetic observers, Mrs. Kulagina produced desired phenomena in five minutes, while in front of a group of skeptics it often took from two to seven hours.

Scientifically we know hardly anything about the nature, condition and energetic basis of mental resonances or other possible extrasensory interactions which are at work in the healer-patient-observer relationship. We are beginning to understand that every person is a highly complicated mental oscillator. The non-physical bodies of the healer, patient and observer all oscillate and can be either in or out of resonance. (*See* Chapter 19, Fig. AA)

There are many analogues in physics. In acoustics some series of notes ring together in harmony, other combinations are not in harmony. Or, one may think of the stacking of waves, where, through interference, new wave patterns can be produced. Such analogues represent resource ideas to help us get a little closer to the paranormal energetic exchanges for which we really possess no scientific "models".

The nature of the energies by which thoughts and emotions are transmitted over long distances are unknown. Over short distances, telepathic transfer might be on an electromagnetic basis but on very long distances the energies involved seem not to follow the known laws in our present space-time concepts. Some scientists are now postulating that velocities faster than light are involved in all of these paranormal and paraphysical phenomena—a concept at variance with our present scientific views.

Perhaps we could begin to make headway in understanding these phenomena—and my research in the Philippines has proven to my satisfaction that they *do* exist—if we knew *what* energy forms are responsible for what we call *consciousness*. Usually the scientists identify our consciousness with the electromagnetic currents in the physical brain, but nothing has been done to date that proves this is correct. It seems far more probable that consciousness involves one or more new kinds of energy with field attributes. Consciousness is being found to have creative power or energetic aspects which can affect so-called physical matter, as shown by the work of Prof. John Taylor with many English children and other scientists working with children in France and Japan.

Biology as a science endeavors to understand phenomena in the animate world in terms of physics and chemistry. It limits itself to the more or less classical physics of this past century. Using this approach, biology has told us very little indeed that throws any light on what is actually going on in the paranormal healing process. Fortunately Soviet scientists have broken out of this limitation and are now looking at biological matters in the light of the latest developments in physics, including plasma physics. In 1944, the biologist Dr. V. S. Gritschenko hypothesized that the fourth state of matter, plasma (after solid, liquid and gas) appeared in biological systems, including the human body.

This was indeed a shocking piece of information because all known processes for generating plasma require very high temperatures or high energies. Yet the human body operates at a low energy level. Nevertheless, the Soviet scientists pursued the studies and concluded that interpenetrating the physical body was another body or matrix, which they named the "bioplasmic" body. This was one of the first scientific endorsements of what mystics and psychics had for centuries described as the etheric or astral body.

The plasma concept may have some relation to the so-called "biological transmutations" which have been the subject of study by French and German scientists. By this term they refer to the fact that plants and other biological systems apparently have the capability of transmutation of elements. By our modern science, it is unthinkable that a plant or a chicken can take in certain elements in its food, and modify the atomic structure of one or more of these elements to create other elements. In the previous century atoms were considered the smallest building stones of matter and to be unsplittable and unchangeable. The discovery of radioactivity by Becquerel in 1896 led to the idea that a few atom types were sufficiently unstable and radioactive that the elements could be transmuted.

Today our nuclear physicists can change every type of atom. They recognize that atoms are not unsplittable and are not compact matter. They have a structure and a nucleus which is circled at a great distance by one or more relatively much smaller negatively charged particles called electrons. The nucleus consists of positively charged protons and neutrons with no charge. A change in the number of protons in the nucleus results in a change to another element, a process called transmutation.

In chemical processes, the atomic nucleus is practically unchanged. The energies are usually in the range of some electron volts. In contrast, the binding energies for the protons and neutrons are much stronger, with binding powers of the magnitude of 8 MEV (million electron volts). As pointed out in the beginning of this chapter this is one of the four basic forces or energies recognized by physics.

Thus, if one wants to implement a change in elements by introducing an additional proton into the core or nucleus, he must use energies which are a million or more times larger than the energies used in chemical reactions. Such energies are achieved with extremely high temperatures such as exist inside fixed stars, for example, our sun. These temperatures are required to create plasma. By comparison, chemical changes can often be accomplished with only the heat of a bunsen burner.

Today's physicists create the conditions for transmutation by artificial acceleration and then shoot the accelerated particle at the atom to be changed. Such processes are exorbitantly expensive and the results are minimal as measured in the weight of matter which is transmuted. At least the scientist has shown that the physics of the previous century was in error in thinking that the elements could not be transmuted. They are also convinced that the alchemists of bygone centuries were in error because they apparently believed in the possibilitiy of transmutation by simple chemical reactions carried through with only modest amounts of energy.

But now we are witnessing research which may show that modern physics has still more to learn about transmutation and that perhaps, just perhaps, the alchemist after all may not have been so foolish in attempting the impossible. German chemist Albrecht von Herzeele of the previous century and the Frenchman Louis C. Kervran of the last decade, have conducted research which seems to indicate that in plants and germinating seeds a transmutation of elements is a daily occurrence.[2] For instance, phosphorus changes to sulphur and sodium to magnesium. We explain this by saying that the *core* of the lightest atom, which is identical with a proton, is built in as the nucleus or core of the phosphorus or sodium atom and changes the element. The biologists say that the energy for the plant comes from normal biochemical action or from sunlight. But such an explanation does not "fit" by a factor of a million to one—if we follow the present theories of physics. The nuclear chemistry formulae are as follows:

$$_{15}^{31}P + {}_1^1H \rightarrow {}_{16}^{32}S \qquad\qquad _{11}^{23}Na + {}_1^1H \rightarrow {}_{12}^{24}Mg$$

Kervran goes further and builds in not only the hydrogen core with its atomic weight of 1, but such relatively large cores as those of oxygen with an atomic weight of 16 and carbon monoxide with an atomic weight of 12.

Magnesium into calcium— $_{12}^{24}Mg + {}_8^{16}O \rightarrow {}_{20}^{40}Ca$

Kervran claims that *this* reaction takes place in the human body

Silicon into calcium— $_{14}^{28}Si + {}_6^{12}C \rightarrow {}_{20}^{40}Ca$

Kervran claims that these reactions are taking place in living systems in weighable amounts, without resulting radioactive side products, without dangerous energy release and without release of ionized rays. If this is true, it would seem that physics and biology laboratories will again have to hang up the sign, "Closed for repairs."

Kervran states that a lowly daisy growing in calcium-poor and silicon-rich soil continuously accomplishes this phenomenon of transmuting silicon to calcium at atmospheric temperatures. To characterize these conditions and processes there is no more appropriate term than the word coined by the Soviet scientists, "bioplasma".

If Kervran's theories are confirmed, another aspect of his theory comes even closer to touching on the subject of paranormal healing. He postulates in the course of epochs of time transmutations have been induced by microorganisms and enzymes at normal ambient temperature. This would produce completely new aspects for geology and mineralogy.

[Ed: While space does not permit development of the rationale, it would seem that the work of Sister Justa Smith who measured the effect of the healing energies of Col. Estebany on enzymes; and the work of Professors Miller and Rinehart in showing that the healing energies from the hands of Olga Worrall, (*see* Chapter 13) loosened the hydrogen bond of water, should be carefully examined for any inter-relation they may bear to the low-termperature transmutation that Kervran is exploring in plants and animals.]

It is obvious that if the statements of Kervran are only partially correct our concepts of the energetic processes of living systems are not only defective and misleading but are guilty of giving us quite a false picture of the nature of living organisms.

In this connection, we may be forced to alter our ideas regarding the efforts of the alchemists and their use of what we considered low-energy reactions. It must be borne in mind that many of the alchemists were very serious students of man's mental and spiritual nature. More and more, our research into the energies involved in paranormal healing are causing us to focus attention on the energies involved in thought and emotion. We can no longer overlook the possibility that the better alchemist was a mentalist or even perhaps a good physical medium.

But perhaps biological transmutation is not the only shock which lies ahead for our scientists. Perhaps many more "holy" or basic concepts of physics will be up for revision. Already in the last century, Albrecht von Herzeele stated that closed systems with sprouting cress seeds were not constant in weight. The German chemist Dr. Rudolph Hauschka[3] claims that during the period 1934-40 he was able to replicate von Herzeele's work, and went on to show a weight gain or loss correlation to the waxing and waning of the moon.

This may cause certain basic conflicts with physics. First is the clash with the conservation of energy and the preservation of the number of baryons as well as of the number of leptons. Toward the end of the eighteenth century, the French chemist Lavoisier postulated the conservation of matter. Einstein at the beginning of this century modified this concept by accepting the reciprocal transformation of matter into energy. Here the factor for the change is given by the square of the speed of light: $E = m.c^2$. This of course means that even the smallest change in the mass of the matter results in an enormous release or consumption of energy. If we consider that Dr. Hauschka measured a mass loss of 3 mg., and if, for conservatism we reduce this to only one mg., then Einstein's formula would indicate that this experiment should have released 20 million Kilocalories or 80×10^9 Joules of energy. This means that in the vicinity of the sprouting cress seeds life would be in danger and the seeds would be carbonized.

Provided the work of von Herzeele and Hauschka turns out to be true and there is a loss or gain of mass in biological processes, either the concept of conservation of energy, including Einstein's formula, does not apply to biological systems, or the enormous quantities of energy should appear in a totally new type of energy which does not react with any of our normal detectors. This last possibility would be not less revolutionary than the first one.

The second large violation of our physical concepts would be that of the conservation of the number of baryons. Protons and neutrons are baryons. If, as von Herzeele and Hauschka are claiming, out of one half gram of sprouting cress seeds in a closed system, three mg. of mass are vanishing or appearing, that seems to indicate that protons or neutrons have "dematerialized" or "materialized", and that is contradictory to the principle of preservation of the number of baryons.

If the experiments of Hauschka and von Herzeele can be duplicated, (I myself cannot decide up to now as I did not yet test it in my own laboratory) I am convinced that the above-cited principles of physics will become shaky. And if we consider the reality of the mediumistic materialization and dematerialization phenomena, we should say this conservation principle is already violated, in the area of paraphysical phenomena, as well as the principle of the conservation of the leptons.

But let us return to the observations of Kervran, which in the last fifteen years are confirmed by some French, Swiss, and Japanese scientists and are contradicted by one English scientist. I myself think that the decision on this point must be determined by very extensive isotopic analysis in biological systems. If the biological transmutations are real, there should be shifts in the proportions of the isotopes of the elements in question. The French theoretical physicist Costa de Beauregard thinks to see a way to explain the Kervran transmutations without violating the fundamental conservation principles of physics. Costa de Beauregard includes the large (great) ubiquitous cosmic energies such as are present in neutrinos, muons, etc. as possibly contributing completely new capabilities to the biological system.

Our basic physical concepts were derived from investigations on inorganic, so-called "dead" matter. Many of our sciences are based equally on the belief that our living systems of plants and animals including man himself, are endowed only with the properties of inorganic matter. Costa de Beauregard says:

> Life is much more clever than we suppose. Life does not only play the game on the atomic and molecular level as we believe, but also on the subatomic level and knows possibilities on this subatomic level that are absolutely unknown to our Western sciences.

Such ideas give new food for thought concerning the understanding of the mediumistic materialization phenomena, and possibly for some forms of psychokinesis. All points of view cited above play a role in this connection. It seems that in living systems something is occurring on the subatomic level which is absolutely new to our physics. It is occurring in an absolutely new way, very smoothly and softly. It collides with our concepts of energy and preservation principles of the number of baryons and leptons.

We are now entering a period of man's history and the evolution of his sciences which indicates that man can never be explained solely by what we think we know about inorganic matter. An immense flood of facts, officially more or less ignored by the sciences, gives indication that the patient's physical body upon which an Arigó in Brazil or a Filipino healer is performing the "magic" of materializing and dematerializing cotton, blood, tissue and organs, simply does not function on the level of what we think we know about our *inorganic* world.

REFERENCES

1. Lyall Watson, *Supernature* (London: Hodder & Stoughton, 1973).
2. C. Louis Kervran, *Prevues En Biologie De Transmutations A Faible Energie* (Paris: Maloine, 1975).

   _____, *Prevues En Geologie Et Physique De Transmutation A Faible Energie* (Paris: Maloine, 1973).

   _____, *Biological Transmutations* (Bristol, England: Crosby Lockswood, 1971).
3. Rudolf Hauschka, *Substanzlehre* (Frankfurt: Vittorio Klostermann, 1972).

   _____, *The Nature Of Substance* (English translation) (London: Vincent Stuart, 1964).

OTHER BACKGROUND BOOKS

Ferman, Richard et al. *The Ferman Lectures on Physics*. Reading, MA.: Addison Wesley, 1963.

Fuller, John G. *Arigó, Surgeon of the Rusty Knife*. New York: Thomas Y. Crowell, 1974.

Komalsi, H. "Sur la Formacion de Sels de Potassium par les Levures et Moissures". In *Rev. De Pathol. Comparee,* Paris, September, 1965.

Konig, L. *Unsichtbare Umwelt*. Munchen: Helmet Moos Verlag, 1975.

Meek, George W. *From Seance to Science*. London: Regency Press, 1973.

Presman, A. S. *Electromagnetic Fields and Life*. New York: Plenum Press, 1970.

Stelter, Alfred. *Psi-Heilung*. Munchen: Scherez-Verlag, 1975.

_____, *Psi-Healing*. New York: Bantam Books, 1976.

Taylor, John. *Superminds*. London: Macmillan, 1975.

SUPPLEMENTARY BIBLIOGRAPHIES

A Paranormal Healing
B Apport and Materialization Phenomena
C Biblical References to Healing, Apport, Materialization and other
Paranormal Phenomena

A
Paranormal Healing

Academy of Parapsychology and Medicine. *Dimensions Of Healing* (a symposium). Los Altos, Calif.: Academy of Parapsychology and Medicine, 1972.

――― *The Varieties Of Healing Experience* (a symposium). Los Altos, Calif.: Academy of Parapsychology and Medicine, 1971.

Bach, Edward. *Heal Thyself.* Rochford, Essex, England: C. W. Daniel Co. 1931

Bailes, Frederick W. *Your Mind Can Heal You.* London: George Allen & Unwin, 1942.

Caillard, Vincent. *A New Conception Of Love.* London: Hider & Co.

Carlson, Rick J. *The Frontiers of Science And Medicine.* London: Wildwood House, 1975.

Chapman, George. *Extraordinary Encounters.* Aylesbury, Bucks. England: Lang Publishing Co., 1973.

Connell, R., and Cummins, Geraldine. *Healing The Mind.* London: Aquarian Publishing Co., 1957.

Cooke, Ivan, ed. *Thy Kingdom Come.* In Arthur Conan Doyle Messages. London: Wright and Brown.

Dresser, Horatio W., ed. *The Quimby Manuscripts.* New Hyde Park, N.Y.: University Books, 1961.

Edwards, Harry. *Agenda To The Understanding And Practice Of Spiritual Healing.* England, Hwaling Pub. Co., 1974.

――― *The Hands Of A Healer.* England: Healing Pub. Co., 1959.

――― *Thirty Years A Spiritual Healer.* London: Herbert Jenkins, 1968.

Elliot, Maurice. *The Psychic Life Of Jesus.* London: Psychic Press, 1938.

Gallert, Mark. *New Light On Therapeutic Energies.* London: James Clark, 1966.

Garrett, Eileen J. *Life Is The Healer.* Philadelphia: Dorrance & Co., 1957.

Gray, Isa. *From Materialization To Healing.* London: Regency Press. 1972.

Hammond, Sally. *We Are All Healers.* London: Turnstone Books, 1973.

Karlins, Marvin, and Andrews, Lewis M. *Biofeedback: Turning on the Power of Your Mind.* New York: J. B. Lippincott, 1972.

Krieger, Dolores. "Therapeutic Touch: The Imprimatur of Nursing". In *American Journal of Nursing,* Vol. 75, No. 5, 1975, pp. 784-787.

Kuhlman, Kathryn. *God Can Do It Again.* Englewood Cliffs, N.J.: Prentice-Hall, 1969.

————— *I Believe In Miracles.*
New York: Pyramid Books, 1969.

Miller, Paul. *Born to Heal: Biography of Harry Edwards.* London: Spiritualist Press, 1948.

Montgomery, Ruth. *Born to Heal.* New York; Coward, McCann & Geoghegan, 1973.

Muramoto, Naboru. *Healing Ourselves.* New York: Swan House, 1973.

Nolen, William A. *Healing, A Doctor in Search of a Miracle.* New York: Random House, 1974.

Podmore, Frank. *From Mesmer to Christian Science.* London: Mehtuen, 1909; New Hyde Park, N.Y.: University Books, 1963.

Ponder, Catherine. *The Dynamic Laws of Healing.* Santa Monica, Calif.: De Vorss & Co., 1966.

————— *The Healing Secret of the Ages.* West Nyac, N.Y.: Parker Publishing Co., 1967.

Ramacharaka, Yogi. *The Science of Psychic Healing.* Chicago: Yogi Publication Society, 1906.

Rosicrucian Fellowship (a student of). *The Mystery of the Ductless Glands.* Oceanside, Calif.: 1940.

Sàmuels, Mike, and Bennett, Hal. *The Well Body Book.* New York: Random House, 1973.

Sanford, Agnes. *The Healing Light.* St. Paul. Minn.: McAlester Park Publishing Co., 1947; Evesham, England: Arthur Jones, 1949.

Sargant, William. *Battle for the Mind.* London: Oan Books, 1959.

Sherman, Harold. *Your Power to Heal.* New York: Harper & Row, 1972.

St. Clair, David. *Psychic Healers.* Garden City, N.Y.: Doubleday, 1974.

Steadman, Alice. *Who's The Matter With Me?* Washington, D.C.: Ex Press, 1966.

Tester, M.H. *The Healing Touch.* London: Barrie & Jenkins, 1970.

Trine, Ralph Waldo. *In Tune With the Universe.* (or *Fullness of Peace Power and Plenty*). London: G. Bell & Sons, 1947.

Trowell, Hugh. *Faith Healing.* London: Institute of Religion and Medicine, 1969.

Turner, Gordon. *An Outline of Spiritual Healing.* London: Max Parrish, 1963; London: Psychic Press, 1970.

Valentine, Tom. *Psychic Surgery.* Chicago: Henry Regnery Co., 1973.

Wilson, Henry B. *The Power to Heal.* Ashville, N.C.: Nazarene Press, 1923.

Worrall, Ambrose A., and Olga N. *The Gift of Healing.* New York: Harper & Row, 1965.

B
Apport and Materialization Phenomena

Crawford, W.J. *Reality of Psychic Phenomena*. London: Watkins, 1916.

———. *Experiments in Psychical Science*. London: Watkins, 1919.

———. *Psychic Structures at the Goligher Circle*. London: Watkins, 1921.

Crookes, William. *Researches in the Phenomena of Spiritualism*. London: James Burns, 1874.

———. *Crookes and the Spirit World*, edited by M. R. Barrington. London: Souvenir Press, 1972.

D'Esperance, E. O. *Shadowland*. London: Redway, 1897.

Dingwall, E. J. *Some Human Oddities*. London: Hoore and Van Tha, 1847, (chapters on D. D. Hoore).

Edwards, Harry. *The Mediumship of Arnold Clare*. London: Rider, 1940

———. *The Mediumship of Jack Webber*. London: Rider, 1940; Guildford, Surrey, England: Healer Publishing Co., 1962.

Fielding, Everard. *Sittings with Eusapia Palladino and Other Studies*. New York: University Books, 1963.

Geley, Gustave. *Clairvoyance and Materialization*. London: Bern, 1927.

Hack, Gwendolyn Kelly. *Modern Psychic Mysteries*. London: Rider, 1929.

———. *Venetian Voices*. London: Rider, 1937.

Holms, A. Campbell. *The Facts of Psychic Science and Philosophy*. London: Kegan Paul, 1925.

Neilsenn Einer. *Solid Proofs of Survival*. London: Spiritualist Press, 1950.

Price, Harry. *Rudi Schneider: A Scientific Examination of His Mediumship*. London: Methuen, 1930.

———. *Stella C: An Account of Some Original Experiments in Psychical Research*. London: Hurst & Blackett, 1925.

Rizzini, Jorge. *Otilia Diogo e a Materlizacion de Uberaba*. San Paulo, Brazil: Editora Cultural Esperita Ltda.

Sudre, Rene. *Traite De Parapsychologie*. Paris: Editions Payot, 1956.

———. *Treatise on Parapsychology*. London: 1961.

C
Biblical References to Paranormal Healing
(and Apport, Materialization, Levitation and other Paranormal Phenomena)

The following index will be of assistance in locating references which include not only the work of Jesus, as it is reported in the four gospels, but also reports of healing work by the apostles, as well as Old Testament references to healing.

	Matthew	Mark	Luke	John
Individual Healings by Jesus				
Nobleman's Son				4:46-54
Unclean Spirit		1:21-28	4:31-37	
Simon's Mother-in-law	8:14-15	1:29-31	4:38-39	
A Leper	8:1-4	1:40-45	5:12-16	
Paralytic carried by four	9:1-8	2:1-12	5:17-26	
Sick man at the pool				5:2-18
Withered hand	12:9-14	3:1-6	6:6-11	
Centurian's Servant	8:5-13		7:1-10	4:46-54
Widow's Son raised			7:11-17	
Demonics(s) at Gadara	8:28-34	5:1-20	8:26-36	
Issue of blood	9:20-22	5:25-34	8:43-48	
Jairus' daughter raised	9:18-26	5:21-43	8:40-56	
Two blind men	9:27-31			
Dumb, devil possessed	9:32-34			
Daughter of Canaan woman	15:21-28	7:24-30		
Deaf, speech impediment		7:32-37		
Blind man of Bethsaida		8:22-26		
Epileptic boy	17:14-21	9:14-29	9:37-42	
Man born blind				9:1-14
Man blind, deaf, possessed	12:22-30		11:14-26	
Woman bent double			13:10-17	
Man with dropsy			14:1-6	
Raising of Lazarus				11:1-44
Ten Lepers			17:11-19	
Blind Bartimaeus	20:29-34	10:46-52	18:35-43	
Malchus' ear			20:50-51	
Multiple Healings by Jesus				
Crowd at Peter's door	8:16-17	1:32-34	4:40-41	
Crowds after leper healed			5:14-16	
Crowd near Capernaum	12:15-21	3:7-12	6:17-19	
Answering John's question	11:2-6		7:18-23	
Before feeding the 5,000	14:13-14		9:11	
At Gennesaret	14:34-36	6:53-55		

Before feeding 4,000	15:29-31		
Crowds beyond the Jordan	19:1-2		
Blind & lame in temple	21:14		
Some sick of Nazareth	13:53-58	6:1-6	
All kinds of sickness	4:23	5:56	
Every sickness & disease	9:35		
All oppressed (Acts 10:38)			
Perfect eternal healing (Rev.21:4)			
Instructions of Jesus	10:7-8	6:7	9:1-2
& promises to Believers		16:14-20	10:8-9
Sending of Twelve	10:1, 7-8	6:7-13	9:1-6
Sending of Seventy			10:1-20
The Lame man from birth		3:1-12	
Paul regains his sight		9:10-22;	22:11-13
Aeneas the paralytic		9:32-35	
Raising of Dorcas		9:36-42	
Crippled man by Lystra		14:8-18	
Girl with a spirit of divination		16:16-18	
Eutychus restored to life		20:7-12	
Paul healed of snake-bite		28:1-6	
Father of Publius healed		28:7-8	

Multiple healings by the Apostles

Many wonders and signs	2:43
Many sick healed in Jerusalem	5:12-16
Stephen performs many miracles	6:8
Philip heals many at Samaria	8:5-13
Paul & Barnabas work signs and wonders	14:3
Paul heals at Ephesus	19:11 12
Sick healed at Melita	28:9

Scriptures of interest in the area of healing

Signs and wonders	Rom. 15:18-19
	II Cor. 12:12; Heb. 2:4
Healing	I Cor. 12:9; 12:28-30
	Rev. 22:2; I Peter 2:24
Annointing	Mark 6:13; James 5:14

Some Old Testament references to healing

None of these diseases	Exodus 15:26
The fiery serpent	Numbers 21:6-9
Schunammite's son raised	II Kings 4:18-37
Naaman healed	II Kings 5:1-14
Hezekiah healed	II Kings 20:1-11
"With His stripes we are healed"	Isaiah 53:5
Some Healing Psalms	Psalm 23, 30, 103

SPIRIT COMMUNICATIONS IN DREAMS

Job	xxxiii-15
Joel	ii-28
Genesis	xxviii-12
Genesis	xxxi-24
Genesis	xxxvii-5
Genesis	xLi-1-8

SPIRIT WRITING

II Chronicles xxi-12
Daniel v-5

INDEPENDENT SPIRIT WRITING

Exodus xxiv-11
Exodus xxxi-18
Exodus xxxii-16
Exodus xxxiv-1
Deuteronomy v-2
Deuteronomy ix-10

TRUMPET SPEAKING

Exodus .... xix 13, 16, 19
Exodus xx-18
Revelations i-10

TRANCE

Genesis xv-12, 17
Daniel viii-18
Daniel x-9
Acts ix-3, 9
Acts xxii-17
II Corinthians xii-2

HEALING—OLD TESTAMENT

Numbers xxi-8, 9
II Kings v-1, 14
I Kings xvii-17, 24
II Kings iv-18, 37

SPIRITUAL GIFTS

I Corinthians xii-1, 12

GIFTS OF HEALING

I Corinthians xii-9, 28

HEALING BY MAGNETIZED ARTICLES

II Kings iv-29
Acts xix-11, 13

INDEPENDENT SPIRIT VOICES

Deuteronomy ix-12, 13
I Samuel iii-3, 9
Ezekiel i-28
Matt. xvii-5
John xii-28, 29, 30
Acts vii-30, 31

SPIRIT LEVITATION

SPIRIT TESTS

DISCIPLES CHARGED TO HEAL THE SICK

BIOGRAPHICAL DATA ON AUTHORS

Gilbert ANDERSON—as Royal Air Force Flying Instructor in World War II sustained spinal injury resulting in loss of use of both legs; after two years of best medical service available given verdict, "Remainder of your life in wheel chair"; Spiritual Healing treatment for ten weeks restored complete mobility; led to investigation of Spiritual Healing in depth; developed abilities as a healer and as a medium of various types, including trance and physical; has served as Spiritual Healer for 29 years; Administrator of National Federation of Spiritual Healers since 1969; Secretary-General of World Federation of Healing which embraces all forms of healing; Principal of five centers for teaching healing.

Forrest J. CIOPPA, M.D.—B.S., Boston College, 1958, M.D., McGill University, 1962; internship at Fairview General Hospital, Cleveland, Ohio; two years as Commanding Officer of 29th Medical Detachment in Goeppingen, Germany; since 1966 engaged in practice of emergency medicine; intensive study of acupuncture in Hong Kong, Seoul, Tokyo, Taiwan and London; directed first symposium on acupuncture at Stanford University in 1972; lectured in U.S. and abroad on acupuncture and gave courses on acupuncture designed specifically for physicians; author of articles dealing with medical hypnotherapy, acupuncture and emergency medicine; made two visits to the Philippines to study the work of the native healers.

David HOY, L.H.D.—degree awarded by University of Recife, Brazil in recognition of his perceptive and objective studies of Voodoo religious practices and philosophy; B.A. degree in radio speech, B.D. degree in Hebrew and Greek theology; internationally-accepted authority, lecturer and author on psychic phenomena; selected for participation in the Philippine "psychic surgery" research based on recommendations from both psychic authorities and leaders in the world of professional magic, for his ability to detect and explain fraudulent and deceptive practices often presented as psychic phenomena rather than the basic manipulative and technical skills of the professional magician and/or illusionist; author of *Psychic and Other ESP Party Games* and *The Meaning of Tarot,* and subject of Charles Godwin's *Super Psychic.*

George W. MEEK—engineering graduate of University of Michigan, 1932; served as Techinal Consultant during World War II in the Combined Production and Resources Board and the Combined Raw Materials Board in London and Washington, D.C.; for twenty-five post-war years designed and supervised industrial and scientific research programs in U.S. and European laboratories; personal inventions relating to air and thermal pollution control processes patented in 13 countries; avocation for many years has been reading in fields of medicine, psychiatry and psychical research; past six years spent in full-time research and in organizing extensive travel for self and teams of specialists to study subjects related to this book; research consultant to the Academy of Parapsychology and Medicine.

Hiroshi MOTOYAMA, Ph.D.—graduated 1951 from Tokyo University of Education; received Ph.D. in philosophy and psychology, 1956; organized and became director of The Institute of Religious Psychology, Tokyo, 1960; worked as visiting research associate at Duke University, U.S.A. and completed Ph.D. studies in psychology and parapsychology, 1962; became President in 1972 of the International Association for Religion and Psychology; made three trips to the Philippines to study the healers and took some of them to his laboratory in Tokyo for study; has studied and practiced acupuncture for 20 years and became advisor to the Japan Acupuncture Association in 1973; reads seven languages, including Sanskrit and Chinese; inventor of electronic equipment for detecting and measuring the energy fields of man.

Hans NAEGELI-OSJORD, M.D.—studied in Lusanne, Zurich, Rome, Hamburg and Munich; medical assistant in psychology and psychiatry in Zurich, in neurology in Paris, in surgery in Lusanne, and in internal medicine in St. Gall; from 1940 to present in private practice of Jungean psychiatry and psychology in Zurich; publications in psychiatry, psychology, mythology and parapsychology; since 1958 president of the Swiss Society of Parapsychology in Zurich; numerous trips to study the work of Filipino healers.

Michael Wynne PARKER—Bakewell, Buxton, London, Sheffield; read theology; despite upbringing as an Anglican, worked for five years in Methodist ministry; parted with Methodism as a result of his theological differences with church leaders, who endeavored to curb his interest in, and involvement with, healing; now a lay Anglican, a firm traditionalist and sacramentalist, believing that the "paranormal" is within the best tradition of the church from its earliest days; lectures all over the world stressing that because of the Church's preoccupation with humanistic philosophy and activity it is not providing spiritual leadership to bewildered peoples of the world; has helped many people through his perceptive and healing gifts; founder of the Foundation for the Wholeness of Man (England and U.S.A.); holder of the Papal Medal received during a recent private audience with Pope Paul.

Leslie PRICE—born Warrington, England; religious studies graduate, University of Sussex; member of council, Society for Psychical Research, London (with special educational responsibilities); formerly librarian, College of Psychic Studies; sometime member of Psychic Phenomena Committee, Churches' Fellowship for Psychical and

Spiritual Fellowship (England); founder member, Research Committee, National Federation of Spiritual Healers; editor, Christian Parapsychologist Publications.

Andrija PUHARICH, M.D.—A.B., M.B., and M.D. degrees from Northwestern University; distinguished career in medicine, neurophysiology, medical electronics, and psychic research; director of research, Round Table Foundation, Glen Cove, Maine; conducted many original experiments in psychical research and studied several of the most outstanding mediumistic personalities of the period; after initial studies in 1963 of the healer, Arigó, he organized and led a team of six physicians and eight paramedical specialists in 1968 to Brazil to investigate the paranormal abilities of Arigó; introduced Uri Geller to Western Laboratory Research at Stanford Research Institute, to London University, to The Max Planck Institute, and to other research centers; pursued the meaning of the "Geller Effects" on a theoretical level; in 1975 organized The Tarrytown Conference on Paraphysics, a colloquium of twenty-seven physicists who had studied the "Geller Effects"; author of *The Sacred Mushroom, Beyond Telepathy, Uri,* and more than three dozen professional papers in the fields of medicine, parapsychology and paraphysics; holder of sixty-two U.S. and foreign patents in medical electronics.

Jeanne Pontius RINDGE—graduate of Ohio Wesleyan University; extensive additional studies in this country and abroad; founder and executive director of the Human Dimensions Institute at Rosary Hill College, Buffalo, New York, and the person-oriented Human Dimensions Center for Spiritual Living at Canandaigua Lake, New York; board member of the research-oriented Human Dimensions Institute/West in Ojai Valley, California, (all holistically-directed "seed centers"); editor of the internationally-circulated magazine, *Human Dimensions;* through Institute and magazine has brought to wide public attention the work of front-rank scientists and scholars in frontier fields of speculation and research, including HDI's own widely acclaimed research in nutrition and paranormal healing; programs or conducts workshops and lectures both in this country and abroad.

Mary SCOTT—M.A. with Honors in Psychology and Philosophy, post-graduate diploma in Social Studies, University of Edinburgh; S.N.R. at St. Thomas Hospital, London; H.V. in Public Health at Royal Society for Promotion of Health; university teacher before entering private practice; awarded in 1974 the first Sir Oliver Lodge Research Grant resulting in "Man, Fields and Physiology" and other papers.

Sigrun SEUTEMANN—licensed as Heilpraktikerin, operates medical and homeopathic treatment clinics in Weingarten and Constance, West Germany; uses her highly developed natural psychic abilities in diagnosing patients' illnesses; at age 29 was healed of a congenital heart condition by Tony Agpaoa in the Philippines; later collaborated with Tony in establishing a Spiritual Center in Baguio City, Luzon, where he and other healers provide help to Filipino and foreign patients; has personally accompanied more than 1,200 patients from central Europe to the Philippines for treatment by healers; has collaborated with scientists, medical doctors, and psychiatrists from U.S.S.R., U.S.A., England, Germany, Switzerland and Italy in their researching of Philippine "psychic surgery".

C. Norman SHEALY, M.D.—Neurosurgeon, Fellow American College of Surgeons; medical degree from Duke University, 1956; Clinical Associate, Department of Psychology, University of Wisconsin; Associate Clinical Professor, University of Wisconsin and University of Minnesota; as Director of the Pain Rehabilitation Center at LaCrosse, Wisconsin, he has had broad experience in alternative therapeutic modalities and speaks internationally on this and related subjects; has recently directed his attention to the study of individuals with paranormal diagnostic ability.

Sir Kelvin SPENCER—served on Western front during World War I and was awarded the Military Cross; entered London University, graduating in physics and engineering; researcher at British Aircraft Establishment; from 1935 to 1950 at Headquarters of State Department dealing with science endeavoring "to administer science and scientists, the latter quite unadministrable"; appointed Chief Scientist in the Ministry of Power in 1950 where he became involved in the early stages of developing nuclear energy for generating electricity; awarded the C.B.E. by King George VI, in part for his services in the aeronautics field during World War II; elected Fellow of a College of London University and a lay member of the Council of Exeter University; during his professional life held foreign assignments in Washington, D.C., Paris, Canada, and New Zealand.

Present address: "Wootans," Branscombe, Seaton, Devon, EX12 3DN, England.

Alfred STELTER—Sc.D., Gutenberg University, Mainz, Germany; specialized in radioactivity at Institute of Inorganic and Nuclear Chemistry, Mainz, until 1960; established Radioactive Isotope courses at Chemical Laboratory Fresenius, Wiesbaden, with the aid of German Atomic Ministry; worked with German Space Research Organization, 1964-1965; lecturer in chemistry and radio-chemistry at Dortmund Engineering College until 1973; since 1973, professor at Fachhochschule, Dortmund; lecturer in paraphysics and parapsychology since 1967; author of *PSI Healing* published in German, French and English; in preparation, *Transmutation of Matter, Energies and Minds*.

William A. TILLER—Ph.D., University of Toronto; nine years in industry as research scientist; from 1966 to 1971, Chairman of the Department of Material Science and Engineering at Stanford University; currently consultant to U.S. Government in fields of metallurgy and solid state physics; Professor at Stanford in the Department of Material Science, and editor of two scientific journals; specializes in fields of crystal growth, surfaces and interfaces, physical metallurgy, biomaterials and psychoenergetics; Guggenheim Fellowship, 1970-

1971; a director of the Academy of Parapsychology and Medicine (California); a director of Health for the New Age Trust (London); has published more than 150 scientific papers; currently active in development of reliable instrumentation for detection and study of psychoenergetic fields.

Lyall WATSON, Ph.D.—born in South Africa; Bachelors and honors degrees in biology from Universities of Witwatersrand and Natal; Doctor of Philosophy degree in ethology from University of London; studied archaeology in Holland; anthropologist to the American School of Oriental Research in Jordan; field work in Nigeria and Saudi Arabia; led marine biological expeditions to Indian Ocean and Indonesia, ornithological expeditions to East Africa and the Amazon; director of Johannesburg Zoo; founder and director of life science consultancy, Biologic of London; author of *Omnivore, Supernature, The Romeo Error,* and *Gifts of Unknown Things;* involved for for past five years in travel and research into the paranormal.

QUEST BOOKS